THREADS OF TIME

The True Story of a Bedford Family

SHELA PORTER

LARGE PRINT

Oxford

First published in Great Britain 1999
by The Book Castle

Published in Large Print 2003 by ISIS Publishing Ltd,
7 Centremead, Osney Mead, Oxford OX2 0ES
by arrangement with The Book Castle

British Library Cataloguing in Publication Data
Porter, Shela
   Threads of time: the true story of a Bedford family
   – Large print ed. – (Isis reminiscence series)
   1. Winch, Agnes
   2. Dressmakers – England – Biography
   3. Large type books
   4. Bedford (England) – Social life and customs –
   20th century
   I. Title
   646.4'0092

ISBN 0–7531–9892–4 (hb)
ISBN 0–7531–9893–2 (pb)

Printed and bound by Antony Rowe, Chippenham

THREADS OF TIME

For my mother who told me the stories;
Bill, my husband, who listened to them,
and Dawn Wells and The Bedford Writers' Circle
who encouraged me to write them down.

Prologue

The pipes beneath the pew were warm against her feet as Agnes settled back to listen to the address. It was always cold in this church, she reflected, and if you sat too close to the door, you caught a draught which seemed to chill your entire body from the feet up.

She would like to kneel for the prayers but was worried that she would be unable to get to her feet again without help. Leaning forward with your seat still on the pew somehow didn't seem to be right. It was too comfortable. Your mind tended to wander if you were comfortable and Agnes wanted to concentrate on the words that George was delivering with his practised expertise in public speaking.

The face of her eldest daughter, on the periphery of her vision, came suddenly into full focus and Agnes was inexplicably shocked to see how lined it was and how her hair was at last beginning to turn grey. Poor Joycey. Such a caring person. Agnes knew she was worried about her and as her daughter's hand covered her own and squeezed comfortingly, she patted it in reply and tried to smile reassurance at the anxious face.

Good old George. He always came up trumps on these occasions. Agnes smiled to herself as her clever second son began to describe some of John's escapades as a lad. There was subdued laughter now and again in the cold church, then silences heavy with collective memories followed by sighs and murmurings as the older brother's achievements were related to his family and friends.

Agnes looked past George, standing aloft in the pulpit, to where parallel rows of lamps above the choirstalls cast separate pools of yellow light on the shining hair and smooth faces of the choirboys below. An old memory of John in the school choir stirred and she tried to suppress a giggle as she recalled his music teacher's acerbic comments on her tone-deaf son's choral efforts.

"Happy landings, John!"

George's voice cracked slightly on the last word of the deftly delivered address and his mother watched anxiously as he removed those comic half-moon spectacles and dabbed quickly at his eyes as he descended the pulpit steps to return to his place behind her.

It was over and now Agnes could stand to sing John's favourite old hymn and afterwards there would be tea and little cakes in the church rooms next door, where people from Britannia Airways and old R.A.F. friends would wait to murmur condolences and barely-recognised faces from the past would smile tenderly at this old lady who had so unexpectedly outlived her eldest son.

At last, when everyone but Joycey had gone, Agnes sat in the comfortable, reclining chair bought for her by the family last Christmas and looked again at the slightly blurred photocopy of John on the cover of the order of service.

A young face smiled back at her as he posed for the photographer with one foot on the wing of his beloved fighter aircraft and one hand grasping the fuselage as he prepared to swing himself up into the tiny cockpit. How like his grandfather he was, she thought as she glanced up at the old sepia print of her father on the wall opposite. And just as stubborn, she reminded herself with a little chuckle.

From the bedroom at the top of the winding staircase, Joycey's anxious voice broke into her thoughts asking about hot-water bottles and suggesting an early bedtime for the old lady who had just endured a stressful day.

"Who's got the ashes, Joycey?"

Agnes knew that they had been beneath the altar during the Memorial Service at St. Mary's Church but the neat little box, concealed inside the conveniently strong carrier bag, had mysteriously disappeared as people began to leave and suddenly she needed to know where it was.

"I told you, Mother. John's girls have taken them to be scattered where their mother's were. In that lovely garden of remembrance. You remember, don't you?"

Yes, Agnes remembered only too well. The dark days of Margaret's illness. The desperate hope that it could somehow be reversed and then quiet despair as they watched her fade away.

Joycey fussed around her mother for longer than was really necessary, not wanting to leave her alone on this day full of old memories and half-forgotten people from her sometimes remote brother's past.

Agnes was almost ashamed to feel, when Joycey finally left, an overwhelming sense of relief that the quiet she'd longed for all day was hers at last.

Now she could remember at will, without fear of upsetting those others who were so concerned for her. She could pick and choose at those memories. She could smile at the funny ones, feel sorrow at the sad ones and wonder afresh how everything always resolved itself in time.

On the day when her family mourned her first-born, Agnes remembered and was comforted.

Contents

PART ONE

1917 to 1926

CHAPTER
ONE

A well-aimed bomb from the biggest Zeppelin raid on London destroyed six massive newspaper presses in Fleet Street. It also killed Agnes's Uncle Joe.

"Poor chap," murmured Emily, who was fond of her brother-in-law although he had been something of a drifter and knew the insides of the local pubs better than most.

Agnes missed him badly, for it was Joe who took her on outings when Mum was working for her ladies in Chelsea and Dad putting in long hours painting those new hotels in Park Lane. It was Joe who introduced the pale-faced London child, who slept badly and had nightmares, to all the great museums and galleries the capital had to offer. And it was Joe, with his shabby clothes and perpetual rolled cigarette hanging from his mouth, who showed Agnes the old city behind its impressive buildings and smart shopping streets.

With Uncle Joe as her guide and companion, Agnes explored ancient courtyards hidden away at the end of narrow alleys and never failed to be surprised on reaching the end of back streets to find they opened out unexpectedly on to small squares or even shady gardens. These oases of green surrounded by tall, old houses seemed to the girl to be the forgotten places of the city and she loved them all the more for it. By the time she was thirteen, Joe's niece knew her way around London as well as any cab-driver did. She was a city child, born to busy, bustling streets and sooty buildings, jellied-eel and pie-and-mash shops and always the distant hubbub of steam trains arriving and departing at King's Cross Station at the end of Gray's Inn Road where the three of them had lived since Agnes was born.

Emily knew that George had worked on right through that last Zeppelin raid and she'd been nearly out of her mind with worry at the thought of him perched up there on the scaffolding, painting away as the bombs fell.

When the first CRUMP THUMP! of explosions came early on a Saturday morning, Emily and Agnes were still in the high double bed where Emily was enjoying a rare lie-in and her daughter was reading the library book she'd brought home from Cromer Street School the day before. Mr Beresford, the headmaster of the old red-brick school just off Gray's Inn Road, insisted that every child take home a book at weekends. Whether they brought them back on Mondays was a different matter, for some of the parents did not hold with too much book-learning and inevitably a number of tattered books found their way into the nearest dustbin on Saturday nights when dad came home from the pub.

A few of the boys in Agnes's class were caned weekly when they failed to produce the wretched books and she had to watch in squirming sympathy as each miscreant was bent over a chair to receive his punishment.

"Old Beresford really lays into them, Mum!" was her protest every Monday evening, "and it's not their fault!"

"No, child, it isn't," agreed Emily stoutly and then, looking at her daughter's worried face, added hastily, "but you mustn't take it all so much to heart, Agnes. We can't do anything about it, now can we?" But long after her cherished only child was asleep, soft-hearted Emily would talk to George about those poor kids who came from homes where books were unknown and unwanted, where the man's word was law and the woman too weary from child-bearing and the weekly grind of coping with debt and drunkenness to do anything about it.

Agnes was just finishing the first chapter when the thumps came again. At first, Emily thought it was Mabel next door thumping hell out of her rag-rugs as if by banging them hard enough she could beat the devil out of the errant husband she was trying to persuade to join her in the Temperance Movement.

Then someone was running hard down the area steps to the basement and there was a loud knocking at the front door as Lizzie's mum from the top flat urged them both to come outside quickly to see the Zeppelin.

Agnes reached the top of the steps to find that most of their neighbours had done the same. All along Gray's Inn Road where the tall four-storeyed houses were home to half-a-dozen families in each, little groups of people stood silently gazing upwards at the monstrous shape above them. In the distance, she could hear the raucous din of an air-raid warning rattle and as a sweating, red-faced man came racing round the corner from Acton Street waving the rattle above his head, Agnes covered her ears against the noise and shrank back behind her mother as if for protection.

"Take cover! Take cover!" the man shouted again and again as he waved the rattle all along the road. Then he was off once more running up towards Holborn and the Ear, Nose and Throat Hospital where Agnes had her tonsils removed when she was four and then on to the next street and Percy Circus where she sometimes played with Lizzie White, and still the crowd gazed silently upwards at the beautiful but deadly craft that had come to bomb their city.

The huge, cigar-shaped airship hung almost motionless above the massive bulk of King's Cross Station, the early-morning sun glinting along its silvery length, only its nose swaying gently from side to side, for all the world, thought Agnes, staring upwards open-mouthed, like a blind whale trying to find its way home.

There was a sudden and universal gasp from the crowd as three small objects, reduced by the distance to black dots against the blue sky, dropped one after the other from the tiny cabin slung beneath the Zeppelin. The bombs, seeming to fall slowly at first, but gathering speed as they fell in a great, curving arc, disappeared behind the high-pillared façade of the station and the road became a corridor of unbearable noise as the force

6

of the explosions broke every pane in that vast roof and shock waves of blast spread outwards past houses and shops, horses and cabs, trams and people and finally spent itself two miles away across the shining, morning rooftops of the city.

Suddenly, emerging from behind the column of thick, black smoke rising above the station, three tiny biplanes from Croydon airfield buzzed angrily after the airship and lights flashed from its cabin as it began to ascend high into the sky and then with a defiant roar of its engines turned away into the sun, headed for the Thames estuary and the open sea.

All along the road, neighbours and passers-by alike cheered on the little planes but Agnes clung weakly to the area railings trying to quell the awful buzzing in her ears and as her stomach lurched again in the old, familiar way and the steep steps wavered before her eyes she sat down suddenly on the top one and was violently sick all down the rest.

"Nerves!" announced Doctor Fuller as he examined Agnes in his cold consulting-room at Monday morning surgery. "You must try to get this child out of London, Mrs Thomas. And the sooner the better. Some country air is what she needs."

Cold but gentle fingertips pulled down Agnes's bottom eyelids in turn and the doctor continued speaking above her head as he wrote out the prescription. "She is rather anaemic and underweight and you say she is sleeping badly?"

Agnes pulled a face at what she read on the prescription. Ugh! Parrish's Food again! That horrible black stuff that made her tongue and teeth black and meant another battle with constipation.

"A shilling, that cost me!" exclaimed Emily later as she and George ate their supper together when Agnes was asleep. "And he only told me what I know already," she grumbled.

George nodded and grinned broadly at Emily's little flash of temper and looked admiringly at her red hair arranged neatly in a bun. His wife caught the look as she began to clear the table and smiled to herself over the washing-up.

"Perhaps old Beresford will come up with something, Em," said George as she poured his third cup of tea. "After all, he's the one with the connections."

"Yes," replied Emily slowly, glancing across to where their daughter was sleeping behind the half-drawn curtain of the little bed-alcove in the corner.

"Now you're not having second thoughts are you, my love?" queried George as he reached across to pat his little wife's hand. "We agreed it was for the best and," he smiled and winked at her worried face, "I can come down at weekends."

"When 'yer leaving then, Agnes?" Lizzie White still couldn't believe that her friend was going to live in the country, for ever since they'd started school together in the infants' class, they'd been inseparable. Both mothers always knew where to look for their children. It was either up on the top floor where three families shared the lavatory or down in the basement where Agnes's family did the same. No one in the house had a bathroom, just a zinc tub by the fire on Saturday nights.

"Cor! Agnes." Lizzie's thin, peaky face suddenly split into a wide grin revealing a gap in her teeth where Mick, her brother, had belted her one when he was drunk. "Can I come to visit? Is it the same place we went to last summer? That was smashing! You're the lucky one!"

Later, as the cold, London, February day turned into foggy night, Agnes snuggled down in the little bed that was a sofa during the day and listened carefully to the soft voices of her parents as they talked about the new life ahead. She and Mum were to go within weeks but Dad must stay on because of his work.

"Can't turn it down, Em. There's enough work in Park Lane for the next five years. And more hotels going up after that, so it's said."

"Yes, and at this rate they'll all need rebuilding before long!" and the anxious look that George had come to dread was back on her face and he knew she was worrying about him working through the raids again.

Three weeks later, just before the end of the Easter term, Emily and Agnes waved goodbye to George as the train pulled out of King's Cross Station bound for a small village nearly thirty miles down the LNER line in Hertfordshire.

"Well away from the bombs, Agnes," comforted Dad as she clung to him and the guard's whistle blew and doors slammed shut along the length of the train. Then they began to move and Agnes pressed her nose to the window to catch a last glimpse of her father before a bend in the track took him out of sight.

Agnes had a brand new book to read on the journey but as the train puffed its way out through the sooty suburbs past rows and rows of small backyards and shrieked beneath countless bridges and rumbled over viaducts into unfamiliar countryside, all she could think of were her old school friends, especially Lizzie and the two boys from next door and even Mr Beresford as he handed her the book on the day she left his school.

"You will do well, Agnes. Don't forget to write to us at your old school." Then, with a rare smile the old, tired headmaster handed her a copy of *Alice in Wonderland* and an envelope containing her school report. "Give that to your new teacher, child. She will need to know what standard you have attained."

Lizzie White didn't say much, but her peaky face lit up at the last moment as Agnes said goodbye at the top of the grubby, area steps and handed her some treacle toffee Mum had made the night before and promised to write to her often. Agnes had left two books for Jed and Sammy with Lizzie's mum, who said they could come round to read on Saturdays if Mick was out. Otherwise it wouldn't do, for when her son was in drink no visitors were tolerated in the flat under the eaves.

"Will Miss Beresford be there to meet us, Mum?" Agnes asked anxiously as she turned from the window where she'd been looking at all those cows again. There must be thousands of them, she thought as she waited for Emily's answer.

10

"Well, she said she would," her mother replied, "but we can always get a bus out to the village." Then glancing at Agnes's anxious face added for the third time since leaving London, "Don't worry, child. It's all been taken care of."

Agnes settled back in the corner seat of the carriage to try to read again but despite the fact that the white rabbit had just appeared and that silly Alice was about to fall down the hole, she found it very difficult to concentrate on the story.

She knew Mum and Dad were anxious to get her out of London away from the air-raids but the further the train chugged through this strange, green landscape, the more she realised how much she would miss her old life in the damp, basement flat. Agnes thought about the Saturday outings on the tram down under Kingsway and out on to The Embankment where you could see the Houses of Parliament and Big Ben and busy little tugs fussing up the river to the Pool of London. She'd really miss those outings with Uncle Joe and then with a sudden lurch low in her stomach, remembered his funeral and how only a handful of people had turned up.

"He was never one to make many friends, child." George's big hand held tightly on to hers as the cheap coffin was lowered into the black hole and all Agnes could think of was Joe's smiling face and the endless supply of bullseyes on their wanderings together through the city.

Hanging her head so Mum wouldn't see she was crying again, Agnes glanced down at the good, woollen stockings and sturdy boots she'd put on for the first time that morning and thought that she'd even miss going to visit the two elderly spinsters Mum had cooked for twice a week. They had a lovely flat looking out over the river at Chelsea Reach and such good clothes they passed on to the hard-working housepainter's wife whose daughter was a year younger than their niece. The boots were half-a-size too big but Mum said Agnes would grow into them.

"Look, Agnes." Emily interrupted the girl's thoughts to point out of the window. "We're just coming in to Knebworth station. There's only two more to go and then we'll be in Hitchin."

She leaned over to tighten the white ribbon which held the thick, dark hair back from her daughter's pale face and said again, "Don't worry, my love, we'll soon be there."

But Agnes's thoughts were back in London again in the dirty, old road which had been her home for the last thirteen years. Where she'd played with Lizzie in Percy Circus Gardens, the only green place near their house. Where the girls' part of Cromer Street Junior School was upstairs and playtime was on the flat roof and you could throw snowballs down on the boys in the playground below. Where she and Lizzie, hidden on either side of Acton Street, stretched black thread across the road and laughed as the cab-drivers swore when it knocked off their top hats. And where she could see, if she leaned far enough out of Lizzie's window, the porters from the Royal Free Hospital along the road, running along with patients on those rickety-wheeled

12

stretchers. And seeing the odd, yellow faces of the women who worked with nitro-glycerine from the bomb-making at Cubitt's ammunition factory in King's Cross Road. And the Police Station further along the same road where Lizzie's Mick sometimes ended up on a drunk and disorderly charge but was always cheerful as he was marched off to the cells singing, "Hail The Conquering Hero Comes", at the top of his voice.

Agnes hoped there would be a jellied-eel or at least a pie-and-mash shop in St. Ippollitts.

"Jellied-eel shop, lass?" laughed George when she asked him. "Not likely, Agnes. But there's bound to be plenty of eggs, seeing that the cottage belongs to the farm."

Agnes remembered last summer and the time she and Lizzie had spent in that funny, little cottage in the country in a place called Little Almshoe. Just a few cottages and a small farm. Something called a hamlet. Old Beresford had organised that as well, through his Country Holiday Scheme. "Sixpence a week starting next term," he announced at assembly, just before Christmas. And somehow Emily had found hers and Lizzie missed some weeks but she still went in the end.

"Mick probably came up on the horses, lass," joked George when she told him the good news.

Oh! It had been lovely! Two weeks sleeping under a thatched roof where you could lie in bed and listen to little animals scratching and scrabbling as you dropped off to sleep. And actually picking real raspberries in the garden and taking the dog for walks along country lanes for miles without meeting another soul. By the end of the holiday, Agnes had just begun to get used to the quietness and all that greenness and all those cows!

Now, here she was again and this time for the duration of the war and it was all like a dream. Except for Lizzie and the old school and jellied-eels and pie-and-mash and Uncle Joe.

The train jolted to a steaming, noisy halt and outside a long board read HITCHIN. They had arrived and in the quiet, dusty road just outside the station, a pony and trap waited for them and as the porter heaved their luggage aboard, Miss Beresford greeted them with an invitation to tea at the vicarage. Agnes hoped it wouldn't be those eggs Dad was talking about, for they made her constipated and that meant syrup-of-figs until your stomach heaved and not going too far away from the lav.

CHAPTER
TWO

The first Christmas in St. Ippollitts was better than Agnes expected for she had made new friends at school and Emily was working for two days a week at the big house up the hill. George came home at weekends and left by the London milk-train from Hitchin station every Monday morning for his job on the hotels near Hyde Park.

It had been decided that he would give up their furnished rooms in Gray's Inn Road and George now lodged with a Jewish family in Acton Street from Monday to Friday.

"They need the money, Em," he explained after his first week with the Blumfelds. "Poor souls, they hardly dare go outside now the neighbours have found out their son is still in Germany."

The tiny, one-bedroomed cottage at the end of the row of three which were also known as the Almshouses backing on to the churchyard, had been quickly but simply furnished and every weekend since Emily and Agnes had arrived, George brought yet another item from the old second-hand furniture shop in High Holborn. Every Wednesday, Agnes waited for the postman to drop a letter with a London postmark into the box set into the wall beside the low front door, for George wrote regularly to his wife and daughter. He missed them badly and found the weekday separation hard to bear.

Now their little home was cosy and warm from the black-leaded stove where Christmas dinner was cooking ready for Emily to serve up to her family when she returned from the Colonel's house.

"I didn't want to work on Christmas Day, George," she declared as she closed the little oven door and shovelled more coal on the fire, "but Cook said she needed another pair of hands for a couple of hours and we're always glad of the extra, love."

Indeed they were, for George, along with many others, had been unexpectedly put on short time and his wages now barely covered the two shillings-and-sixpence weekly rent on the cottage and the family's food bills.

"There's no sense in staying on in London, Em," he had announced at the beginning of December. "We can't afford the fares or my lodgings."

And soft-hearted Emily thought about the old Jewish couple and hoped that they would soon get another decent lodger like her George.

"I'll see about that Henlow job after the holiday," he promised, "and if I can get hold of a second-hand bike that'll save the bus fare to the camp. It's only about six miles."

Emily nodded and patted her worried husband's cheek as she buttoned up the good overcoat the Miss Dentons had sent down for Christmas. What a good, old pair they were! She sometimes wondered how things would be without the regular parcels from the well-to-do ladies who were so sorry to see her leave their employ.

"Don't forget, Mrs Thomas, if you should ever need anything for yourself or the child, please let us know!"

With her thoughts on the two kindly spinsters she'd left behind in London, Emily walked past the churchyard, up the hill and then turned into the Ponsonbys' driveway. If she worked hard, she knew she could finish all the vegetables for their big, Christmas dinner party in two hours and then she'd be home in time to dish up her own small one.

For Agnes, busy with the length of pretty material Dad had picked up cheaply in Tottenham Market, the next two hours flew past and by the time Emily got back she had already tacked her new skirt together.

"Just like her grandmother, that little lass," smiled George proudly as Agnes held up the skirt for them to admire. "She'll make her living with a needle, you mark my words!"

By Easter, when Agnes was nearly fourteen, George had regular work at Henlow Camp which was expanding to take in R.F.C. recruits and his daughter had to sleep across the road in old Mrs Wrigley's spare bedroom under the thatched eaves of her little house. It was a nuisance on cold nights but the big, old bed had a feather mattress and Agnes was allowed to read by the light of an oil lamp.

"Why can't I sleep in the kitchen like I did in London?" she complained when the new arrangement was first suggested. But Emily only smiled and replied that she was a big girl now and too old to sleep on the sofa. She didn't add that she and George needed their privacy in the tiny cottage where every sound could be heard from next door, never mind from the bedroom above. Emily hoped Agnes would understand and anyway, the old woman over the road asked only a shilling a week for the room.

Both George and Emily knew that this arrangement couldn't go on for very long and although Agnes was doing well at the village school, just across the road from their cottage, the time was not far off when they would all have to move again.

As things turned out, the move became suddenly urgent for old Mrs Wrigley died peacefully in her sleep about a month after Easter and it was Agnes who found her.

"I just thought she was having a lie-in, Mum!" Agnes shivered as she sat in George's old armchair near the warm stove and thought about the still shape beneath the faded, quilted bedspread which had been a wedding gift fifty years ago and the round, white face with its mouth grotesquely open, revealing toothless gums in all the indignity of old age.

"Will they put her teeth in for the funeral, Mum?" Suddenly it seemed important to Agnes that others should not see the old woman like that, for she had been kind to the pale-faced child from London whose nightmares about Zeppelins had kept her awake more than once since she arrived in the village.

18

"Reverend Beresford says it's a tied cottage, George," sighed Emily the day after the funeral. "The old woman was allowed to stay on after her husband went but now a new farm-labourer's family will move in."

"Never mind, lass," George consoled his wife. "I told you not to count on it too much. Still," he added thoughtfully, "you were right, Em. It would have been just the place for us with two bedrooms and all."

So Agnes was back to sleeping on the sofa again and George began to make enquiries about another place to live, this time hopefully with two bedrooms. It didn't matter about a bathroom for only the gentry had those and the little housemaids to haul buckets of water up the service stairs twice a day.

Emily knew all about that kind of drudgery for, until she met George when she was thirty-three, it had been a daily task for her to take hot water up to the nursery in a big house in Liverpool. Oh! Those steep stairs and such heavy buckets and here she was now with a deformed hip and losing three bairns before Agnes came late, when Emily was nearly forty.

Agnes was happy at St. Ippollitts school and had made special friends with Gladys Fairey who walked in every day from her farm at Redcoats Green. Together the two girls would take their sewing down to Five Acres field near the vicarage in Sperberry Lane where the new vicar, old "Cocky" Foster was now in residence. On those long summer afternoons they talked endlessly about what they wanted to do when they left school.

"Mr Parkes-Cole thinks I should go into service like most of the other girls, Gladys."

Agnes sat under the big oak tree by the river carefully completing the smocking on a new blouse for her mother's birthday.

"But Joseph Jehosophat Parkes-Cole has another think coming!" she laughed as she thought, not unkindly, about the fair-haired headmaster with those weird rimless glasses who was strict but fair and his gentle wife who taught the little ones behind the big curtain drawn across the school hall.

The school holidays had just started when George found the house.

"You'll like it, Em. It's at the end of a row of six with the lav at the bottom of the garden and we have to share that with next door. And the night-soil men call every other night. It's in Gosmore, just down the road."

Emily smiled at the enthusiasm in George's voice and told him that no matter what condition it was in they'd take it if it had two bedrooms. They'd manage with sharing the lav and a new, zinc tub from Hitchin market would cost only one and elevenpence halfpenny. Somehow they'd manage as long as they could all be together.

Two weeks later, the Thomas family said goodbye to their neighbours in St. Ippollitts and moved on a horse-drawn cart to their new home at No. 4 Maidencroft Lane, Gosmore. Agnes said goodbye to the school and Gladys who still had another year of schooling to do.

And now Agnes was turned fourteen and the war to end all wars had been raging for four of them. In the newspaper that George hid behind every evening, she read with horrified fascination of the terrible slaughter of the soldiers in the trenches and someone called General Haig who was now in command.

"That chap will see it through," stated her father as he watched Agnes trying to make sense of the blurred photographs of tanks and drawn faces of tommies and "messages from the front line".

Further down the road in St. Paul's Walden Bury, the Bowes-Lyon family were trying to come to terms with the loss of their son Fergus on active duty and Elizabeth, his sister, sat sad and white-faced in church at his memorial service.

"That makes sixteen from this village alone, Em," murmured George as they walked home afterwards. "God knows how it will all end. At this rate there'll be no young-'uns left to carry on afterwards."

Emily didn't answer but in her prayers that morning she had not only thought about those who had gone but thanked God and fate that her man was too old for the draft and was employed safely on government work at Henlow.

Just across the road at The Bull, where George called in regularly for his Saturday night pint of bitter, the talk was mostly about potatoes and brussels sprouts and only the marked absence of any young faces in the public bar served as a grim reminder that across the Channel the carnage continued unabated.

Jim, the young potman, often tried to help Mr Weston, the landlord, behind the bar as best he could but with the loss of a leg and his hearing and the obvious signs of shell-shock, he made a sorry sight with unsteady hands and a twitching face that if it was not so pitiable would have been truly comical.

"Poor young devil!" George exclaimed to Emily regularly every Sunday morning as he cleared the grate and stoked up the fire in the range. "What future is there for him and those like him?"

"Well, dear, the Government promised to care for the wounded," replied Emily soothingly. She didn't like to see her man upset like this for his heart was not as strong as it should be and those turns during the past year worried her more than she cared to admit.

"Beattie and Dolly help their father quite a lot, Dad," said Agnes as she set out the table for breakfast.

"Yes, but what happens when they leave home? And by the look of things that won't be long either. There's always one or the other of them up at The Grange, pushing those young officer convalescents around in their wheelchairs. You mark my words, Em! And you, young lady," George pointed a stern finger at Agnes's cheeky grin, "are not to go up there with them again. Do you hear?"

"Hush, George," said Emily hastily, looking anxiously at his flushed face. "Agnes is still a child with another year at school to do. Perhaps it will be all over by then."

Another whole year at school! Not if I can help it, thought Agnes later that evening as she put the finishing touches to her new dress. Most of the other girls in her class had already left at the end of last term.

"Yes, and gone into service, lass. That's not for my daughter!"

George was adamant that his only child should not be an underpaid skivvy in some big house where the privileged few ordered the lives of the many they considered beneath them.

"Times are changing, my love," Emily assured him after one of his outbursts over Agnes's future. "The colonel's wife reckons girls won't want to come back into service after making such good money in munitions. And if they do, the wages will have to be a lot better."

"Who says I want to be a skivvy anyway?" protested Agnes. "What I really want is a dressmaking apprenticeship. Then I can get a good job in one of those big shops in London."

Emily looked again at her husband's worried face and thought how he had aged so much over these last four years and then she realised with a sudden shock that he was not a young father who could cope easily with a high-spirited girl like their Agnes. This good man she had married late in life was not far off sixty and the years were beginning to show.

George retreated behind his newspaper once more and Emily put her finger to her lips and frowned at Agnes as she began to tidy up her sewing things. Later, as they prepared for bed, she told him she'd have a word with the colonel's lady who she knew was a good customer at Spurrs, the big ladies'-wear shop in

Hitchin which catered for the clothing requirements of many old county families.

"Well, Mrs Thomas," announced the colonel's lady two days later, "the workroom supervisor will see your daughter next week with a view to offering her an apprenticeship after Easter next year. It seems that one of the girls is leaving then and there will be a vacancy." Mrs Ponsonby smiled and waved away Emily's thanks, then added slowly, "Actually, I was hoping Agnes would come to me as a lady's-maid. I'll be without one after Enid leaves to marry her milkman."

All the way home, Emily debated with herself as to whether she should tell Agnes about Mrs Ponsonby's offer of a job up at the big house. It would be easy work, she knew, compared with her own start as a nursery maid all those years ago. And it would mean Agnes might give up her grand ideas about working in London.

It was the look on her daughter's face when she broke the news about the apprenticeship that made Emily keep the other job offer to herself. And George, she knew, was happy at the decision to give Agnes a good start in life, even if it meant she could not contribute anything to the household budget for the next three years.

On the ninth of November that year, Kaiser Bill abdicated and two days later, Dolly, who was keeping company with a young officer while he was still in his wheelchair, came rushing over from The Bull with the news that the Armistice had been signed. In the morning, George's newspaper was headlined in enormous black letters, GUNS FALL SILENT ON ALL FRONTS. And next door, Mrs Allen mourned her Billy, just eighteen and killed a week earlier at Valenciennes.

CHAPTER
THREE

Agnes had not changed her mind about not going back to school but the fact was that the promised apprenticeship would not start for another six months and already she was bored and restless in the little house all day.

Twice more before Christmas that year, Mrs Ponsonby tried to persuade Agnes to come to her as a lady's-maid and then gave up and took on another girl.

"You could have helped her out for a few months, Agnes!" Emily reasoned with her daughter. She did not add that they could have done with the extra money in the little household, for in the damp winter months George was often so unwell that he could only sit by the fire and fret to see his Emily going off to work leaving him at home. For no work meant no money for either of them.

It was Beattie Weston who told Agnes about temporary work her friend could get in some of the big, local houses.

"Some of the parlourmaids come into the pub with their gentlemen friends, Agnes. They are always complaining about having to do sewing jobs on top of their normal duties. I'm sure you could get something for a few months if you asked around."

That evening, Emily and Agnes made a list of the big houses they knew in the vicinity of Gosmore and by the end of the week, Agnes had secured three mornings' work a week at one of them and two afternoons at another.

The nearest was just a short distance away from Maidencroft Lane at Gosmore Ley, the home of Colonel and Mrs Sowerby in Hitchin Road on the outskirts of the village.

"I need someone to sew for the household and look after my clothes, Miss Thomas," smiled the Colonel's lady as she led Agnes through the wide, oak-panelled hallway and into a small room at the back of the house. "I do hope you will be happy with us."

The work was mainly repairs to linen and making up the servants' new uniforms in time for Christmas for that would be their Christmas present from their employer.

On her first morning in her new job, Agnes was delighted to find that one of her old school friends from St. Ippollitts was the new parlourmaid at Gosmore Ley and it was Daisy Bell who first took the younger girl up to her mistress's dressing-room to view the long rails of fashionable clothes which hung from end to end of the heavy, oak wardrobe.

"However can she need all these at once, Daisy?" gasped Agnes as she tenderly stroked the soft velvets and gently lifted delicate tulle frills of beautiful evening gowns.

Never in her life before had she seen such wonderful clothes at close quarters but on that day in early December 1918, when she was not yet fifteen, Agnes knew that her future lay in working with garments like these and she was impatient for her apprenticeship at Spurrs to begin.

"It was incredible, Mum!" You should have seen those dresses! But Mrs Sowerby says I can only do simple repairs on the children's clothes and that she'll find plenty of socks for me to darn! And of course I will be making up the servants' Christmas uniforms for a start."

Emily and her daughter sat in their little kitchen after supper that night while Agnes enthused over her new job and Emily smiled and remembered the two kind, spinster ladies she'd worked for in Chelsea and the good clothes they always passed on to her which she still wore for rare outings to London or for church.

"Well, Agnes. Mrs Ponsonby tells me that the Amos household is much the same as the Sowerbys', so you should be well suited between now and Easter."

So the time passed quickly for Agnes and she was able to pay her mother a small amount for her keep. The rest she spent on new materials for decent clothes for herself for she was now fast becoming a fashionable young woman intent on keeping up with all the latest smart trends like those ladies she sewed for in their big houses.

The first few months of Agnes's apprenticeship were very nearly the last. For a high-spirited girl in her sixteenth year who could already cut out and sew all her own clothes, the tedium and seeming pointlessness of her duties was almost more than she could bear.

"All I do, Mum," she exploded at the end of the first week, "is pick up pins, dust the shelves and fetch buttons and petersham ribbon from the shop below. And that awful carpet in the workroom! Dark brown and shows every tiny bit of cotton and fluff. Doris and I have to dust-pan and brush it first thing every morning and there's dust everywhere!"

George, hiding behind his newspaper as usual, winked at Emily as they listened to the complaints and she smiled back as she remembered his tales about the carpentry apprenticeship he'd taken many years before. The never-ending sawdust to be swept up, the interminable and finger-bruising task of nail-straightening and worst of all, clearing out nests of wriggling, pink, baby rats whose parents thought they were safe behind the wood shavings.

So George let Agnes have her moan and Emily murmured sympathy and assurances that things would improve. She was right, for at the year's end, in the week that the body of the Unknown Warrior was brought home from France for interment in Westminster Abbey, Agnes began to work under the supervision of the chief skirt-hand at Spurrs, a middle-aged, bosomy woman by the name of Miss Goody who had a sharp tongue but a kind heart. In later years, Agnes would remember this skilled and patient dressmaker with a degree of fondness which belied the caustic remarks she'd made about her when she was a girl.

"She's a real task-master, Mum. Nothing I do is ever right for her. Nothing short of perfection will do on her workbench!"

Agnes complained regularly and bitterly about this paragon of excellence but as the months went by amid growing newspaper reports of two million out of work, the gauche girl became used to long hours bent over petersham waist-bands, double inverted pleats and hidden plackets and all the other mysteries of a superbly fitting skirt. And she knew without being told, that she was learning from a mistress of her craft and the knowledge served her well for the rest of her life.

In the workroom the apprentices sang the new songs of the year above the whirr and clatter of the heavy machinery.

"Margie, you are my inspiration, Margie," could always be guaranteed to bring a smile to the chief skirt-hand's plain features. How had those girls found out her name was Marjorie?

Agnes had now made new friends with some of the other apprentices and as they worked away at the heavy, old treadle machines or sat quietly at the big work tables hand-stitching at some county lady's new evening gown, she began to enjoy the company of talented girls who, like herself, would stitch for a living for the rest of their lives.

By the time she was eighteen and within sight of her dressmaking certificate, Agnes had a good grounding in all aspects of the trade.

"I only wish we could ask Agnes to stay on with us after she finishes her apprenticeship, Mrs Thomas," the workroom supervisor enthused to Emily when she met her one day on the market square. "But I'm afraid there won't be a vacancy for a fully-trained dressmaker for at least another year and I expect your daughter will have found other employment by then."

"Yes, you bet they do," laughed Agnes, confident now in her ability to cut out, fit and sew anything any woman would wear. "But I've done my time there, Mum and I've more than paid for the apprenticeship. They've been selling my skills for more than a year now. Anyway," she added scornfully, "the starting pay they are offering is not much more than apprentices' wages."

That evening, as George sat fiddling with his precious crystal-set wireless, trying to tune in to the new B.B.C. broadcasts from Marconi House about the discovery of the tomb of Tutankhamun in Egypt, Emily looked thoughtfully at her daughter as she sat smocking a child's dress by the light of the oil lamp and wondered yet again where the nimble fingers and flair for style had come from. Not from herself, of that she was certain. Or from her own mother who had difficulty threading a needle, never mind making dresses.

Then Emily remembered George's words in the little one-down-one-up cottage that was their home when they first left London. "This child will earn her living with a needle." And if Agnes's ambitions were to be realised, that meant leaving home to live and work in London again.

It was five years now since the family had left London and nearly two since Emily took Agnes up to the great city for the day, to visit her old employers. The girl was appalled by the noise and dirt and upset to see so many war-wounded begging in the streets. Every few yards, it seemed, another amputee offered matches for sale or tried to squeeze a tune from an old accordian or mouth-organ. Some had small children with them to hold up a tin mug or greasy cap to collect pennies from indifferent passers-by.

"It's disgraceful, George!" Emily protested as she strained potatoes for supper that night. "What happened to all the promises to look after those poor men?"

Agnes remembered the pointing, accusing finger of Lord Kitchener on those posters from her childhood declaring, "Your Country Needs You!" And then she remembered Lizzie's Mick and Mabel's husband who had responded to it. Both long dead now, one at Ypres and the other in the Dardanelles. And Uncle Joe. Dear Uncle Joe in his cold grave in a sooty London cemetery.

"Don't upset yourself, lass," comforted George quietly as the tears threatened to fall down Emily's soft cheeks. "The unions will put things right now that Lloyd-George has gone. Though he was a trier, I'll say that for him. A man of the people if ever there was one."

Supper that evening was an unusually quiet affair in the Thomas household and as Emily looked across the table at her daughter's thoughtful face, she guessed it was only a matter of time before Agnes told them what was on her mind.

Over the washing-up and when George had left for his pint in the Bull, Agnes enquired casually, "How's the new girl doing up at the house, Mum?"

Lily had started work for Mrs Ponsonby a month previously as the new lady's-maid and the colonel's wife was having a hard time training her in the required routine.

"She can't sew on a button in the right place, Mrs Thomas," her employer confided after an exasperating first week with the new girl. "And as for my hair — well I've never met anyone before with such clumsy fingers. My girls won't let her near them!" And the good lady sighed as she handed over Emily's wage packet. "What I need," she continued, "is a girl who can sew and be my dresser and who is willing to help at table sometimes. Someone, in fact," added Mrs Ponsonby slowly, "like your Agnes."

"I don't think she'll be interested, madam," smiled Emily. "She's finished her apprenticeship and is set on going to London to find work." And now it was Emily's turn to sigh at the thought of her only child living alone in the city.

Agnes was drying the last plate as Emily answered her question about Lily. "Not very well as it happens. Poor Mrs P's giving up on her I shouldn't wonder. She's a nice little thing and very willing but if you ask me, a bit lacking in the upper storey. Housemaid maybe. Lady's-maid, never!"

Agnes looked more thoughtful than ever as they prepared for bed and as Emily reached the top of the narrow stairs, she called to her mother to come in for a minute before she went to her own bed.

"I've been thinking, Mum," began Agnes slowly, as she brushed her dark hair carefully before the tiny dressing-table mirror. "Perhaps I won't go to London. Not just yet anyway," she added hastily, catching sight of her mother's surprised face reflected in the mirror. "Oh, yes, I know I always said that's what I'd do but . . ." Agnes stopped speaking, put the brush firmly down on the dressing-table and turned to her mother with a big smile on her face.

"The fact is, Mum, I don't fancy it any more. It seems so dirty and noisy and there's no-one left who we knew in the old days. Even Lizzie's gone off into service and the old ladies have moved to Brighton."

"Well!" exclaimed Emily, trying not to look as delighted as she felt. "Your father will be relieved I can tell you, Agnes. But what about your apprenticeship? And all that hard work?"

"It's all right, Mum. I've got plans! Mrs Sowerby came into the fitting-room last week and she's asked me to go back to her again as her personal maid. Just sewing for her and helping with the girls' clothes. And perhaps helping out when they give a dinner party. Of course, she'll want me to live in this time. But just think about it, Mum. I'll be earning a good wage and with all found! And," she added gently, "I'll be just down the road."

"Well, I don't know what your father will have to say about all this, Agnes." Emily shook her head doubtfully over her daughter's new idea. "He always hated you working in service when you left school and here you are talking about it all over again!"

"But things have changed since I was there before," persuaded Agnes softly. "The pay is so much better for a start. And," she went on, as her mother continued to look so worried, "it's only until I've saved enough to set up on my own. Perhaps in another year or two."

So George grumbled and Emily worried but two weeks later Agnes was installed in the Sowerby household again and the Colonel's lady welcomed her back at the start of the new summer social season of 1922.

Also newly installed at Gosmore Ley was a smart, wind-up gramophone and often, when the Sowerbys were out for the day, Daisy and Agnes played all their latest records and danced around the sitting-room to "The Sheik of Araby" and "Look For The Silver Lining", until the cook called loudly from the kitchen for them to turn off that infernal noise before it drove her crazy.

On the frequent weekends when the family was in London, Daisy sometimes dressed up in Colonel Sowerby's best dress uniform and Agnes donned one of Mrs Sowerby's lovely, low-waisted evening gowns and her favourite beaded headband complete with its long osprey feather and together the two girls would dance to the new square tango they had learned at the village hop in the Men's Memorial Hall the week before.

"You two will cop it if she finds out!" Cook laughed every time she heard dance music coming from the sitting-room. But, as she confided to her friend, the cook at Major Amos's house, "They are only young once, Gertie. Let them enjoy themselves!"

Outside, in the lovely, old walled garden, the gardener and his boy cut fresh flowers every day for the hall and dining-room and on summer evenings it was Agnes's task to help the old man set up a magnificent display of chrysanthemums and vast potted geraniums beside the French windows looking out onto the smooth lawns beyond. Here the dinner guests would sit to drink their after-dinner sherry while Agnes took note of all the ladies' latest finery and looked critically at the fit and finish of each expensive garment through the changing social seasons.

In her opinion, Agnes considered that she could match anything the ladies wore for flair and style and it was during this time of transition from girlhood into young womanhood that the great idea finally began to take shape. After a year with Mrs Sowerby, the good lady agreed reluctantly to let Agnes go but in the girl's little notebook were carefully penned the names and addresses of all those affluent guests she'd looked after so carefully during her days in service at the big house.

"Now I'm ready, Mum," she announced on her day off just before her notice was worked out. And she told Emily all about the small room to let just off Bancroft in Hitchin.

"It's above the Employment Exchange at the back of the building. You know, near Russells, that smelly old tannery just past the Police Station and the newspaper office. That's how I found it. In the Rooms to Let section. It's exactly right for a one-woman workroom!

I'm setting up on my own, Mum. We'll get my sewing machine down there next week and look for a comfortable sofa and a couple of pretty rugs. Then I'll run up some curtains for the fitting-alcove and I'll be in business! I've had lots of enquiries already from old customers at Spurrs. Mrs Sowerby knows a lot of them. There's a big demand for a dressmaker who will do alterations. The big shops only alter their own clothes."

The rest of the weekend was spent in excited discussions about the new venture and Emily could see that George was as keen as his daughter when he offered to build a cutting-out bench and make a sign for the door onto the street. By the end of the week, Agnes was ready for business. Adverts had been placed in the local paper and polite notes sent out to all old customers. Small, discreet cards were placed in shop windows in the town centre and even the Sun Hotel agreed to display one on their reception desk.

"We must encourage enterprise, young lady," the manager told Agnes with a smile as she presented him with the card. "And good luck to your new venture."

It was a very different Agnes who closed the cottage door quietly behind her on Monday morning. Quite suddenly she felt really grown up and she certainly looked it, for the long, dark hair of which her father was so proud had been cut short into a fashionable bob beneath the cloche hat pulled low down over her brow. A visit to Freeman, Hardy and Willis on the corner of the Market Square and the only decent shoe shop in Hitchin, had produced the T-bar court shoes with Louis heels that all her ladies at Spurrs and Sowerby's were now wearing and Agnes herself had made the smart, grey, dropped waistline dress and matching coat and the little silk scarf secured at the neck with a pretty brooch.

It was a mild, spring day as she coasted slowly down Hitchin Hill on the sit-up-and-beg bicycle she'd bought from the daughter of Holland's the fish-and-chip shop people in Queen Street and who had started her apprenticeship at Spurrs on the same day as Agnes.

As she turned into Bridge Street and pedalled purposefully over the Hiz into Sun Street past the Sun Hotel, where that nice manager had displayed her new advertisements and made her way carefully across Market Square, down the High Street past Moss's Corner and into Bancroft, Agnes knew that she would never again make this journey with the bursting anticipation she felt on this special day.

Ransome's, the lavender distillers, was just opening its doors for business and the sun shone warmly on the old brick wall of Seebohm's, the Quaker family who lived in the big house on the corner of Bancroft and Hermitage Road as Agnes began to climb the stairs behind the Employment Exchange.

As she turned the key in the door and stepped into the bright new workroom, she had the odd feeling that she was also stepping from her old life into another strange but exciting one.

CHAPTER
FOUR

"So, my dear, I hope you can help me."

Mrs Sowerby smiled as she opened the long box bearing a famous London store name and carefully took out the top layers of tissue paper.

"Oh, Mrs Sowerby. It's beautiful!"

Agnes stared in awe at the shimmering, black, bugle-beaded dress that the colonel's wife was holding up for her to see. It must have cost the earth, she thought to herself, as her new customer stepped behind the curtains to change into her latest purchase.

A few minutes later, Agnes was on her knees at Mrs Sowerby's feet, deftly pinning up the hem of the skirt lining.

"They should have done this at your final fitting, madam," the girl advised as Mrs Sowerby turned slowly round while Agnes continued her pinning.

"You're right, my dear, of course, but it was all done in such a rush," Mrs Sowerby explained with a little smile. "You know, the colonel and I were so surprised to get the invitation and there wasn't much time to choose the right dress. Imagine," she continued as Agnes helped her to slip out of the dress, "Lady Elizabeth Bowes-Lyon to wed the Duke of York! I always think of her as our Lady Elizabeth and of course the colonel knew her brother in the army."

It had been headline news in the papers for over a week now and the people living near St. Paul's Walden Bury were just as excited at the prospect of the pretty young girl from the large family down the road marrying into royalty, as if she had been a local village girl.

"We are so looking forward to the garden party at the palace. The colonel's brother will be there of course, with his wife and daughters."

Mrs Sowerby chattered happily on as Agnes finished the pinning-up and then helped her new customer out of the ankle-length dress before hanging it carefully on a padded hanger on the long rail behind her.

There were several other garments there awaiting alteration for their owners but none of these would be going to a royal garden party. Mostly they belonged to local women who had learned about Agnes's skills through their friends and neighbours. The rail was always half full and the work kept her busy every day and even on the last few weekends.

One very special outfit, designed and made by Agnes, hung separately and carefully covered by a dust-sheet at the end of the rail.

The low-waisted dress of deep-red chiffon with a handkerchief-point hemline had been commissioned by a young actress to wear at auditions for parts in new London productions.

"I need the right colour to set off my dark hair, Agnes," the young woman stated. "And something that's the latest fashion to make them sit up and take notice!"

So Agnes worked late every night for a week on the outfit, for hand-sewing the hundreds of beads on to the matching jacket was a painstaking task and she was thankful when the last one was attached to the delicate fabric.

Now the outfit was ready and Miss Flora Robson was coming in to the workshop for a final fitting that very afternoon.

"Why, it's lovely, Agnes!" she exclaimed as she studied herself from every angle in the long mirror. "Exactly what I had in mind and so right for me. What luck my little sister worked with you at Spurrs, otherwise I'd never have known about your new business."

It was as Agnes was folding the new dress and jacket before carefully placing it in the long box her customer brought with her, that Flora asked whether Agnes had ever thought of going into theatrical costume design?

"You mean as a career, Miss Robson?" she asked as she tied thin twine carefully around the box and placed the bill on top of it.

"Why of course, my dear," the actress replied, with the charming smile which would, in time, be seen in theatres and films around the world. "You are so creative with material and your cutting and fitting is first-class!"

Agnes had been in the audience with Shela Robson at several of the productions which her sister, Flora, had put on for The Barnstormers Theatre Company during the years the young actress had worked for The Shredded Wheat Company in Welwyn Garden City and now, it appeared, she was ready to spread her wings wider and fly further afield, for the London theatre beckoned.

"Give it some serious thought, Agnes," were Flora's parting words as she paid the modest bill and picked up the box ready to dash for the London train. "You have the talent to succeed and the theatre can always do with more of that!"

Once planted, the seed of the idea that she could someday be responsible for costumes in the professional theatre took root and Agnes began to visit the library to borrow books on costume design and in her few idle moments started a sketch-book of her own of designs for everything from revue to serious drama.

In the next few months, Agnes made up several more outfits for Flora Robson and always the rising young actress was delighted with the results and never failed to remind the girl of her potential for success in the theatre. It became, in time, a dream she would cherish in secret for that is what it remained — a dream that eventually gave way to the reality of earning her living in the present at the craft she loved.

The workroom had been open for just over a year and although things were slow to begin with, word soon spread that one of the Spurrs-trained girls was doing alterations at reasonable cost. Soon, a trickle became a steady stream as customers found their way up the steep stairs to the small room above the Employment Exchange. In later life, Agnes would think of that busy little workroom with its one window open onto the courtyard below and smile at the recollection of the heady combination of the scent of lavender from the distillery down the road and the sharp smell of the old tannery further down the alley, which in the summer months was sometimes hard to bear.

"You'll have to take on an assistant if things get any busier."

George watched his pretty daughter with concern as she danced around their small living-room showing off her new dress for the dance that evening and singing the latest song from the wireless, "Fascinating Rhythm".

"Never mind fascinating rhythm, my girl," interrupted George with a laugh. "It won't be so fascinating if you are ill from overwork, now will it?"

George was proud of his daughter's progress but worried about the long hours she spent alone in the workshop, sometimes working until nine or ten at night if there was a rush order to be completed. He had often cycled down into Hitchin in the dark, at the end of his own long, working day to accompany Agnes home along the lonely road up Hitchin Hill and past Priory Park.

Agnes did not mind the long hours bent over her sewing machine or hand-stitching at some delicate, fluted hem. She loved the work but she loved her independence even more. Agnes was her own boss and answerable to no-one. That's the way she liked it.

Emily called in to the workroom sometimes if she was out shopping in the town. It was convenient, for

Bancroft was only a few minutes' walk away from the old church of St. Mary's, flanked on one side by market stalls and on the other by the ancient tombstones of past worthies of the little market town.

Such an ordered life they had lived, thought Emily one sunny, August day as she picked her way through the leaning headstones. And so different from the bustle and noise of London where vast cemeteries waited patiently to receive the inhabitants of teeming streets and crowded tenements at the end of their hard, working lives. At least here, in this small place, people lived longer in retirement even though they must rely completely on their children or on charity for a living. With only one child Emily knew both she and George would have to keep working into old age.

She sighed and shrugged off these depressing thoughts as she turned into Bancroft and walked slowly along the busy street until she reached the street door at the foot of the stairs up to the workroom. It stood wide open to let some air circulate in the room above and it was as she climbed slowly upwards that Emily heard the deep tones of a man talking to Agnes.

As she walked quietly into the sunny room, Emily realised that she knew the young man who stood by the window laughing down at her daughter's animated face.

"Oh, Mum!" Agnes looked up quickly and laughed nervously as she patted her smooth hair in a gesture that Emily knew so well. Agnes was embarrassed.

"You know Albert, don't you, Mum?"

"Well I should think so, after six years with Mrs Ponsonby," replied Emily with a little edge to her voice that made Agnes blush even more. "And what are you doing here, young man?" she demanded, looking pointedly at the smiling, self-confident face of the colonel's manservant-cum-chauffeur.

"Just called in for madam's alterations, Mrs Thomas. She's in London today but she needs the things for the weekend."

Then, with a cheeky grin, the chauffeur picked up the parcel from the cutting-out table and with a cheerful nod at both women went clattering down the stairs two at a time singing at the top of his voice, "Show Me The Way To Go Home".

Emily watched as the big saloon car pulled away from the kerb and began its journey up High Street and across Market Square on its way back to Gosmore. Then she turned to her red-faced daughter.

"And how long has this been going on?"

"Oh, Mum! Albert's alright really," the girl replied, trying to cover her confusion with a nervous laugh. "I can't stop him coming for the work, can I?" she added, glancing at her mother's straight face.

"No, dear, you can't, if Mrs P. sends him but you don't want to stand any nonsense from him either. He's a sharp one is that young man. And did you know," Emily asked quietly, "that he's walking out with Lily?"

"But he told me that they'd fallen out and she's more interested in the butcher's boy!"

"Not true, Agnes!" Emily retorted. "Lily thinks he's the cat's whiskers by all accounts. Poor girl," she added thoughtfully and then more deliberately, looking at her daughter's concerned face, "he's just two-timing you both, it seems, Agnes. Not to be trusted, that chap!"

No more was said on the subject but over the next few days, when George remarked more than once how quiet Agnes was, Emily kept her own counsel and hoped things would blow over. No sense in giving her George any more worry, she thought. His gout always played him up in the hot weather and quite suddenly, the fit energetic man she'd married seemed somehow to have grown old before her eyes. Poor man, she thought sadly, looking with concern at his thinning hair and narrow, lined face. You've had a hard life.

Within a few weeks, Agnes was back to her old cheerful self again and as Emily watched her practising the new dance craze, the Charleston, before the next Saturday night dance, she knew the girl's innate common sense had overcome whatever infatuation she'd had for the unsuitable Albert.

Agnes continued to work long hours in her little business but as the days went by and Albert began to fade from her mind, something else began to take root in his place.

It was a few weeks later when Agnes closed the workshop early, at one o'clock, and caught the bus back to the village in time to meet her mother out of work. While she waited for her in the large kitchen, talking to Cook, the green baize door opened suddenly and Albert swung in carrying a silver tray.

In the next few minutes, Agnes told him exactly what she thought of him and although he tried to bluster his way out of the situation, by the time she'd finished, the self-sufficient girl felt much better than she had done for some weeks.

It was not that Agnes had really believed all those flattering things Albert told her on his frequent visits to the workroom. It was just that she'd allowed herself to enjoy it and actually began to look forward to his visits. How could she have been so silly about a good-looking, silver-tongued rogue?

Cook disappeared into the pantry when Albert arrived in the kitchen and she wisely stayed there until he retreated again through the baize door.

"Good for you, Agnes love!" Cook beamed, wiping floury hands on her big, white apron. "That young man has all the girls in a right tizzy. If the missus knew he'd get the sack. And poor Lily's heartbroken," she added as she handed Mrs Thomas's pretty daughter a cup of tea.

"Is she here today, Cook?" asked Agnes, sipping her tea appreciatively.

"Oh yes, but she's laid up with a nasty cold, so the missus said," Cook replied with a heavy sigh. Then she added sharply, "The poor girl's been really down over all this, I can tell you. And she's a nice little thing. So willing and all. Taken quite a while to learn the ropes but madam says she's improving at last."

In Lily's small, attic room, Agnes looked down at the white face on the pillow. "Why don't you tell her, Lily? You'll have to sooner or later and I think she'd appreciate it sooner."

"Because she'll dismiss me without a reference, that's why!" And the young maid started crying again at the hopelessness of it all.

Lily was pregnant with Albert's child and the young chauffeur denied that he was the father.

"But Mrs P. will have to know some time," Agnes said gently as Lily rubbed at her red, swollen eyes with the edge of the sheet. "Then she will see that you are looked after. That Albert must be brought to heel, the cheeky devil." And Agnes thought of how he had hung around the workroom ever since they'd first met at the dance, pestering her to go out with him. She had not liked his cocky attitude and, now that she was over him, she admitted to herself that she'd liked even less his wandering hands. Ugh!

"He's a real ladies' man and no mistake," Emily confided to George that night after Agnes had left to visit her friend at The Bull.

"Good thing our girl's got her head screwed on right, that's all I can say, lass," replied George, shaking his newspaper into place. "Could have been her, you know!"

"Oh, no, not our Agnes, George. She's got her sights set on better things than marriage and babies. Why — she's only twenty!"

"And Lily's just eighteen," replied George heavily. "Well, he'll have to marry her, that's all. Otherwise it's the naughty girls' home for her and no job prospects afterwards."

A month later, Mrs Ponsonby reluctantly informed Lily that she'd have to leave before the growing bulge beneath the white apron became too obvious.

"Why don't you marry him, my dear?" the colonel had asked the girl more than once after he was told the news. "He's admitted he's the father and he's willing, now that he knows his job depends on it."

"But that's just it, sir," Lily replied tearfully. "If he marries me now, it'll only be to save his job."

Just after Whitsun the next year, Lily's baby was born in the big, old Victorian house known in Hitchin as "the naughty girls' home". Six weeks later, she signed the adoption papers and handed over the little blue-eyed girl to a young couple from London.

"She'll be well cared for, Lily," Agnes said gently as she led the weeping girl down the steps of the old house. "They seem like good people. Come on now, don't cry any more."

As they reached the bottom of the steps, the taxi carrying the baby and her new parents was just drawing away on the short journey to the railway station and Lily clung to Agnes again in another fit of weeping until long after it was out of sight.

Back in the workroom, Agnes put the kettle on for tea and told Lily about her new idea.

"I've been thinking about taking on an assistant for some time and, as you can see, there's plenty of work for both of us."

Lily looked round at the full rail of garments all down one side of the room and then at Agnes. The tears threatened again as she saw the concern on the older girl's face and as Agnes hastily poured the tea, she wailed, "But where am I going to live? I have to be out of the home by the end of the week, now that the baby's . . . gone."

Agnes put an extra spoonful of sugar in the girl's tea and then, stirring it quickly as if trying to ward off any more tears, said quickly, "You can stay with us at home for a while. After that, if you like, you can move in with my friend Belle and me. We'll soon be renting rooms just down the road from here. It will be much more convenient for us both to live in the town and Belle can walk to her teaching post easily from there."

Things were a bit cramped in Agnes's little room in the cottage but Lily soon settled in to the family routine and she was so willing to help in every way she could that Emily declared it was like having two daughters instead of one. Then she sighed as she remembered her first little one who had died from diphtheria in her first year and the others who were still-born, one after the other until at last Agnes arrived safely after seven years of marriage.

Neither George nor Emily liked the idea of Agnes moving into rooms with Belle and Lily but at twenty-one, they knew she could do as she pleased and although this did not stop the heartache, they both realised that their support would do more to keep their daughter near than any amount of opposition.

"Better than London, lass," George reminded Emily more than once. And she agreed, for the new move meant Agnes was only a twopenny bus ride away from the village.

As the summer months turned slowly into a mild and misty autumn and Lily settled into her new job and her new home, Agnes began to realise that she had taken on quite a heavy responsibility. The younger girl was not exactly simple-minded, just "not very quick on the uptake", as she told Emily on numerous occasions. But Lily's work improved almost daily and although Agnes gave her straightforward jobs like hemming and pressing to do, she knew her assistant was keen to do bigger things.

One of Agnes's best customers was the wife of the editor of the local newspaper and a near neighbour in Bancroft. Since their first meeting two years previously, this lady had produced first twins and more recently, a new baby boy.

"Would you consider making the twins' dresses, Miss Thomas?" the editor's wife asked one day. "Reginald likes to see the girls dressed nicely and I've seen some of the work you did at Spurrs. Such beautiful smocking and so well finished."

Later, Agnes discussed the request with Lily who was still sighing and sad over the sudden death of her film hero, Rudolph Valentino and had sung "Bye-Bye, Blackbird" incessantly for the past week until Agnes, in exasperation told her in no uncertain terms, to, for goodness sake, change the tune before everyone went mad!

To her surprise, Lily stopped the singing in mid-flow to reply eagerly, "I can do smocking, Agnes. That's one thing I'm any good at. Embroidery too. The nuns taught us all those things at the convent."

Agnes knew Lily was an orphan but had never realised that she'd been brought up in a convent orphanage. Poor girl, what a sad start in life, she thought as she looked across the workroom at the dark head bent over a small scrap of material on which the girl was demonstrating her smocking skills.

The result was far better than Agnes had expected from someone who had been accused of having "such clumsy fingers" by Mrs Ponsonby.

"Why, that's excellent, Lily. As good as I can manage any day!"

The compliment brought a rare blush to Lily's pale cheeks but as Agnes handed her the newly-finished, pink silk dresses for the twins and the girl began to pick up the delicate material in an intricate smocking pattern, a new confidence seemed to grow in her with every stitch.

"Don't strain your eyes too much over that, Lily," murmured Agnes gently. "You can finish it tomorrow, you know. It's not being collected until the end of the week."

But Lily had found her niche in the little business and soon all the baby work was put aside for her, for customers began to ask for her services as her skills became known around the little market town.

Even Mrs Ponsonby asked Lily to make and embroider half-a-dozen dresses for her new grand-daughter, born just after Christmas.

"Who would have thought it?" the good lady confided in Agnes one day when Lily was out buying silk thread from the wholesalers. "When she came to me she was hopeless!"

52

"Yes, madam," replied Agnes with a small smile at the expression on her customer's face, "but that was because Lily had no interest in patching sheets and darning socks. She needs to create things. And see what she's achieved," she announced proudly, indicating a low clothes rack on which hung half-a-dozen tiny dresses, all beautifully smocked or embroidered.

"Is she . . . er . . . keeping herself to herself?" whispered Mrs Ponsonby delicately, although there was no one else in the workroom apart from herself and Mrs Thomas's girl. "What an upset that all was. Albert has left our employ, of course. The last my husband heard of him, that scallywag was working as a bookie's runner somewhere near Letchworth. No doubt charming some other young girl out of her senses, I should imagine."

Agnes avoided Mrs Ponsonby's eyes as she began to wrap up the barathea skirt she'd just completed for the Ponsonby family holiday in Scotland.

"Well, Lily has a regular young man now, madam. I believe he has a steady job as a groundsman at the Grammar School and he seems to be very fond of her. But," Agnes added hastily as she saw her customer's eyebrows rise, "I make sure she's home at a reasonable hour. This one's a decent chap, I'm sure."

Satisfied, Mrs Ponsonby smiled and nodded goodbye as Lily came panting up the stairs and into the workroom.

"Would you ever want to go back into service, Lily?" Agnes asked casually as the girl laid out her purchases carefully along the ironing-board.

Startled by the question, Lily dropped the brown paper bag of assorted mother-of-pearl buttons and swung round with such an anxious expression on her face that Agnes hastened to add, "It's alright — Mrs P. has found another girl, Lily!" Then, seeing the panic still on the girl's face, added quickly, "And I need you here. You're good for business!"

CHAPTER
FIVE

"I don't know what we shall do, Agnes!"

Emily sat at the kitchen table warming her hands round a cup of tea. Agnes looked at the drawn face of her mother and decided that she didn't know either. She tried to sound cheerful as she reassured the older woman.

"It's alright, Mum. I'm bringing in enough for the three of us now. We'll manage somehow."

Yes. Agnes would work until her eyes stung and her back ached from the constant bending over the old treadle sewing-machine and always she knew she would never desert her elderly parents. But the independent spirit which had carried her through the first hard weeks and months in the fledgling business railed bitterly against fate as she thought of her father lying helpless in the little bedroom above.

"We must get him down here, Mum. We'll make up a bed in the front room and keep the fire going in there. It will be easier to look after him that way."

While Agnes and her mother were at work the previous afternoon George's workmates had found him lying collapsed and unable to move or speak, on the floor of the administration office at Henlow Camp where he had been painting all week.

"It looks like a stroke, Mrs Thomas," the old doctor sympathised with the distraught woman as her husband was carried up the narrow stairs and placed gently on the big, brass bedstead. "Just keep him warm and comfortable, my dear. There's not much more we can do now."

Within a week, Agnes had moved back into the little cottage and Belle and Lily had found a new flatmate to take her place. Agnes tried hard not to think of her old, spacious room in Hermitage Road or the freedom she'd given up when she moved back but the dreadful, trapped feeling persisted and was firmly repressed each time she closed the workshop door behind her and ran for the bus back to her old home.

George was nearly seventy and although the tiny insurance policy would mature early in the new year, the only other income must now come from his wife and daughter. Emily was well over sixty herself and finding it increasingly hard to work the hours required up at the big house.

Christmas in that year of 1925 was a quiet affair, with the little family making the best of things in the tiny, front room where George was propped up on a narrow bed lent by the landlord of The Bull. "Keep it as long as necessary, Mrs Thomas," the good man said cheerfully as he put the iron frame together for his old friend.

But the words had an ominous ring to them. What did he mean by necessary? Would George ever be able to walk again and how could he manage if he was unable to speak properly?

It was on her first day back at work after Christmas that the colonel asked to see Emily in his study.

"Has your husband been in work all his life, Mrs Thomas?" he wanted to know.

"Since he was thirteen, sir," replied Emily with some spirit. Then added, "And none worked harder!" But her eyes filled with tears again as she thought of her George lying helpless on his bed and alone until she could get back to him.

"Then," the colonel spoke gently to the grey-haired, distraught woman, "we must apply for the new pension the Government has just brought in. It's called the old-age pension, and your husband should be eligible to draw it. He is over seventy I take it?"

"He'll be seventy next month, sir," replied Emily slowly, wondering what this pension was that the colonel was talking about. "And I've been on at him for the last five years to stop but he always said he'd work as long as possible. Now this is the result." Then, to her horror, and in front of the colonel and all, Emily felt the tears begin to slide uncontrollably down her cheeks yet again.

Three weeks later, Agnes joined the queue at the General Post Office in Brand Street to collect her father's pension. It was a pitifully small sum, just a few shillings a week, but it meant all the difference to the overstretched budget of her mother's little household.

"If I can put in just a few hours a week, we'll manage, Agnes," she declared as her daughter put the first week's money down on the kitchen table.

Agnes shook her head at her mother's stubbornness. "I told you, Mum, there's no need for it. You'll be ill yourself soon."

But Emily would not hear of Agnes paying in to the household more than the cost of her own board and lodging. "You need to put any extra back into the business, child," were her last words on the subject before she took George's tea in to him.

For most of the time that Emily was at work, George slept but as soon as he heard the front door open and her quick steps through the little house, he was wide awake and needing her attention. He was not a heavy man, but it was sometimes more than Emily could manage alone, to turn and wash him regularly and she liked to keep him clean and fresh in the narrow bed. So it was with help from poor, shell-shocked Jim from The Bull that she managed to care for the loving husband who had cared for her and Agnes for so many years.

After a few months, during which George was as helpless as a baby and completely dependent on others for everything in his life, his speech began slowly to return but the left side of his body was paralysed from the waist down and his left arm was practically useless.

Agnes felt guilty about leaving her mother on the one evening a week when Emily urged her to go out with her friends.

"Come on, Agnes," beseeched Belle, looking down with concern at her friend's too-thin figure bent over the sewing-machine. "You'll work yourself to death and then where will they be?"

58

The girls had joined the Hitchin Tennis Club in Portmill Lane the previous summer. Not particularly for the tennis, but as Belle laughed, "for the dances".

Agnes found to her surprise that most of the other members were young people about her own age from middle-class homes who didn't have to work for their living. A few had mothers or older sisters who were her customers. And some were downright snobs and fond of looking down their noses at those new girls from outside their own circle.

"Take no notice, Agnes. We pay our subs just like them!" Belle exclaimed defiantly after her friend overheard a catty remark from a rather plump, young lady and her spotty partner in the pairs competition. But there were others who went out of their way to befriend the two girls and try to make them feel welcome. One of them was Bernie, who always looked so dashing in spotless tennis whites, striped club blazer and a dickie-bow tie for evening socials.

Agnes quickly decided that he was very pleasant, although not really her type and that he probably didn't have to work either. Oh well, she thought wearily as she walked slowly up the hill past Priory Park one evening. Some people have all the luck.

It was late autumn and Agnes was feeling quite sorry for herself, having missed the bus home yet again after working well past closing time. It was as she quickened her steps past the dark expanse of the park on her right that she became aware of the sound of an engine behind her. Then someone shouted her name and she turned to see a motor-bike and sidecar drawing up to the kerb beside her. It was almost dark and although Agnes was not usually frightened at the prospect of the lonely walk home, she was not looking forward to doing it on her own all through the coming winter months. Dad had always cycled down to meet her in the early days at the workshop.

"Hi, Agnes! Want a lift?"

At first she did not recognise the tall, uniformed figure as he swung his leg over the bike and came round onto the path to greet her. She took in the peaked cap, khaki jacket and breeches, the polished Sam Browne belt and the leather boots and gaiters. Then she saw the sign on the side of the yellow sidecar and in the same moment recognised the smiling face of Bernie. He was an AA patrolman!

"You should have seen your face, Agnes," Bernie laughed as he drank his third cup of tea in Emily's little kitchen later. Then he added gleefully, "Some of us also have to work for a living, you know. It's not all beer and skittles for me or a monthly allowance from daddy either."

Agnes learned a valuable lesson that night and vowed that never again would she take people at face value.

"A posh accent doesn't mean much these days," George managed slowly after listening to the tale of the snobs at the club and Agnes's surprise at Bernie's job. "There's plenty out of work now, lass, and some of those never expected to be in the same boat as working men."

It was true enough, for the news in George's daily newspaper and on the cat's-whiskers wireless Jim had set up for the old man, became daily more alarming.

60

Miners in South Wales were striking for better pay and conditions and many lost their jobs during that year of social unrest fostered by the unions.

"God knows where it will all end, Em," George sighed and closed his eyes. He could not bear to think of his brother's family back in Wales, suffering and half-starved. He had not seen them for some years but blood-ties are strong and George wished with all his heart that he could do something to help them.

"Try not to worry yourself, my love," Emily urged him after one of his anguished outbursts. "There's nothing we can do. It's up to the Government now."

Agnes's friendship with Bernie blossomed over the next few months and although the lift home on dark evenings may have had something to do with it, she nevertheless enjoyed his company at the club for he was a good dancer and soon they were regular partners both at the supper dances and on the tennis courts. So when Bernie proposed, Agnes was not too surprised.

"Will you, Agnes? Think about it I mean," pleaded Bernie after producing a small garnet and pearl ring during the interval at Saturday's dance. Afterwards, as she allowed him to kiss her goodnight, he begged her again to marry him.

Gently, Agnes turned him down, explaining that she was very fond of him but that was not enough to even become engaged. Bernie was optimistic as he climbed back onto the smart combination motor-bike and sidecar.

"I'll ask you again, sweetheart — by the end of the month. The ring will keep until then!"

"You could do a lot worse, my girl," was George's opinion, unasked for but nevertheless received with much heart-searching by his daughter. "That lad's going places. He's told me he won't be a patrolman for ever. He's got his sights set on a car sales business. That's where the money is, he reckons."

Later, when she and Agnes were alone after George had been settled for the night, Emily listened quietly as the girl assured her mother that she would not be getting married until she was at least thirty and then only if she really loved the man.

"That's the problem, Mum," she explained. "Bernie's nice and good fun without being pushy. But I don't love him. I can't imagine living with him and as for . . . well, you know what I mean, don't you?"

Emily knew only too well. She also knew that somehow her young daughter considered herself to be responsible for her parents in their old age. Oh, if only there had been others to share the burden. And now Agnes had turned down that steady chap and who knows how many more chances would pass her by until she was an old maid and all alone?

No amount of reasoning would change Agnes's mind however and not long after the month was up she was catching the bus home again and although she missed the lifts from Bernie and his combination and still sometimes met him at the club, she knew she had made the right decision.

"How could I have married a chap who wears a brown, tweed suit with a bowler hat, Belle?" Agnes laughed, not unkindly, about the way Bernie was dressed when she last saw him walking out with the girl from the Post Office.

A few months later, a wedding announcement appeared in the local newspaper and Emily and Agnes stood in the crowd to watch as Bernie and his new bride came out of St. Mary's church to be photographed against a background of weeping willows beside the old river Hiz.

"No regrets then?" questioned Emily quietly as the wedding car, bedecked with ribbons, glided away from the church to a tasteful reception at the Sun Hotel.

"No, Mum!" exclaimed Agnes, smiling at the anxious look on her mother's face. "I told you. He wasn't the one for me. Oh, I just hope they'll be happy and have lots of little combinations!"

Then she changed the subject quickly as she noticed a tall, dark-haired man dressed in a well-cut, double-breasted suit, grey Homburg hat and pearl-grey spats strolling towards them across the crowded Market Square. The well-dressed figure, looking, in Agnes's opinion, completely out of place in a small market town, carried a silver-topped malacca cane in one fashionably-gloved hand.

"How is your husband these days, Mrs Thomas?" the man asked as he tipped his hat and smiled politely down at the two women.

Agnes noticed that one of the man's front teeth was gold-tipped and that the pearl of the pin fastening his cravat was bigger than a blackberry. Then she realised that she was staring and looked away, trying to avoid the man's amused gaze from behind his steel-rimmed spectacles. She felt the colour burn in her cheeks as her mother introduced her blushing daughter to the foreign-looking stranger.

"You remember Jim's pal, don't you, Agnes? Ted, this is my girl Agnes. All grown up since you were last home, I expect."

"Pleased to meet you, my dear," returned Ted smoothly and then, giving a small bow which somehow made Agnes feel very special, added quickly, "but I mustn't keep you, ladies. I'll be at The Bull for the next few weeks so I expect we'll meet again. I'm home to see my mother and brothers. Goodbye for now."

Then the tall man was gone, leaving behind him a whiff of perfumed tobacco smoke from the small, black cheroot he was smoking.

"Fancy Ted Winch turning up again, George!"

Emily was preparing supper in the little kitchen and George was fiddling with the cat's-whiskers radio again, trying to get the latest news about Malcolm Campbell's attempt to break the land-speed record.

"I quite thought we'd seen the last of him," Emily chatted on, as she sat down and reached for the teapot. "With his poor wife being taken so suddenly with the flu epidemic after the war. Of course, his old mother still lives in the village and I believe there's a half-brother and sister somewhere."

All through the meal, Agnes kept quiet and learned more about that dark-haired chap they'd met outside the church. He had, apparently, married very young. "Oh, about eighteen or so, Agnes," Emily remembered being told by Mr Weston. "She was cook up at the Grange before the war and he was a stable lad there."

"A stable lad? Only a stable lad, Mum?" asked Agnes incredulously, thinking about the expensively-suited Ted. And that cravat pin!

"Yes, dear. A stable lad. Anyway," continued her mother, smiling at Agnes's astonishment, "then the war came and he joined up and went off to France. Jim only saw him two or three times after that and of course once more at his poor wife's funeral. She was quite a bit older than him though. About thirty I think."

"But where's he been since then?" Agnes asked curiously. Somehow the stable lad image did not fit in with the man she'd met earlier.

"He went back to Paris in 1919 and learned to speak French well and then, when he left the army, got a position in the British Embassy. Passport Office, I think. After that, so I'm told, he sold Bacardi Rum all over Europe for a company in Paris. Stayed with them for six years. I expect that's how he learned to dress so well, Agnes."

"And now he looks like a real Froggy," laughed Agnes as she began to clear the table for washing up. Then she added thoughtfully, "But he's a bit out of place here, Mum, isn't he?"

Then Ted Winch was forgotten as Emily and her daughter hurried to get ready in time to see the latest, talking Al Jolson film in the newly-opened picturehouse, The Playhouse in Market Street next to the Corn Exchange in Hitchin.

"Enjoy yourselves now, don't worry about me," called George as they hurried out to catch the last bus down the hill. "Young Jim's coming over for a game of poker."

Emily couldn't help but see that Agnes was interested in Ted Winch but she did her best not to encourage the girl, for she reasoned that soon he would be off back to Paris and their lives would return to normal again. She did not, however, reckon on Agnes's single-mindedness and as the weeks slipped by and there was no sign of Ted's departure it became a regular thing for Agnes and Belle to sit together in the lounge-bar at The Bull. Sometimes, Jim collected George in an old, wicker bath-chair and wheeled him over the road for a pint of bitter. Once or twice they persuaded Emily herself to take a glass of sherry with them.

Each time, Ted was there, treating the locals to pints of ale and the landlord to a brandy. His own tipple was whisky and Agnes watched fascinated as he downed several every night to no apparent ill-effect.

"Apparently they drink wine like water in France," Belle stated one evening, eyeing the young potman's friend at the bar ordering yet another round of drinks. Then she added quietly, so only Agnes caught the quick words, "Jim's told me quite a bit about Ted. He said that he had a bad time in the trenches. Got caught in gas attacks several times and had personally to shoot wounded horses from his gun-carriage. In Ypres that was, Jim said. Ted thought more of those animals than of any human being. When Jim was invalided out, he left Ted in a field hospital where they found he had a damaged lung. Still, he survived the war more or less intact. More than can be said for poor Jim, though."

Agnes looked at Ted Winch in a new light after that whispered explanation from Belle and although she did not care for his drinking, she tried to understand why he did it.

"Don't get carried away, lass," advised George as he watched his daughter getting more and more interested in the visitor from Paris. "He'll not change now at his age."

"Why, Dad, he's only thirty-one. And think what he's been through," replied Agnes sadly. Already she was making excuses for this man who fascinated her and George and Emily waited anxiously for him to leave their girl alone and go back to his life in France.

Another girl had been taken on in the workshop, for Agnes and Lily could no longer cope with all the work coming in.

"I'm so thankful to get this job, Lily," confided Dolly on her first day. "My dad's out of work along with half his mates now that Billings has cut back. It was a case of last in, first out there."

"Agnes is glad to have you, I'm sure, Dolly," replied the younger girl. "Didn't you train with her at Spurrs?"

Dolly nodded as she bent her fair head to thread black Sylko through the sewing machine needle. "Yes, that's true but she's a much better dressmaker than I'll ever be. I'm quite good at cutting out though," she added hastily as Lily began to sing the latest song from a London show. "Among My Souvenirs," she warbled

67

and Agnes smiled as she caught the last few words on her way up the steep stairs to her little kingdom.

So the little workroom was now a complete unit with each girl specialising in her own skill and all three working happily together. It was a small, safe world where hard work brought its own reward but in the big world beyond the workroom, a million or more were out of work and the queues for poor-relief grew longer. In Wales and the North-East, children went hungry and their fathers marched to London in a protest that eventually was to take the Prince of Wales to visit them with vague promises that "something must be done".

Every night after supper, Agnes listened to her parents discussing the worsening situation.

"'A land fit for heroes,' they said," declared Emily angrily, "and look at those poor lads now, with wives and bairns to feed and a pittance coming in. God help them, that's all I can say."

"The T.U.C. supported the General Strike, Em," George stated, as his red-haired wife, with a temper to match, began to cut up his tripe and onions into the small pieces he could manage with one hand. "And look where that got them. The poor devils are back down the pits now working longer hours for the same pay. And now a general strike is illegal. Baldwin must act soon, or there'll be riots in every town, mark my words."

Listening to all this Agnes found herself wondering where Ted Winch would fit in if he decided not to return to Paris. He knew no other trade, apart from selling wine abroad, than stable work but somehow, she could not imagine the fastidious chap she was beginning to know better every week becoming a stable lad again.

Agnes was impatient with herself over her feelings for Ted but at the same time she knew she was intrigued more than she cared to admit. He was so different from the other men she knew, most of them little more than boys in comparison. Some were thorough gentlemen, though, as she had more than once remarked to Belle, "still too wet behind the ears for my taste." Others were true sons of the soil, rough and hardworking with weathered faces and hands to match. Many a time after the village hop down at the Memorial Hall, Agnes had limped home suffering the effects of the clod-hopping efforts of some of these lads. "Good-natured they may be, Mum," she complained as she eased her shoes from bruised feet, "but dancers — never!"

Agnes had only danced with Ted Winch two or three times. He did not, he explained in her ear as he guided her carefully around the floor, care too much for dancing and would rather sit at the bar and watch the others.

In fact, Ted was watching Agnes most of the time. Now and again she would catch him observing her through those continental-style spectacles he wore occasionally and once he intervened when two country boys asked her to dance at the same time.

"This one's mine I think, my dear," he announced quietly as he put an arm around her slim waist and, taking her hand, led her away into a foxtrot.

Agnes was silent all through that dance but by the end of it, the attraction she felt for this older, more worldly man had developed into an overwhelming love that never left her for the rest of her life.

On the following Saturday, Ted met Agnes out of work and together they walked back to the village through Priory Park. In the fading light of an early summer evening, they stopped and Ted kissed her for the first time. Before the walk was over Agnes had accepted his proposal of marriage.

"We'll get the ring next week," Ted assured her as Agnes opened the front door to break the news to her parents. "Then we can get married in August."

Later, as she lay in bed unable to sleep, Agnes suddenly remembered her little bed in London as she listened to Emily and George talking in low voices in the room below. As then, they were still concerned for their only child but now it was for a different reason. Their Agnes was finally leaving home and this time it was for good.

PART TWO

1926 to 1940

CHAPTER
SIX

"Bedford, Agnes? You'll be living in Bedford?"

Emily tried to hide her dismay as she looked at her daughter's happy face.

"Yes, Mum. Ted's just started his new job and he's been given Bedfordshire, Northamptonshire and Buckinghamshire to work. We decided that Bedford would be the most central town."

Emily took a deep breath before asking her next question.

"But . . . what about the business, child?"

"Ted's taking care of everything," Agnes quickly reassured her mother who she could see was clearly shocked by the sudden announcement of the imminent move to a town which was a great deal further than a twopenny bus ride away. "He says you are not to worry. Dolly's parents have offered to buy me out and then they'll just get another girl in to share the work."

Emily sat down quickly and Agnes came round the table to put her arms around the thin shoulders of her mother.

"It's alright, Mum. This time I'm sure. And anyway," she continued hastily as she saw the tears in the older woman's eyes, "Bedford's not that far away. Ted says he'll be having a new company car so we'll be able to visit often."

But it won't be the same, thought Emily bleakly. Then looking again at Agnes's happy smile she knew she must make the best of things once again. Ted was not a bad sort really, though she'd heard the tales about his drinking from both George and Belle. He'd probably settle down once he was married and if he made their Agnes a good husband what more could they ask?

"It's to be a very quiet do, George," Emily confided later. "Agnes says it will be at the registry office and then a nice meal at The Sun before they go off to their new flat." And then she sighed over the pastry she was rolling out for a beef and kidney pie and wiped a floury hand across her eyes, trying to hide the tears from her George, who had enough to bear as it was.

Ted's new job, at The Shredded Wheat Company in Welwyn Garden City, where Flora Robson had worked before going off to London, had been secured despite strong competition from other, more experienced men in the wholesale cereal trade.

"It'll be the gift of the gab that got him there!"

Belle was helping out in the bar of The Bull one Saturday in late August, for this was Agnes's wedding day and the landlord was acting as a witness at the ceremony in Hitchin.

"Did you see the car, Belle? It's brand new and apart from the Colonel's Bentley and the Vicar's old Morris, it's the only other car in the village."

Belle heard the envy in Jim's voice and reaching over quickly to take a pint pot from the boy's shaking hand

74

she replied so quietly that the couple of old men playing dominoes in the public bar could not hear the words. "Not for much longer, Jim. They'll be out of it by nightfall and Agnes will be Mrs Ted Winch. Fancy! She always told me she'd not get spliced before thirty. It must be real love, that's all I can say!" And Belle polished away at the already sparkling beer-mug even harder and thought about her friend and how she would miss her now that she was a married woman living miles away in a strange town. Oh well! Perhaps her own chap would pop the question soon and then she'd be off like a shot from this small community where nothing much seemed to happen from one year's end to another. Tony was a deputy headmaster after all and with good prospects of better things to come.

At The Sun Hotel, where two years earlier Agnes had asked the manager to display her little card about the new workshop, the wedding luncheon was nearly over and, to give him his due, Ted only drank wine during the course of it. Emily and George sat watching their daughter's shining eyes and listened to the talk and laughter between the landlord of The Bull and the other witness, Ted's younger brother, Harry.

"Time you thought about retirement, Emily," Ted observed, looking keenly through steel-rimmed spectacles at his new mother-in-law. "The pensions have improved quite a lot this year and Agnes and I can make you a small allowance now I've secured this new job."

"We'll see about that, lad." George's voice rose above his wife's as she started to reply. "We've always been self-sufficient and I can't see there's any need for change now."

Emily looked down at her plate and thought about the new flat full of the lovely furniture Agnes's new husband had bought. Nothing in Hitchin was good enough for his wife, he'd declared to anyone who was prepared to listen, so most of it came from Maples, the big London shop. And now everything was ready for them in their comfortable home in De Parys Avenue, just down the road from Bedford Park.

Soon the meal was over and with the waiter tipped generously and the bill settled quickly, they all piled into the big, brown Ford with "The Shredded Wheat Company" emblazoned down each side as Ted pulled on his new driving gloves that matched the car and with a cheerful wave at the smiling manager drove back up Hitchin Hill and on to Gosmore for a final drink at The Bull before leaving.

"Goodbye, Agnes," whispered Belle as she gave her friend a last hug. "Be happy."

"Goodbye, child," murmured Emily as her daughter climbed into the car beside her new husband.

"And good luck to you both," added George from his old wheelchair at the kerbside.

Already, they thought, Agnes is different. This one day has changed her for ever and from now on the little cottage will seem a quieter and a lonelier place.

For Agnes, life was new and exciting. She was mistress in her own home and Ted was faithful and loving. Too loving at times, she thought to herself, smiling over the washing-up after he had left for work

76

and glad that no one could see her suddenly burning cheeks. Oh well, perhaps he'd calm down when the honeymoon period was over.

The only thing Agnes had taken from her little business was her old Singer treadle sewing machine and during the long hours when Ted was on the road calling on customers all over the Home Counties, she made good use of her spare time. In the first month of married life, she sewed all the new curtains and cushion covers for the flat and, in the second, secured a commission from Gladys Clayton's Outfitters, on the corner of Tavistock Street and Harpur Street in Bedford, to make up babies' dresses for 6d a time. Bundles of them now lay on a shelf in the spare bedroom and a row of finished garments hung from a rail above, just like in her old workshop.

"You should ask for 9d at least, Agnes," exclaimed Ted when she told him the terms of the contract. "And a shilling if you can get it!" he added cheerfully. But Agnes was content just to be sewing again and each week she was adding to a small nest-egg in an account she'd opened at the General Post Office just around the corner from Clayton's in Dame Alice Street.

True to his word, and despite protests from George and Emily, Ted posted off a one pound postal order for them every Friday evening and Emily thankfully cut her working hours down to two a day.

"Your father is grateful, of course," she confided to Agnes on one of their visits, "but he is a proud man and it grieves him to accept charity from anyone."

"But it's from us, Mum. We're not just anyone!" And Agnes looked closely at her mother and saw that the lovely red hair was fast losing its colour and that soon it would be a washed-out pale shadow of the hair she had loved to brush as a child. Then she looked again at her father as he sat propped up in the old bath-chair and she could see that he was struggling and suspected that his cheerful manner was reserved only for their visits.

"Why not consider moving a bit closer to us, Mum?" Agnes asked gently before turning wearily away to fill the kettle again for tea. "There's bound to be something suitable in Bedford and I could give you a hand now and again."

"No, child, no more moves for your father and me. Besides, he has his friends here and a regular lifestyle of sorts. Things are better now that I work less hours. So you see, you are giving us a hand already."

It was just before Easter the following year when Emily received the news that she and George were to be grandparents.

"I'm two months gone, Mum, and I feel so sick every blessed morning. Ugh! It's horrible."

"Why, that will wear off soon, child," Emily reassured the pale-faced girl who looked so sorry for herself. Then she added quietly, "And what does that husband of yours say? Is he pleased?"

"Oh, Mum, of course he's pleased. Although," Agnes sighed, "he did say that another year on our own would have been better management."

"Well, he should have thought about that sooner," Emily replied a little tartly and then patted Agnes's hand as she looked up in surprise at her mother's sharp tone.

Ted had appeared pleased when she first told him the results of Dr Chillingworth's examination but that evening he stayed on longer than usual at the Conservative Club.

Agnes was in bed by ten o'clock, with her head under the blankets trying to shut out the sounds of the pigs squealing as they were slaughtered behind Linger's the butcher's just along the road from the flat.

She pretended to be asleep when Ted slipped carefully in beside her and soon his snores told her that once again he'd given way to what she thought of as his weakness. Belle would have called it selfishness no doubt, but Agnes loved her husband dearly and so was prepared to accept the bad with the good. For now, there was more of the latter and perhaps with a baby there would be even more. Yes, she admitted to herself one evening as she watched Ted leave the house to walk down the road to the big club in St. Peter's Street, sometimes she felt lonely but he was nearly always home by nine and although not always entirely sober, at least he was cheerful and full of jokes and intent on making her laugh at them.

"Guess what old Dudeney said to me in the shop this morning, Agnes," he'd grinned as she served up his supper on the dining table in the big bay window. "He said he had a message for me from his wife. Would I please be sure not to park the car too near their driveway as neighbours might think it belonged to one of the family! So I told him that next week I'd be having a new one without 'The Shredded Wheat Company' written on it and then his wife's friends would think it belonged to her!"

Agnes laughed as she thought of the well-to-do family in the big house next door to them in De Parys Avenue and then reminded Ted that Dudeney & Johnston's, the big grocer's shop in Bedford High Street, was one of his best customers and perhaps they should not upset Mrs Dudeney or Ted might lose their business!

"Not much chance of that, Agnes. Shredded Wheat is taking on in a big way and old Dudeney is too keen a businessman to let his wife's self-righteousness stand in the way of that!"

As her pregnancy advanced and the nursery was finished with the same care as the rest of their home, Agnes counted her blessings and told herself, as her father had told her long ago, that she could have done a lot worse.

It was in Linger's, the butcher's shop in The Broadway where she'd listened to those pigs squealing every Sunday night, and where she'd called in for some chops for dinner on the way home from seeing a matinée of the new American cartoon of Mickey Mouse, that Agnes felt the baby quicken for the first time. Quite suddenly, beneath her bulging skirtband, there came a strange fluttering and then a beating as of tiny wings somewhere within her body. At the same moment, she became very aware of the overpowering smell of blood on the half-sides of beef hanging from a rail at the back of the shop and the next thing she knew,

80

she was lying on the floor in the sawdust with the red face of Mr Linger peering anxiously down at her from behind the chopping block.

"Well, Mrs Winch, you did give me a fright! Now just you lie still a minute. You fainted clean away. Must be the hot weather." And the good man sent his assistant to the back room to fetch his white-faced, young customer a glass of water.

After a few minutes on the floor and when the shop had stopped whirling around her head at a fine rate of knots, Agnes was helped to her feet and a little chair was placed by the door where she could get some fresh air and rest until she had fully recovered. To say she felt foolish would be an understatement, for Agnes knew that the butcher was the father of a strapping son of his own, who would one day take over the business and so he probably guessed her condition and was also quite used to young mothers passing out in his shop.

As she related the story later to Ted, who was home early for a change, Agnes tried to pass the incident off as lightly as she could manage for she did not want to alarm him unnecessarily.

"All I can remember is the smell of blood and Mr Linger singing 'Old Man River', then I was lying there on the floor in front of all those customers! I did feel an idiot, Ted!"

Ted made her sit with her feet up for the rest of the evening but apart from telling her that she should see the doctor in the morning to tell him what had happened, he did not mention the incident again and

Agnes knew that he had put it from his mind as he'd done with so many things in his life.

Over the months since their marriage, Agnes had learned that when her husband was under stress he drank more than he should and although this habit was not as bad as in the old days at The Bull, she knew he still overdid it from time to time.

Agnes also learned more about her husband's childhood and early years but even so, she found it difficult to understand why he spent so much time with his friends at the club. Surely, now that he was starting in this new life with her and with a baby on the way, he should be able to put the past behind him?

This worldly and knowledgeable man who was her husband had been born on the "wrong side of the blanket". Like so many of his generation, her Ted was the result of a brief relationship between a young housemaid and the son of the house where she was in service. When her condition was discovered, Ted's mother was packed off home, without a reference, to bear the shame of unmarried motherhood with no support from the father of her child, who was, in any case, about to be married to the daughter of a big county family.

When Ted was seven, his mother married Harry Winch, who worked for Carter Paterson, the carriers, and from then on he was treated badly by his bullying stepfather. By the time three more children came along in quick succession, Ted was thirteen and after a rudimentary education at The Hitchin British School in

Queen Street, he left and was expected to work for his keep.

With no regrets, he walked away from the crowded two-up-two-down cottage in Portmill Lane and was taken on as a stable-boy for a big estate near Gosmore. Here he lived above the stables in a small but cosy room where the smell of sweating horses mingled with the pungent odour of manure from the heap below the tiny window.

These animals were the only family Ted had for the next five years and he grew to understand them better than any human being.

The marriage to the cook from the big house when he was eighteen meant he could at last live in a decent cottage on the estate and when she died, only a year later, Ted took the King's Shilling and joined the army. "It was," he said, "better than going back to the room over the stable."

"Life in the army was tough but secure," he told Agnes. "And I made some good friends, especially when I transferred to the artillery on the gun-carriages. Most of those heavy pieces were horse-drawn and always a soldier rode the lead-horse as the team pulled the gun up to the front line. Poor creatures," Ted's face softened as he remembered his charges under shellfire. "They were always terrified of the noise and the death-rate was almost as high as the men in the trenches in the early days of the war. I had to shoot some of them at Ypres to put them out of their misery. Poor creatures," he said again.

On November the eleventh in that year of nineteen twenty-seven, Ted Winch first stood with head bowed, standing shoulder to shoulder with other old soldiers at the War Memorial on Bedford Embankment as the members of his club, The Warriors, laid their wreath of poppies on Remembrance Day. In later years he never missed the simple ceremony by the river but after that first time, his terrible experiences in the trenches were never discussed with the family again.

"It's a local club he's joined, Mum," Agnes explained to Emily on her next visit. "You know — they talk about the war and drink to absent friends every week. Better there than with that Alf up at the Conservative Club anyway."

The incident in the butcher's shop was the only time Agnes felt faint or unwell during the pregnancy and by November, when her time was almost due, she was, as Emily reported to George after a Saturday visit, "In blooming health and better than she's looked for years."

George smiled at the news as Emily tucked him up for the night and his mind was at rest about his girl as he drifted off to sleep.

Emily found him there the next morning and noticed with a mixture of shock and pity that in death, her husband's face had lost that look of strain and illness which had so aged him during his last few years.

Now her good man had gone and she must go on alone but oh! how she would miss him and as the tears came Emily realised that her George would never be a grandfather after all.

84

Ten days later and a week after her father's funeral, Agnes gave birth to her first born, a golden-haired, beautiful baby who was to be named John after his father, David after his grandfather and Vernon after his Shakespearean actor great-grandfather.

CHAPTER
SEVEN

"Are you awake, Agnes?" queried Ted as he poked his head around the bedroom door. "You've got a visitor," he continued, as Agnes stirred in the big bed and then Emily was coming towards her smiling and holding out a big bunch of yellow chrysanthemums.

"Oh, Mum," murmured Agnes sleepily, "you shouldn't have come over so soon."

Emily knew she meant so soon after the funeral but through all the days since George was laid to rest in the little village churchyard and even more after the baby came, she had been longing to talk to her girl and hold her new grandson in her empty arms. And the wise words of the vicar kept coming back to her mind.

"One door closes and another one opens, Mrs Thomas."

"I wanted to see my new grandson, child," said Emily, as Ted went off to put the kettle on for tea. "And here he is!" And she leaned over the little crib frilled round with white lace ruffles and smiled as the sleeping baby curled one tiny fist around her little finger.

"Is your milk in yet, dear?" she asked as she helped her daughter to sit up in bed and plumped the pillows energetically behind her head.

"Yes, Mum, and so much of it!" laughed Agnes, looking down at her swollen breasts resting on the eiderdown. "The midwife tells me that your grandson has a powerful suck and that I should breastfeed for as long as possible." She didn't add that the midwife had also told her that this was a good way of avoiding another pregnancy too soon after a birth.

Agnes's labour had lasted sixteen hours and throughout all of them she had resisted Ted's suggestion that he should fetch Emily over.

"No, Ted," she gasped through clenched teeth in the wake of another pain, "she needs to be on her own for a while. Belle pops in every day and Mrs Ponsonby has been very good to her."

Later, as the waves of pain levelled out and became a sudden urgent desire to push, Agnes would have given anything to see her mother's kind face and to hold on to a familiar hand as Ted was hustled quickly out of the room. And she had no breath to spare for anything but a desperate plea to the midwife as to how long it would be now?

"You're doing fine, mother," was the calm reply. "Baby will be here by teatime."

At six o'clock, with her son sleeping peacefully beside her Agnes drank gratefully from a cup of tea and wondered where Ted had got to.

"I told him to go for a long walk in the park," smiled the midwife, "and not to come back until at least seven o'clock. That gave me time to tidy up both baby and mother. Fathers are not much use at times like these, I'm afraid."

Agnes was asleep when Ted came home but when she awoke, the first thing she set eyes on was a great, hairy coconut perched on the end of the bed where he had placed it so carefully after winning it at the Autumn Fair down in Mill Meadows next to the river.

A grinning and not quite sober Ted told how he had first wetted the baby's head round at the club and then gone on to the fair, which Agnes knew he loved.

"And I won this for him, Agnes," he announced proudly, producing a tiny, fluffy, toy rabbit.

"Oh, Ted!" It hurt her stomach to laugh but what else could she do at a husband who went to the fair as his baby was being born? Afterwards she wondered if the tears that followed were of weakness or despair.

Emily stayed on for two weeks. "Just to see her on her feet again, Ted." But at the end of that time, the thought of leaving the little family to go back to her own empty home was almost more than she could bear and on the way back to Gosmore, her son-in-law persuaded her to give up the little cottage and come to live in Bedford.

"Stay with us for a bit, Emily. Then we'll find you somewhere suitable near to us. Agnes will like that."

Ted didn't add that it meant Agnes would have company when he was at work or stayed late at the club. For Ted, fatherhood was one thing, but giving up his own interests was quite another and after Emily moved in three weeks later, he began to stay out until nine o'clock on most evenings without any qualms of conscience at all.

"Why does he do it, Agnes?" asked Emily one evening as Ted left the flat straight after supper. "He's out all day and still he has to go out again. Your father was only too glad to get back to his home and only went across to The Bull once a week."

Agnes didn't reply for there was no answer to her mother's question. The pattern of her marriage had been set from the first days in their new home and she knew, beyond any doubt, that nothing would change her husband. She comforted herself with the thought that her son was healthy and thriving and that they were both well cared for and that her mother was no longer alone. For Emily never did move into her own place and soon their lives settled down into a daily routine in which Ted played a constant but somehow separate part.

It was on the way back from a matinée of "Popeye" and news vendors along the High Street were shouting about the Wall Street Crash, that Agnes suddenly felt very sick and giddy and it was as much as she could manage to reach home and the bathroom before she threw up the chocolates she'd eaten during the film. John was thirteen months old and Agnes was pregnant again.

"There are things you can use, Mrs Winch. If you want to limit the size of your family, that is."

Dr Chillingworth looked quizically at his patient and saw a pale-faced, young woman in the second month of pregnancy.

"Another year would have been better but you are young and healthy and there should be no complications. I'll see you in three months' time, then."

As she settled John into the handsome, grey Swan Baby Coach that Ted had bought as a surprise just before the baby's birth and turned towards home, Agnes wondered vaguely what the doctor meant by "things". She remembered reading something in a women's magazine that the means were now available to prevent married women from having too many babies. It was called 'birth control' but all Agnes could think of were those little packets Ted brought home sometimes but which he hardly ever used.

"They're not foolproof, anyway," he assured her every time he left them in his waistcoat pocket.

So, here she was again but as the morning sickness gave way to a healthy appetite and the summer came at last, Agnes began to feel better about a second baby so soon and the good feeling grew into optimism that this time she would be able to cope more easily. Emily was there to help and Ted's job provided them all with a good living, so there was nothing to fear.

"There's lots worse things than having babies, Mum," she reassured Emily when the news about number two was discussed over tea. But she avoided her mother's eyes as she picked up John's bottle for his six o'clock feed and began to sing, "Tip-Toe Through The Tulips", while Emily held her tongue and privately longed to give that Ted a piece of her mind. Two babies in less than two years! And she looked across the table at her daughter and knew she must not say a word to upset her.

In early October and just two weeks away from her time, Agnes tried to persuade her husband to take her to the pictures. "It'll be the last time for months, Ted," she pleaded as he thought of every excuse for not going. All week Agnes had waited for him to get home early enough to take her to see the new Lon Chaney film at the Picturedrome just over the town bridge off St. Mary's Street.

"Belle says it's a good one, Mum. She saw it last week at the Hermitage," explained Agnes and looked yet again out of the window to see if Ted was in sight. "He promised me, Mum. He really promised me that he'd be home in time."

There was no reply from Emily who sat rocking John to sleep in her rocking-chair brought from her old home at the last minute.

"There won't be room for much, Emily," Ted had explained as he struggled to fit the chair in the back of the car. "The rest will have to go, I'm afraid. Apart from your bed of course."

"He's asleep now, Agnes. I'll just put him down," said Emily softly. Then looking at her daughter's tense expression, added gently, "You might just as well take your coat off, child. He won't come now."

But Agnes was turning from the window with a big smile on her face as Ted's car came to a halt outside in the tree-lined road.

"I told you, Mum! He'll have had his tea at the Black Cat."

Then, pulling her red felt hat down over her dark hair, she moved heavily over to her mother to kiss her goodnight. "Don't wait up for us, Mum. You go to bed when John is really settled."

The Hunchback of Notre Dame was halfway through and the piano accompanist really excelling herself in the belfry scene, when Agnes's first daughter announced her impending arrival in the fifth row of the circle.

"It's strong, Ted. Really strong!" gasped Agnes as the usherette flashed her torch to guide them out of the picturehouse. "Oh, why couldn't it have waited until tomorrow? I did want to see this film!"

Later, when the small, dark-haired baby girl lay beside her in the big bed and just before blessed sleep came at last, Agnes suddenly thought that if Ted hadn't left things until the last minute she'd have seen all of the film instead of only half. "Continuous showing, Mum," she murmured as her eyes closed.

The new baby was christened at St. Cuthbert's church at the junction of Mill Street and Newnham Street on a cold October day and Ted arrived late to find an impatient vicar waiting for him.

"So glad you could make it, Mr Winch. Shall we get on then?"

He's been at the club again, thought Agnes, looking carefully at Ted's smart grey, double-breasted suit and polished black shoes. Not a hair out of place as usual, she noted as the good vicar named their daughter Joyce Anne and the baby's father dropped a ten-shilling note on the offertory plate.

"Render unto Caesar the things that are Caesar's," intoned Ted solemnly.

"And unto God the things that are God's," replied the vicar, smiling down at the plate.

92

"Ted, how could you?" exploded Agnes later as they shared Emily's homemade christening cake with Belle and her fiancé. Poor old Belle. He was her third and hopefully her last now the wedding day had been fixed. Whatever happened to the deputy head she was so set on? wondered Emily as she took a tired baby from Agnes's arms so her daughter could pour out some sherry for the guests.

Joyce Anne was a baby who didn't sleep much. Or so it seemed to her exhausted mother and thank goodness John was through his teething now or she'd never get any rest at all. At six months the little girl was still underweight and already plagued with the ear infections that she would suffer all through her childhood.

"Poor little mite," District Nurse Rogers sympathised as she dipped cotton-wool into warm oil and gently placed a piece inside each tiny, red ear. Joyce's face was as red as her inflamed ears as Emily picked her up and tried to soothe the pain with a dummy coated in Lyle's Golden Syrup.

It had been an exhausting winter for both women and as the baby began to pick up and respond to the spring sunshine when the pram was placed outside in the tiny garden, Agnes looked often round the flat that seemed to have shrunk in size with the arrival of her second child.

"We need a house, Ted," she announced that evening when the children were at last asleep. "A proper house with our own garden. And anyway, we'll need another bedroom when John is older."

Agnes knew that her mother never complained about sharing her bedroom with the little boy but lately, when the older woman went for her afternoon nap, John tried to climb up beside her and although Emily always told her to leave him, Agnes realised that her mother needed her rest even more than herself.

So it was that in August the family moved into a roomy bay-windowed house near the church on the corner of St. Cuthbert's Street and Grove Place.

"There you are, Agnes, will that suit?" laughed Ted as he opened the French windows onto a good-sized walled garden with a lawn and a shady tree in the centre.

Agnes loved it. There were three bedrooms and a surprisingly spacious attic room which she planned to turn into a bed-sitting-room for her mother.

"You'll get some peace and quiet up here, Mum," she assured Emily as they measured up for curtains and planned where to place the furniture.

Emily looked slowly round the cosy room, then walked across to the dormer window which gave a good view as far as the big houses on St. Peter's Green.

"Well, it's handy for the shops, anyway," she said, placing the old sepia photograph of George carefully on the mantelpiece. I wonder what he'd have made of all this, she mused, thinking wistfully of her own little home when her good man was alive and Agnes still at school in St. Ippollitts where they had settled after the Zeppelin raids that drove them out of London. Such a long time ago it seemed now.

The attic room was up two flights of stairs and for Emily the climb was sometimes as much as she could manage but over the next few months she grew to love that small place which was her own and where she could keep and cherish her photographs and ornaments from the past. Increasingly, when the children were asleep and Ted was home, Emily climbed the stairs and thankfully shut the door behind her. She loved her daughter and the children, but always at the end of the day, her own comfortable bed beckoned and a library book waited for her on the bedside table.

The old, brass bedstead with a screw-on knob at each corner had been her marriage bed and her mother's before her and each night, as Emily pulled the eiderdown up to her chin and settled down to sleep, she thought about her life with George and smiled as she turned off the oil lamp. What was it he said every night? Oh yes. "Goodnight, sleep tight, don't let the bed-bugs bite."

And she slept with the memory of his arms holding her safe in the old bed they'd shared for over thirty years.

CHAPTER
EIGHT

"It came over the town again today, Mum." Agnes was feeding Joyce who was teething badly.

"Just look at this child's gums!" she exclaimed. "And her chin and bottom are so sore, poor little mite."

Agnes soothed zinc-and-castor-oil ointment onto the angry rash on the baby's tender skin then, balancing her expertly on her knees, folded a warmed nappy into a triangle and pinned it carefully around the tiny form.

Joyce was still underweight but with the cod-liver-oil-and-malt prescribed by the doctor was slowly beginning to catch up and Agnes looked across at her chubby little boy playing with his new toy airplane and wondered for the thousandth time how the two children could be so different.

"She's just like you were, Agnes," smiled Emily whenever her daughter voiced her concerns over the baby. "Delicate when young, but tough as old boots when you grew up." Privately, Emily thought that it was just as well.

The R101 airship was on its trial flights all through that summer and Bedfordians were becoming familiar with the huge, grey shape floating overhead when its flight path took it over the little town.

"Ted told me that Alf's son will be on the maiden flight to India."

Agnes didn't like Alf. He was much older than Ted and apart from membership of the Conservative Club, the two men had nothing at all in common.

"He never seems to do a full day's work, Ted!" she complained one evening after a prolonged visit from his drinking friend that day. "He arrived for coffee at eleven," she continued hotly, "and left after tea-time."

Emily kept her own counsel over the subject of Alf Parker for she did not trust him. Why would a man old enough to be her father, hang around Agnes so often? In her opinion, there was only one answer. He fancied her daughter and if Ted had any sense he should warn him off.

"He's managed to swap places with one of the cabin stewards," continued Agnes, pretending not to notice the disapproval on her mother's face. "Ted said it cost him fifty pounds but he reckons it will be worth it, for the publicity he gets will double his business by next year."

Alf's son ran a small cafe in Tavistock Street near the long wall of Bedford Prison and, in these days of depression and unemployment, was finding it hard going.

The airship was due to leave on her long voyage to India early in October and Agnes wanted to be there at the send-off from the huge airship sheds out at Cardington airfield.

"We'll get nowhere near it, Agnes!" protested Ted as a cold, wet September drew to a close and excitement began to mount in Bedford. "The roads will be jammed solid with cars and buses. Everyone I know has the same idea as you."

But Agnes persisted in her aim to see the great airship take off and in the end Ted reluctantly promised to get back from work in time to drive the three miles out to the little village of Cardington.

"Didn't you have enough of airships in London, child?" asked Emily as Agnes tucked Joyce up in her cot and started to lay the table for tea.

"That was different, Mum," Agnes replied as her thoughts returned to that awful day in Gray's Inn Road and the bombing of King's Cross Station. "This one is ours. *The Beds Times* reckons that Cardington could become the English end of an Imperial Airship Service between England and India. Just imagine," Agnes laughed, as she concentrated on slicing the quartern-loaf held tight against the bodice of her apron, "by this time next year we might see men wearing turbans and women in saris buying their groceries in Sainsbury's!" And she wondered again at the courage of women like Amy Johnson, who had just flown solo even further than India, all the way to Australia.

By three o'clock on the afternoon of the fourth of October, Ted was still not home and Agnes was beginning to fret. Take-off was reported to be set for late afternoon and all day lines of charabancs and cars streamed away from the railway station in Ashburnham Road and the bus station in Tavistock Street, over the town bridge along St. Mary's Street and through St.

John's Street and headed for Cardington, three miles down the road.

"I'll be sharing your bed tonight, Mum, if he doesn't get here in time," Agnes said crossly and then her eyes lit up as the door opened and Ted came in bringing a flurry of cold, damp air with him.

"You surely don't want to go out in this lot, do you?" he asked as he removed his Homburg hat and shook it over the fender. Drops of water sizzled on the grate as Agnes poured his tea and Emily flashed her daughter a warning look as Ted pushed away his plate and lit up one of his habitual Player's Medium Cut cigarettes.

An hour later, with both children safely in bed and Ted dozing in his armchair, Agnes stepped off the last bus out to Cardington into a fine drizzle that soaked through her coat and felt hat in minutes.

Cars and charabancs, parked bumper to bumper, lined the narrow road leading up to the airfield perimeter while across the wet expanse of grass beyond, the two massive sheds towered into the darkening sky. A great crowd of people stood, shoulders hunched against the persistent rain all along the muddy verges of the road, straining to see the huge shape floating high above them, secured by its nose to the mooring mast.

Lights gleamed through the windows of the cabin beneath the vast envelope of the airship and as she peered through the gloom of a dismal, early October evening, Agnes saw men struggling across the airfield carrying heavy trunks and boxes towards the lift which would take them up to the boarding platform high above.

As the last of the light faded from the desolate, rain-swept field, a convoy of shining, black cars turned in at the main gates and there were cheers from the excited crowd as a small knot of dignitaries gathered at the foot of the lift.

Agnes shivered and hugged her arms closer to her body as the great airship finally slipped its moorings and after a breathtaking moment when its nose dipped perilously close to the ground, began to rise slowly into the night sky. Then it turned away towards the town and disappeared from view over the dark horizon.

"It's too low!" a voice behind her shouted and the cry was taken up by the crowd as first one then another commented on the amount of baggage taken on board and the huge supplies of food and drink necessary for the first leg of the journey.

"God help them!" A woman nearby expressed the feelings of much of the crowd which was slowly beginning to disperse. And Agnes marvelled again at the courage and loyalty of the men on that flying beast now making its way towards Hertfordshire and eastwards to the coast.

"Sooner them than me, sweetheart." A rough voice spoke in her ear as she turned to begin the long walk back to the town. It was Alf and judging from his slurred speech and the smell of whisky on his breath he must have been on the bottle all day.

"You'll not get on a bus now, little girl," the man continued as Agnes tried to walk on ahead and ignore him. "Come on, my car's just down the road." Then Agnes's arm was gripped tightly as this man she disliked so intensely opened the car door and almost thrust her onto the front passenger seat.

It was a slow ride back into the town for the road in was still jammed with traffic and people returning from the airship take-off. Alf talked about his son for most of the way home and Agnes remembered that he was somewhere up there on the R101 and she thought with compassion about the young wife waiting at home for news of a safe landing.

"Silly young fool," Alf muttered as he manoeuvred the big car across the narrow town bridge and pulled it sharply round to the left on to St. Paul's Square and turned off the engine. "Told him not to go. The word's out that the ship wasn't ready to fly. The only trials have been in good weather and look at this lot!" And Alf nodded at the wind-lashed trees in the churchyard as Agnes, murmuring her thanks, opened the door to get out.

"Don't I get a kiss as a thank-you, sweetheart?" Alf grinned at her through the window. When there was no reply, he added cheerfully, "You should tell that husband of yours to pay you more attention. He's a lucky devil to have a girl like you."

Then the car pulled away across the square and disappeared down Harpur Street. As Agnes turned in the opposite direction to hurry along the High Street towards home, she noted that the time on the big clock beneath the gold bull of John Bull, Goldsmith and Jeweller's, read ten minutes past seven and she quickened her steps round Mill Street corner and past *The Bedfordshire Times* office halfway along the road. If she was lucky she might just get back before Ted went out to his club for the evening. She was still shaking from revulsion and cold as she let herself in the front door.

Emily was sitting half-asleep in the living-room but of Ted there was no sign and Agnes knew she had missed him.

On the wireless next day came the shocking news of the airship's crash in France.

"Only six men survived, Mum!" Agnes hugged little Joyce closer as she bent her head nearer to Ted's wireless to listen to the solemn voice of the B.B.C. announcer.

"And Alf's boy wasn't one of them." Ted had come home early from the club, full of the news about the airship. "I left old Alf on a real blinder. Offered to get him home but he was downing doubles like nobody's business. He'll have a rotten hangover tomorrow, poor devil!"

What about the young wife? thought Agnes as she settled the baby down for the night and made up her mind to visit the girl in a few days' time in the little cafe where she worked such long hours to build up the business.

A week later, Agnes and her mother stood outside the Swan Hotel near the town bridge as the procession of forty-eight coffins, each carried on a horse-drawn gun-carriage and draped with a Union Jack, passed by on its way to a communal grave in Cardington cemetery.

"The whole town was at a standstill, Ted," she told him over supper that evening. "And it was so quiet. I remember hearing St. Paul's clock striking three as the last of the carriages crossed over the bridge. Oh! It's dreadful to think of all those men killed. I'll go to see Mary tomorrow — that is if the cafe is still open."

Over the next few months, tea in the little cafe became a regular stop for Agnes after shopping in the market on Wednesdays and Saturdays and soon Mary was the friend she confided in about her marriage problems.

"He's promised we'll go to the Licensed Victuallers' Ball this year," Agnes sighed and remembered Ted's many promises, most of which he broke. Admittedly, there were compensations, for Agnes's husband did have, as she hastened to add to her friend, a conscience, although sometimes he was curiously reluctant to show it.

On Sundays, after his forty winks in the afternoon, it was now a ritual for the little family to go out in the car for a ride round the countryside. In the summer months, although on increasingly rare occasions, they finished up in Gosmore, where Ted's mother was now living after her drunken husband finally deserted her, leaving her with the three younger children to bring up alone.

The small house on the corner of Gosmore Road and Waterdell Lane, with its combined smell of camphor and paraffin and the sharper smell from the sty at the bottom of the yard where the children fed cucumbers to fat, pink pigs, belonging to Moss's farm, became a place of wonder to Agnes's children who loved to visit Grandma Winch and eat homemade scones with strawberry jam and thick, yellow cream for Sunday tea.

Sometimes, Ted's younger brothers Harry and Len were there and while the older pair went off to The Bull for an early evening drink, gentle Len, who was almost blind, played games with the children and gave Agnes combs or basket-work he had made in the blind-school in Letchworth.

Emily never went with the family on these outings for she looked forward to an afternoon of peace and quiet and in good weather the chance to visit an old friend from her London days, lately arrived in Bedford and now in service at one of the big houses facing the river on The Embankment.

"I don't know how my girl puts up with it!" Emily exclaimed to Kitty one Sunday over tea and scones in the big kitchen.

"Seems to me that she has no choice, Emily," replied Kitty, whose husband had been killed in the war, leaving her to fend for herself. Thank God the children were off her hands at last although the boy was out of work and her girl married to a soldier and stationed in South Africa.

"She's dead set on going to this Licensed Victuallers' Ball, Kitty," said Emily, helping herself to one of her friend's homemade shortcakes. "You should see the dress she's made for it. My Agnes is such a clever girl with a needle, and to think she gave it all up for him!"

So the old friends gossiped and drank another cup of tea and then it was time for Emily to leave.

"I like to get back before them, you see," she explained when Kitty said she must stay longer next time. "I'll just have time to make some ginger parkin for their tea. It's Ted's favourite."

Christmas that year passed quietly enough in the snug, little house near the church in St. Cuthbert's Street and to give him his due, Ted spent most of his Christmas bonus on toys for the children and new shoes for Agnes and his mother-in-law.

On the morning of Christmas Day Agnes took John to church while Emily began the dinner preparations. "Happy Christmas, Mrs Winch." The vicar smiled as he shook hands with her in the porch as she was leaving and Agnes felt the hot colour rise in her cheeks as she wondered if he remembered Ted's behaviour at Joyce's christening.

She was surprised to find that Ted was still there when she arrived home until she remembered that the Conservative Club was closed on Christmas Day, as were The Peacock in Mill Street and The Ship, just down the road in St. Cuthbert's Street, usually his last two ports of call on the way home from the club. Ted never kept strong drink in the house apart from the decanter of good sherry on the sideboard and this was used only on the rare occasions when he brought business colleagues back for a meal.

Ted and his little boy spent most of that day in the pretty, little front room where the track of John's new Hornby train set was laid out all around the carpet square. When Agnes called them for dinner, they were both crouched down watching in rapt concentration as the green and gold locomotive chugged its way round the sofa and passed beneath the table before it came to a stop in its tiny station in the window bay.

"I never had one of these, son," Agnes heard Ted say, as he stood up and lifted his son carefully over the tracks before following her into the dining-room for dinner.

As they all tucked in to the goose and afterwards the Christmas pudding, in which Emily had hidden silver threepenny bits and bachelor buttons when it was made in late September, Agnes looked with a renewed fondness and better understanding at the man she had married for love but who was still sometimes a puzzle to her. And she recalled tales she'd heard of his deprived childhood and the struggle to make his own way in the world. Yes, he was difficult sometimes and hard to tolerate at others when he stayed at the club too long, but thank God he was never violent, like Lizzie's Mick had been all those years ago.

If only, she thought, looking again at the still handsome face opposite, he would spend more time with us and less in the company of drinking companions. And Agnes sighed as she spooned mashed potato into Joyce's mouth and tried hard to count her blessings.

That night, as Ted took her in his arms murmuring, "This is my best Christmas present, Agnes," she was truly happy and more optimistic about the future than she'd been since the very early days of their marriage.

106

A week into 1931 and with the weather so bitterly cold that the children were restless through lack of fresh air, Agnes booked an appointment at Lane's, the little hairdresser's salon round the corner in Newnham Street, for a Marcel wave. The new dress of blue chiffon with bows on each shoulder hung ready and waiting in the wardrobe and only the day before she'd managed to buy a pair of blue satin evening shoes with Louis heels, in the January sales.

"You look lovely, dear!"

Emily watched fondly, as her slim, dark-haired girl tried on all the new finery and applied Tangee lipstick for the first time in her life.

"Not too much, now!" Emily warned. "You don't want to look like those overpainted filmstars."

"Oh, Mum!" Agnes laughed, "that's only stage make-up for the cameras. Belle says that without it they'd look really washed out and plain."

"Maybe," muttered Emily, "but some of those girls pile it on. They'll all ruin their complexions," she added. For Emily still viewed any kind of make-up as a tool of the devil.

But Agnes was not listening to her mother's fears about her complexion or indeed to very much at all at this moment. She was busy twirling in front of the cheval mirror, singing the song from Ted's latest record, "On The Sunny Side Of The Street", and admiring her new dress.

The annual Licensed Victuallers' Ball, held in the Bedford Corn Exchange facing St. Paul's Square, was one of the biggest social occasions of the year and tickets were hard to come by. But each year, Ted used his connections at the Conservative Club to produce tickets for two.

This was the third ball they'd attended so Agnes knew what to expect. The mayor and mayoress would be there and so too would the M.P. for Bedford and his lady wife. There would be a lovely, buffet supper and a good dance-band brought down specially from London for the occasion.

Agnes still loved dancing but she knew that, after the first set, Ted would leave her with friends and then disappear into the bar with his club friends.

"It's no use, Agnes," he used the same excuse every time, "I've got a stiff toe and you don't want me treading all over your new shoes!"

Agnes and Mary sat together at a little table in the company of two or three other couples and the men were kept busy partnering their wives and only occasionally, when these ladies went to the powder room, the two girls.

When a slim, dark-haired young man approached to ask Agnes to tango with him, she was on her feet at once and away round the floor dancing her heart out to the tune of "Jealousy". When it was over, her partner escorted her politely back to her seat, bowed slightly and thanked her for the dance then with a smile for both girls, strolled back to rejoin a small group of men standing near the door.

Later, as they piled their plates with prawn vol-au-vents, tiny sausage rolls and dainty sandwiches, Agnes kept her eyes open for her tango partner.

"Talk about Rudolph Valentino, Ted!" she laughed as he led the way back to their table. "He's a lovely dancer. I wonder why his girl-friend's not with him?"

"I suspect it's because he doesn't have one," replied Ted. Then, looking at Agnes's surprised face, he added quickly, "You know, Agnes. He prefers boys."

Agnes stared at Ted in silence and then, as a vague memory of an overheard, puzzling conversation as a child stirred, she glanced quickly across to Mary who was deep in conversation with one of the young men from the group near the door.

"Do you mean . . .?" was all she could say and Ted nodded and Agnes thought she must warn Mary, who was lonely and too young to be widowed for long.

"Just my luck," groaned her friend ruefully. But both girls happily danced the evening away with their new dancing-partners and by the end of it Agnes wondered why she'd felt so concerned.

"Well, one thing is certain," Ted had said as he went back to the bar. "You'll both be quite safe with them!"

"I really didn't know what he was talking about, Mum," she confided to Emily as they sipped the first cup of tea of the day together, early the next morning.

"Then you'd better ask him, dear," replied Emily, hastily closing a discussion which she found embarrassing.

When Ted finally gave her all the explicit details about homosexuality, Agnes was truly astounded, for never in her life had she heard anything like it before.

"You mean you never knew about your Uncle Joe?" asked Ted incredulously.

Agnes had not known, but with the knowledge came some understanding of Joe's way of life and the restlessness that drove him into the pubs and kept him isolated from family life. And she wondered why her father had never told her. Was it because he was ashamed of his brother or because he wanted to protect his only child?

Agnes didn't know the answer but in later years, whenever she read anything about these men in the newspapers, she always tried to understand and in doing so was able to accept the difference as just another puzzling but inescapable part of nature.

CHAPTER
NINE

The big gramophone in Agnes's pretty front room was playing "Dancing On The Ceiling" and Jessie Matthews was giving it her best as Emily said goodbye and closed the front door behind her on her way to visit Kitty.

Since before Christmas John had asked every day when were they going to see the pantomime at the Royal County Theatre? "Puss In Boots" was now in its last week and Ted, as usual, had managed to get circle seats for the family from a friend at the club.

"*The Bedfordshire Times* has given it a good review, Mum," Agnes had said as she buttoned up Joyce's new coat and tied her bonnet ribbons more securely.

And now it was after two o'clock as John stood by the window looking anxiously for his father and Agnes prayed that he'd be home in time to get them all to the theatre for the three o'clock matinée.

By ten to three, she finally realised that Ted wouldn't show up with the tickets in his pocket. But the sight of her little boy still standing hopefully by the window, his eager face waiting for the treat to begin, was suddenly more than Agnes could bear and a great, swelling anger began slowly to fill her head with such intensity that she actually contemplated smashing every one of Ted's precious record collection.

John turned from the window with tears on his cheeks and the little girl, not understanding, ran to him to play.

"Go away, Joycey, you're too little," he shouted and pushed his sister roughly away and then both children were crying. He from disappointment and the baby because she didn't understand.

Agnes stood quite still in the middle of her sitting-room and thought of the hours of work it had taken to make the soft covers on the furniture and the curtains at the windows. How each finished piece had been lovingly fitted and proudly shown to Ted as he came home at night. Now she looked slowly around the familiar room and knew she loved her little home but she thought bleakly as she bent to comfort the children it was obvious to her at last, that Ted did not. She knew he was still at the club and probably wouldn't get back until after six. The day was ruined yet again.

Suddenly, Agnes was glad that her mother had gone out for she knew she would try to stop her from carrying out the plan that was beginning to take shape in her distraught daughter's head.

Where was that envelope that had come through the letter-box just before Ted had left this morning? Where had he put it? Agnes knew it was from The Shredded Wheat Company and she also knew that it contained his salary cheque for the month.

"Well, I'll just show him," she muttered to herself through tightly clenched teeth as she began to look

112

through the desk drawers. She'd searched every one without success when she suddenly remembered Ted's habit of slipping things beneath the big blotter on the green, leather-topped desk.

Lifting the blotter quickly, Agnes stared breathlessly at the long, buff envelope addressed to E. J. Winch Esq. and then, trembling as she did so, picked up the silver letter-knife he'd brought back from Paris and carefully slit along the entire length of the letter.

The cheque was for sixty pounds. A month's salary plus a generous Christmas bonus, for Ted was a good salesman and his boss acknowledged this fact every year.

Glancing quickly at the carriage clock on the mantelpiece, Agnes sat down at the desk and slowly opened the lid of the heavy glass inkpot on its ornate silver stand in front of her. She'd have to use one of the nib pens in the top drawer, for Ted always carried his Waterman fountain pen with him.

Carefully, she dipped the pen in the inkpot and turning the cheque over, painstakingly traced a passable replica of Ted's signature on the back. Then she blotted it carefully on the pink blotter pad and slipped it quickly into her handbag.

Hurry now, she thought, as she packed clothing quickly into one of Ted's big, leather suitcases and then ushered the children before her into the hall.

The grandfather clock stood at three-thirty as she opened the door and walked down the path to the front gate, leaving the suitcase between the hedge and the wall. Carrying Joyce in her arms and with John trotting beside her, Agnes walked quickly down St. Cuthbert's Street and round the corner to the little grocer's shop in Newnham Street where she'd bought her weekly groceries since moving into the house two years before.

"Do you think you could cash this for me, Mrs Wooding? My husband couldn't get to the bank in time yesterday."

Agnes surprised herself as she calmly asked the grocer's wife to accept the endorsed cheque and as she waited for the twelve five-pound notes to be counted out wondered why her hands were not shaking like her legs.

"There you are, Mrs Winch. No trouble at all for a good customer like yourself."

The round-cheeked little woman waved cheerily at the children as they left the shop and then they were back at the house and Agnes quickly picked up the suitcase and shut the gate firmly behind her.

An hour later, as Joyce slept on the carriage seat and John stood on his toes to peer out of the train window, Agnes thankfully heaved the suitcase up on to the luggage racks then sank down beside the baby and closed her eyes.

It had been a long trek from the house down St. Cuthbert's Street past The Ship where Ted sometimes had a last drink on the way home and then O'Dells the cobbler's and round the corner and by the time she was halfway along Mill Street, Agnes was thankful to rest the heavy suitcase on the step of *The Bedfordshire Times* office and get her breath back. She rested again outside Dynes the fruiterer's in Midland Road but when they at last reached the railway station at the end of it she was distraught to find they had missed the four-forty-five train to Liverpool by only five minutes.

The next train north, at six-thirty, was running on time and though they'd have to change at Crewe, she could rest for an hour or so and try to quell the bilious attack that was threatening to make her sick and making it difficult to see across the carriage.

"Can I get you anything, my dear?"

Agnes opened her eyes to find an elderly woman bending over her. Her first thought was for the baby but Joyce was still asleep and John sat quietly beside her looking at his comic. She must have dozed off, she thought in sudden panic and then, as the bitter bile rose in her mouth once more and she gagged into one of Ted's big handkerchiefs, the kindly woman reached into her handbag and offered smelling salts to the young mother who was clearly not well at all.

"Thank you. Thank you," Agnes managed at last as the seat opposite swayed then settled once more and the smelling salts began to take effect. "It's travel-sickness, I'm afraid. I'm always like this."

"Well, I change at Crewe," the woman continued, looking keenly at Agnes's drawn face and then as the girl's eyes closed again, added gently, "but I'll keep an eye on the children until then. You try to rest, my dear."

By the time the train to Liverpool pulled out of the big station at Crewe, Agnes felt a little better but if her kind travelling companion had not found a porter to help, she doubted if she and the children would have been on it at all.

When they arrived at Lime Street station, Joyce was crying for her bottle and John was asking incessantly when would tea be ready? Outside, a long line of taxis waited and regardless of the cost, Agnes, hugging the baby close, climbed thankfully into one of them and settling John in the corner directed the driver to Aunty Nancy's address in Grassendale.

"What happened, Agnes?"

Aunty Nancy had swiftly sized up the situation when she opened the door to find her sister's girl and her young family huddled on the doorstep.

On the rare occasions she'd seen Emily since George died, Nancy gathered that all was not well with her niece's marriage and although her sister was not one for telling tales, the sight of Ted arriving home late every night was enough to tell its own story during her brief visits.

Now, as she waited for an explanation and looked closely at the pale face before her, Nancy suspected that the situation was about to get a great deal worse. When Agnes fainted at Sainsbury's three days later, her aunt, who had borne eleven children to a hard-working but harder-drinking docker who died in his fifties, knew that her suspicions were well-founded.

"You'll have to go back, my little lass," she announced shortly, as Agnes wept tears of frustration at the new turn of events. "And when you've had this one, go to your doctor for that advice he offered you before. Else you'll end up with a football team, like me!"

"The Peanut Vendor" was playing on Nancy's wireless a week later and Agnes was washing the nappies in a big, galvanised metal bucket in the tiny kitchen, when a telegram boy appeared on the doorstep with a telegram for Mrs E. J. Winch.

"Shall I wait for an answer, missus?" he asked cheerfully.

The telegram read, "If you are still my wife, please come home", signed E. J. Winch.

"Well, at least he said please, Agnes," laughed Nancy as she closed the door on the telegram boy. "But why don't you stay a few more days, my love? Then we'll get you back on that train."

That night, as Agnes lay waiting for sleep in the big bed that had been used by so many of her cousins down the years, she thought about her Aunty Nancy's hard life and compared it with her own. Had she loved her young husband as much as Agnes loved Ted? And was that why there had been so many children? Then she thought of her own mother and the little ones she had lost before Agnes herself came along. It seemed that women didn't have much say on how many children to bear. They just did the hard work without complaining. Surely that couldn't be right? Or was it, in the end, up to the men?

Agnes sighed and turned over again as sleep still refused to come and she thought over her aunt's advice about the doctor and determined that she would never be like her with a football team and probably more if Uncle Peter had lived longer.

Another week went by and as Agnes began to regain her usual good health and cousins of all ages visited and exclaimed over her children, she gradually became resigned to the fact that she was pregnant again.

It was on the way home, after the change at Crewe, that Agnes remembered her aunt's parting words which seemed strangely at odds with her earlier advice.

"There's lots worse than babies, lass." And Agnes smiled to herself and felt her tummy as she wondered whether this one would be a brother or a sister for her pigeon-pair.

To her great surprise, Ted was waiting at Bedford station in his smart new Ford car and when she opened the front door of the house, a bowl of hyacinths, just beginning to bloom, stood in the centre of the polished table.

"He went just about everywhere for those flowers, my girl," Emily informed her as she helped her daughter to unpack. "And," she whispered, "he's been home by six every night since you left."

"Well, it must have done him some good then," retorted Agnes shortly. Then looking at her mother's concerned face added quickly, "I suppose you've been waiting on him hand and foot, Mum?"

"Oh, Agnes! A man needs to be cared for," replied Emily with a sigh. "But he's really missed you, dear."

"I'll bet he has," laughed Agnes. And for the first time, Emily heard a hard note in the laughter and had no answer when her daughter added, "And a good thing too."

Emily kept her own counsel about the telegram she'd received from Nancy the day after Agnes arrived on her doorstep. But Agnes found the second one her aunt sent, advising Ted when his absent wife would be home again.

"She's a wise old bird, is my sister," smiled Emily.

"And a very kind one, Mum," replied Agnes softly.

As they prepared for bed that night, Agnes waited for Ted to ask about the cheque but it was not until the following morning that he said, quite casually, just before leaving for work, "If there's anything left, Agnes, you'd better put it into your Post Office savings account. I didn't realise that my wife was such a good forger!"

Over the next few weeks, as her waistband tightened and spring gave way to summer, Agnes noticed a subtle change in Ted's behaviour. Could he have really learned his lesson, she thought incredulously? Or at least have begun to mend his ways?

It was early in June and two months before the baby was due that Ted arrived home at his now earlier time of six and announced that they were all going away to the coast for the weekend.

"Pack enough things for two nights, Agnes. Maybe three," he continued, pleased at the astonishment on his wife's face. "Tell your mother she's to come with us."

"But where are we staying, Ted?" Agnes wanted to know as the big car was loaded up the next morning and they pulled away from the kerb and turned right into Goldington Road towards Newmarket and the coast.

"Wait and see, my girl," was Ted's cheerful answer. Then by way of more explanation, "If you like it, we can come every summer."

He would say no more and Agnes had to wait until she read the sign for Hemsby, near Great Yarmouth before she knew where they were headed.

"What's at Hemsby, Mum?" she asked Emily in a whisper, and then stared in wonder as they stopped beside a smart, green and white bungalow in a little pebbly road winding down to the beach.

"Old Bill Hutchings rents it out every year for the summer months and I got it at a special price if we take it for a full month," Ted said triumphantly as he switched off the engine and opened the door.

"But ... the baby's due in August, Ted!" gasped Agnes, staring at him as if he had lost his mind.

"Yes, I know. But you are going into a nursing-home this time, my dear," Ted answered firmly. "I thought it would be a good idea for your mother to be here with the others for those two weeks and we can join them later."

The bungalow was quite new when Agnes first stayed there and the little seaside village was so quiet with Fakes General Stores at one end of the road and a pub at the other with only half-a-dozen other bungalows besides theirs. But best of all was a great stretch of golden beach where paddling was safe and the children could play all day outside in the fresh sea air.

In Bedford, the first week of August was so hot that Agnes could hardly drag herself out to the shop let alone run about after the children. John, usually a quiet little boy content to play in the garden with his airplanes was irritable and bad-tempered with Joyce who at nearly two was into everything. The new baby was due at any time and Agnes was so heavy and uncomfortable that she just wished it was all over and done with.

On the night of the sixth of August, when the thunderstorm that had been threatening all day finally broke over the town, Agnes went into labour.

"Hurry, Ted! This one won't take long!" she gasped as another, sharper pain rose to a crescendo and then died away, leaving her bathed in sweat and shaking uncontrollably with the nervous tension that every woman experiences as she prepares for birth.

The suitcase had been packed for two weeks and everything Emily would need for the children's stay in Hemsby lay in neat piles on the old trunk in her room.

"Don't forget John's airplane," were Agnes's last words to her mother as Ted put the car deftly into gear and pulled smoothly away from the house.

The nursing-home was five minutes away in Union Street, off Bromham Road in Bedford and that was just as well, for less than an hour later Agnes gave uncomplicated birth to another girl who weighed in at nearly nine pounds and then gratefully did as she was told by matron and took full advantage of the rest the home offered for the next ten days.

During that time, Agnes thought long and hard about her marriage and when on the sixth day Belle arrived with flowers for her old friend and a beautifully crocheted shawl for the baby, who was to be named Shela after Flora Robson's sister, she was more than ready to talk about her problems.

"Count your blessings, Agnes!" exclaimed Belle as she rocked the baby to sleep after her afternoon feed. "At least you have a nice home and your mum being cared for. So what if Ted does like the booze? He's in work, which is more than can be said for my Ned. And now they've cut his dole money again!"

After Belle failed to net her deputy head, here she was married to an out-of-work brewery foreman with a child of two and another on the way.

"He's applying for a job at the new Ford plant in Dagenham when it opens in December," her friend stated cheerfully and Agnes could only marvel at Belle's optimism and enquire how she was able to manage on the dole and offer her some of John's outgrown clothes if the new baby was a boy.

"You must get your Ted to bring you all down for a visit as soon as we're settled in the new house," were almost Belle's final words before she left. Then, with a last look around the pretty, private room, she said again, "Don't forget to count your blessings, Agnes!"

Then she was gone and a few days later Agnes told her mother all about it as they sat together in the little walled garden while the new baby slept peacefully in the big London Baby Coach that Ted had bought on the day she came back from the nursing-home.

"She said I should count my blessings, Mum, and I think she's right."

Agnes's deft fingers were completing the hem of a new dress for Joyce as she spoke and then she continued without taking her eyes off the work, "Ted says that there are still so many men out of work and his orders have dropped by a third this summer alone."

Emily nodded and looked at the clever daughter who always seemed to bounce back from whatever happened in her life. And the older woman sighed and thought back to the years before Agnes was born and the struggles she and George went through in order to make a bare living in the rooms in London.

"I'll put the kettle on, dear," she said brightly as she stood up and adjusted the fringed sunshade over the pram. "Ted will be back from the zoo soon and we'll have a very tired little boy to tell us all about it before he goes to bed."

John and his father arrived back from the newly-opened Whipsnade Zoo half-an-hour later and then Agnes was kept busy until all three children were tucked into bed.

Emily had cooked Ted's favourite supper of baked macaroni cheese and it was waiting for him in the oven as later she climbed the stairs to her little room beneath the eaves and she could hear the strains of his new record coming faintly from the living-room two floors below. "Walking My Baby Back Home", sang Nat King Cole and Emily smiled to herself as she turned out the oil-lamp and plumped up her pillow for sleep. Her baby *was* home and had learned at last to make the best of it.

CHAPTER
TEN

"Three is a nice little family, Mrs Winch," advised Dr Chillingworth. "More is too many."

The busy G.P. who had become a friend to Agnes through her childbearing smiled warmly at the young woman who sat nursing her bonny, fair-haired baby in his dark little consulting room in Duke Street, just round the corner from home.

Shela was nearly nine months old and the doctor knew that when Agnes stopped breast-feeding the child the chances were that she would again become pregnant.

"Have you spoken to your husband yet, my dear?" Agnes knew he meant had she told Ted about the birth-control device she'd been offered on her last visit. "It's in both your interests after all," Dr Chillingworth continued as he told her how to use the rubber contraption in the plain black box on the desk beside him.

Ted laughed when Agnes showed him the Dutch Cap and remarked that she didn't need it because he'd see there were no more children if that was what she wanted. What about those packets in his waistcoat pocket? she thought as she hid the black box in her undies drawer. Why can't he use them? Agnes had yet to learn about the selfishness of some men in bed, however heavily disguised as love it might be.

But now it was late April and Agnes dismissed all these worrying thoughts from her mind as she walked slowly along The Embankment by the river, where the almond-blossom trees were in full bloom, wheeling the big, grey pram towards Russell Park and the children's playground.

"Let's stop at the bowling green, Mum!" pleaded John, who loved to watch the old gentlemen bowling and walking solemnly up and down in their white trousers and shirts and panama hats with the club hatband matching smart red ties.

John and Joyce were getting more and more excited as August 1932 approached, for it would be the first full month's holiday at the bungalow in Hemsby.

"Can we really paddle in the sea again?" John asked his mother at least six times a day. The little boy remembered the ten days he'd spent there last summer with Emily and he was eager to get back to bucket and spade, sandcastles and dashing in and out of the sea with Susie, Ted's little Sealyham dog.

"Ted's planning to come down at weekends and we'll be able to stock up from that little shop during the week, Mum." Agnes chatted away as she began to pack the suitcases and count out enough nappies for the two little ones and Emily was pleased to see her girl so well and happy again after having her family in such a rush.

The bungalow at Hemsby, one of a row of a dozen or so, was less than two minutes' walk from the beach.

And what a beach! A short, steep climb up through tussocky sand-dunes and then down a narrow gully straight out onto a wide stretch of fine, pale sand. At low tide, the sea glittered in the distance and at high tide was still shallow enough for the children to paddle in safety.

Half-a-dozen families occupied the best places near the dunes and Agnes and Emily returned smiling greetings with them as they staked out their own place further along the beach. That first long, sunny afternoon at Hemsby became the pattern of their days as the children grew brown and Shela slept peacefully between feeds in the old clothes basket Emily had discovered in the shed behind the bungalow.

"What's that funny smell, Gang-Gang?" John wanted to know as Agnes unpacked the children's clothes on their arrival at the bungalow and looked anxiously for their woollen swimsuits she was sure she'd put in last night.

Susie had already found the fenced-in cesspit at the bottom of the sandy garden and was busily chasing bluebottle flies when Emily called the little Sealyham in for her dinner.

"We'll have to keep the children away from that, Mum!" Agnes exclaimed, wrinkling her nose at the Elsan smell from the lean-to lavatory just outside the back door. And Emily laughed and reminded her about the communal lavatory behind her cottage in Gosmore and the night-soil men who emptied it twice a week.

"We'll just have to get used to it, I suppose," Agnes said with a grimace, then added with a laugh, "The lady at the store tells me it's a healthy smell and that all the bungalows have one because there's no sewerage system here at all."

Inside, the bungalow was surprisingly spacious with three small bedrooms, a good-sized living-room and a kitchen-cum-outhouse tacked on to the back, where Emily worked wonders with a cooker fuelled by bottled gas and Agnes boiled the baby's nappies in a big zinc bucket every night after the children had gone to bed.

After a week's good weather, the weekend of Ted's first visit was disappointingly overcast and Agnes was thankful that she could pile everyone into the big car for a day at the funfair in Great Yarmouth, just down the coast.

She'd missed Ted beside her at night and apparently he felt the same for their first lovemaking in the bungalow was urgent though satisfying and it was not until the next morning that Agnes realised that the Dutch Cap had remained in its little, black box and Ted's packets had remained in his waistcoat pocket yet again.

By Sunday night, as she watched the big Ford bump away down the stony road towards Newmarket and home, Agnes told herself that perhaps one slip didn't matter and that she'd see it didn't happen again.

It didn't, but at the end of that first August by the sea and plans forming in her head about new school clothes for John's first term at Goldington Road Infants' School in September, Agnes's period was overdue and Emily heard her being sick in the Elsan toilet before breakfast.

"The Sun Has Got His Hat On", sang Agnes a week later as they began the journey home and her mother recognised something like desperation in her girl's determinedly cheerful voice. "Surely not another one so quickly!"

John had been at his new school for nearly two months and Emily was wheeling Joyce and Shela down the road to Wooding's the grocers, when the first pain struck, low down in Agnes's stomach. Then she was on all fours on the kitchen floor and screaming for her mother as a menacing, red wetness soaked through her dress and ran down her new lisle stockings and into the T-bar shoes Ted had bought for her birthday.

"A three-month miscarriage can be very dangerous, Mr Winch."

The tired doctor removed his spectacles and glanced shrewdly at Ted as he felt for Agnes's wrist and with steady fingers noted that her pulse was racing and her skin was clammy to the touch.

Agnes could not remember what happened after she passed out on the kitchen floor for when Emily found her she had lost several pints of blood and with it the child conceived in Hemsby. Now she lay, white-faced and silent in the big, double bed, trying to ride each wave of pain as her womb rid itself of the remains of a human life.

"I'll stay with her, Mrs Thomas," Dr Chillingworth assured Emily, "but I shall need this from my dispensary. Perhaps Mr Winch could go for it straight away?" he added shortly, handing Ted a prescription for the powerful painkillers which would help his patient through the next few hours.

The kind doctor proved as good as his word for he never left Agnes's side for the rest of that day and when evening came and Nurse Rogers took over, promised to be back in the morning.

To Agnes, the miscarriage was far worse than any of her confinements. When she drifted, helpless and too weak to turn her head or speak or even open her eyes, it seemed that her only precious link with reality was Dr Chillingworth's cool touch as he held her small hand in his gentle, large one and it was only his voice she responded to each time she surfaced desperately from another trough of pain.

Emily kept the two little ones quiet as best she could and Ted took John to school for the rest of that awful week and by the end of it Agnes was sitting up in bed, pale and spent but so thankful that the pain had stopped. No doubt Ted thought her ready tears were for their lost child and at first they were, but as Agnes regained her strength and the children cuddled up to her before Emily took them for their morning walk to Russell Park, she admitted to herself that they were also tears of thankfulness that Mother Nature had given her a hard-earned rest.

By Christmas that year, Agnes was her old, cheerful self again and the Dutch Cap was in regular use, for Ted, like most men, did not like using the contents of the little packets in his waistcoat pocket.

The Licensed Victuallers' Association Ball at the Bedford Corn Exchange in January of 1933 was the best that Agnes could remember and she was happy now to dance the evening away with the same young man from last year's event.

"He's a lovely dancer, Mum, and his tango is better than Rudolph Valentino's any day," she told Emily the next day as they set up the washboard in the sink and shaved off pieces of Sunlight Soap to go in the copper waiting in the corner to boil the family sheets.

Since the miscarriage, Ted had become more considerate to his wife, often taking John with him on short journeys during the school holidays and not spending every evening in the club. But old habits die hard and before the end of the year, as Agnes and her mother listened to nightly wireless reports about Herr Hitler taking over as Chancellor of the Third German Reich, Ted began to stay out late again.

"The orders are not as good as they were," Agnes confided to her mother as the door closed behind Ted one late March evening in 1934. "He's worried about his job."

Emily kept her thoughts to herself for she could see that her girl was upset enough at Ted's behaviour and with yet another child on the way had more than enough to contend with as it was. The baby was overdue and there was no sense in giving her opinion of her son-in-law who sought his answers in the company of drinking friends rather than with his patient wife.

Two weeks later another girl was born to Agnes and the Vicar smiled again as he christened her Joan and old Dr Chillingworth sighed and shook his head and then did his best for mother and child.

It was at the end of the summer when Fred Perry became the Wimbledon Champion and the family had just returned from their bungalow holiday, that Ted picked up the long, buff envelope from the front-door mat to learn that he had lost his good job with The Shredded Wheat Company.

Afterwards, Agnes remembered that "Smoke Gets In Your Eyes" was playing softly on Ted's new radiogram as he opened the envelope and read out its contents.

"The territories are being re-distributed," he stated as the awful news began to sink in. "And mine has disappeared, Agnes!" Then as the car was returned, together with the regular supplies of free Shredded Wheat, Agnes watched anxiously as her worried man did his best to cope with a situation that many found themselves in during that year of recession and lost jobs.

At the end of it, with Ted working on an irregular basis for a contact made through his previous employment, he announced that they would have to give up the house and move to a smaller one with no attic room for Emily.

"Then where is she to live, Ted?" Agnes wanted to know as they discussed the situation one evening after her mother had gone up to bed.

"Well, she'll come with us, of course," Ted reassured his worried wife. "But there are only three bedrooms, Agnes. She'll have to share with the girls for now. Then when things improve, we'll look for another, bigger house again."

So the move was made and to her mother's consternation, Agnes was being sick again every morning and another baby was on the way and due to arrive in July 1935.

"Why on earth didn't you go back to Dr Chillingworth again?" Emily pleaded, as Agnes tried to keep her breakfast down and Ted kept well out of the way every evening. "He tried to help you before, child and he'll help you again if you ask him."

This was the nearest Emily ever got to discussing birth control with her daughter for she was of the generation where such things were only whispered about and then only between man and wife in the privacy of the bedroom.

But Agnes was blooming in this fifth pregnancy. And as she worked around her little home at 14 Newnham Street, not far from the spacious house they'd just left, or sat at her old treadle sewing machine singing the latest Fred Astaire song, "Dancing Cheek To Cheek", and mended the children's clothes and made new ones for the coming baby, she was content. For after all, she reasoned, they were still all together and she believed that Ted, with all his failings, would care for them to the best of his ability.

Her faith in her husband was justified, for by the time her second son George was born, weighing in at a hefty nine and a half pounds, his father was working full time again for The Hilmar Trading Company based in north London and although he had to drive much further afield, the pay was better than before and the family owned their first car. For Christmas that year of

1935, Ted presented Agnes with a beautiful silver fox fur and she wore it proudly draped over one shoulder of the smart, grey suit she had made for the British Legion reunion concert at the Granada cinema.

Now cases of Daw's Fruit Cordials lined the hallway as Ted brought his samples home and the bathroom cupboard was stacked high with white sample toilet-rolls. The younger children learned the alphabet through reading Avery's Macaroni Letters For Soup and John and Joyce learned strange words like "vermicelli" and "spaghetti" as they sat beside their father while the orders were entered in his book and played at "commercial travellers" with discarded sheets of carbon paper from the wastepaper-basket.

In that Silver Jubilee year, Agnes's oldest child was doing well at school and was looking forward to going into the scholarship class where his mother hoped he would win a place to the Bedford Boys Modern School. Already, John's interest in flying was establishing itself as the boy began to make model airplanes from balsa wood to hang from his bedroom ceiling and all his pocket money went on tubes of glue and little pots of paint to make each one authentic.

With the oldest three children now at school, Agnes's life settled down once more into a routine of washing, ironing and the constant sewing, for Emily continued to cook for the family as she had from the earliest days.

It was in the year that John achieved his ambition and won a place at the big secondary school in Harpur Street and King George V died and the new King Edward abdicated, that Agnes first became concerned

133

about her mother. She knew that Emily sorely missed her little room beneath the eaves in the old house but she had tried to make the older woman as comfortable as possible in the smaller one.

"If you have Joyce in with you, Mum," she explained, "the younger girls can share the other bed."

So Gang-Gang and Joyce shared the old, brass-knobbed bedstead and Shela and Joan slept top and bottom in a single bed in the corner. But it was very cramped in the small bedroom and Emily missed the privacy of her old one where she could go in the evenings after a long day spent with the family and where she could think about George and their old life together.

Agnes was making up new summer dresses for the three girls and singing "When I'm Cleaning Windows" along with George Formby on the wireless, when Emily dropped her bombshell.

"I've tried really hard for your sake, Agnes, but I'm getting on now and I need my own room. I've applied for a job as a cook in that big house at the corner of Bromham Road and Shakespeare Road on the other side of the town."

Before her startled daughter could protest she added hastily, "I'll have my own room there and the job's not at all hard for the Howards are away for a lot of the time because of his poor health. Do you remember, he was the mayor of Bedford some years ago, Agnes? So the job won't be hard at all. And I'll be able to come often to give you a hand with the children."

134

Before Christmas, Emily was installed in her new position and Agnes missed her mother badly.

"She's not far off seventy, Ted," she sighed over supper on the evening of her mother's departure. "And she shouldn't be working for anyone at her age!"

Agnes didn't add that her own workload would almost double now that Emily had gone, for that extra pair of hands had made all the difference with five children to care for. But she made the best of things as the bedroom space was eased and counted her blessings when she heard of those poor folk who came south on the Jarrow March in desperate search of help from the Government for jobs.

On the wireless the next year, Agnes and Emily listened enthralled, as the coronation of King George VI and Queen Elizabeth — their own Lady Elizabeth from the old days at Gosmore — was broadcast live from Westminster Abbey and, on the newsreels at the new Granada cinema, watched a smiling Duke of Windsor wave from a balcony in France after his marriage to Wallis Simpson.

Emily was as good as her word, for she came nearly every day to give Agnes a hand and her daughter needed that help now more than ever. For she was pregnant yet again and in the third month it was suspected to be an ectopic pregnancy which meant a stay in hospital for a whole month after a major operation only to find it was constipation after all.

"Imagine that, Ted!" Agnes laughed weakly as he visited her in the big, gynaecology ward at the South Wing of Bedford General Hospital in Kempston Road.

135

"A good dose of syrup of figs would have saved all this!" And she placed her small hand gingerly on the great swathe of wadding and bandages across her stomach. "The baby's fine though, thank goodness. And I'll be the same once I get home."

But she was far from fine for a long time after that operation and in desperation, Ted found a young girl from the next street to come in and help Agnes as her pregnancy progressed and after Agnes's fourth daughter, Mary, arrived safely, stood with bowed head as Dr Chillingworth gave him a dressing-down and told him he had put his wife's life at risk and there were to be no more babies.

Ted listened and agreed with the old doctor. But within the next two years, yet another child was born to Agnes and now the house was bulging at the seams and she was so tired every evening that she no longer noticed or cared when Ted went off to the club.

"The Folks That Live On The Hill", crooned the band-singer on the wireless as Agnes tried to keep her eyes open in order to finish off new dresses for Mary and Beryl, her two little ones asleep in the bedroom above.

It was ten o'clock and Ted was still out as she turned off the light in the living-room and wearily climbed the stairs to feed Beryl before she thankfully got to her own bed.

Lying there in the darkened room with the baby sleeping peacefully in the crib beside her, Agnes asked herself, not for the first time, how it had all come to this. It was true to say that she still loved Ted and she knew that in his own way he loved her and the children and she realised that their life together was better than many others in the late Thirties, when so many men were out of work and the dole was so pitifully small. But there must be more to life than this, the rebel in her thought wistfully. And then the baby stirred and coughed and Agnes leaned across to soothe her and pop the dummy back in her tiny mouth.

"You are my last baby," she whispered softly as the child settled again to sleep. Then she smiled as she recalled Ted's words when he handed out Easter eggs to her and the children the month before.

"Snow-White and the seven dwarfs!"

As long as it remains seven, she thought as sleep overcame her tired eyes and she heard Ted coming in through the front door.

So Agnes persevered while the orders on Ted's books grew smaller by the week as the retail market became uneasy at the way things were going in Europe and the National Socialist Party swayed the German people ever nearer to war.

Beryl was three months old when the family prepared to move yet again, this time to a larger house at 152 Castle Road, a few minutes' walk away from the smaller one near St. Cuthbert's church.

Agnes knew she would really miss the small community of shopkeepers and neighbours who had become her friends since the move into Newnham Street. Mrs Pateman, across the road, was now godmother to the three oldest children and "Pate-Pate" could always be relied upon in any small emergency or for providing Saturday sweets to any little Winch child who wandered away from their busy mother across the quiet street to her house.

Almost next door to Mrs Pateman was Billy Whiffin the barber's shop where Ted regularly had his hair cut short-back-and-sides and then John had all those golden curls cut just before he started school. "So he doesn't look like a girl any more!" his father had stated when Agnes protested about the shorn locks of her little son.

Stevens', the small confectioner's and general store opposite the house, was the Saturday destination of all the children, who spent their twopence a week pocket money there on sherbet dabs and bullseyes and Mrs Stevens had to go into the small room at the back to wash her hands after Emily called in on Fridays for paraffin to keep the Calor stove going in the girls' bedroom on cold winter nights. And it was in this small shop that Agnes bought her clothes-pegs and candles and the little night-lights that floated in a saucer of water and flickered away all night on a table on the landing in case she had to go to one of the children in the dark.

It was on a never-to-be-forgotten morning in summer 1937 that a distraught Agnes took her two oldest girls to Lane's the hairdresser's to have most of their hair cut off after Joyce brought home headlice from school and for weeks afterwards all the children were regularly shampooed with nasty-smelling medicated shampoo and the nit-comb pulled out the small eggs to drop with a satisfying "ping" onto sheets of newspaper spread on the kitchen floor.

Further along Newnham Street near the entrance to Featherstone Buildings where Mr Brittain, the St. Cuthbert's church sexton lived with his daughter Beryl, was White's shop where Agnes bought delicious, home-made ice-cream and Sunday teas in the summer months were not complete without a bowlful to go with strawberries or the apricots which Ted liked so much.

Linger's the butcher's, who had now moved from The Broadway to the corner of St. Cuthbert's Street opposite the church, was where Ted had bought the goose every Christmas since the family lived in the little street. And on Christmas Eve the back garden at number fourteen would be blowing with white feathers as Emily sat in the kitchen doorway to pluck the bird before it was stuffed ready for the oven early next day. And it was at the bottom of the garden, one cold day early in December that Ted caught a fine, fat hen that had somehow managed to flutter over the high fence from the coop at the back of The Ship.

"We'll have that for dinner on Sunday, Agnes!" he grinned as he wrung its neck in front of his horrified wife before placing the bird firmly down on the kitchen table. "Serves the landlord right. He should make sure the hen-coop door is fastened properly at night."

As Ted had promised, the new house had four bedrooms and Emily gave up her job and Agnes thankfully welcomed her mother back into family life once more.

"The room is all ready for you," she said as she hugged her mother in the doorway of the room at the end of the long corridor. And Emily unpacked her suitcase and looked at Agnes's drawn face and then quickly down at her belly and prayed silently that there would be no more little ones to make an old woman of her daughter before she was forty.

As Ted's orders fell, so his hours spent at the club increased and although he was never violent like Lizzie's Mick had been in the old days in London, there were times when he wandered about the house half the night, disturbing the babies and frightening the older children.

It became a regular event for Agnes to wake the children late at night and gather them all together in Emily's room, which was the only one with a lock on the door and here they would sleep in and on the big, brass bed as best they could until Ted fell at last into his own bed and they could go back to theirs for what was left of the night.

Always, the next morning, Agnes listened to the familiar outpourings of remorse from a sore-headed Ted and promises of reform which were doomed to be broken within a week of making them.

And now Agnes was taking in sewing alterations to make up for the shortfall in Ted's wages and although the hours spent at her old Singer treadle machine were hard on her, she still enjoyed the thrill of creating a new garment from an old one and practising the skills she'd learned so long ago at Spurrs.

By the end of the next summer, after a last holiday at Hemsby, the beaches were ringed with barbed wire and Mr Chamberlain told the waiting country that its young men were once again needed to fight for its freedom.

At the Plaza cinema by the river, Walt Disney's *Snow-White And The Seven Dwarfs* was showing and Emily queued for an hour with the older children to see the matinée, then cared for them all one Saturday evening while her daughter and Ted went to the last showing.

Three weeks later, Ted was once again out of work, this time voluntarily, for he was running the car at a loss in his efforts to obtain orders for the firm.

"Everyone's hanging back, Agnes," he sighed as he displayed yet another empty order page. "The shops are fearful of what's coming and there is bound to be rationing by next year. Jobs like mine are finished!"

Alone again that evening after Emily had gone up to her room, Agnes laid out the children's clothes for Sunday School the next day and made up her mind to approach Gladys Clayton's in the town for another contract to make babies' dresses again.

"Do you propose to sit up *all* night sewing, then?" asked Emily a few nights later as her daughter worked her way through a bundle of cut out baby dresses. But she volunteered to iron each one as it was finished for she knew that money was tighter now than it had ever been in the household and even her own pension of ten shillings a week went regularly on porridge oats and bread flour from Mayes, the big corn merchants in St. Paul's Square.

"You should keep some for yourself, Mum!" Agnes protested every week but nevertheless was glad of the extra, when Emily made all the bread needed for seven children with hearty appetites.

"I don't know what we'd do without her now, Ted," she told him one evening when her mother was visiting Kitty. And Ted looked at his wife's worried face and didn't go to the club that night.

Three days later and the day after the German navy scuttled its mighty battleship *Graf Spee* in the River Plate and the song played incessantly on the wireless was "We're Going To Hang Out The Washing On The Siegfried Line", the man who had fought in the trenches over twenty years earlier and now existed with a damaged lung and terrible memories returning as nightmares however much he drank, enlisted in the army and became a private in The Royal Army Service Corps.

Ted Winch spent his forty-fourth birthday on a bleak parade ground in Yorkshire, learning all over again how to be a soldier.

PART THREE

1940 to 1957

CHAPTER
ELEVEN

The first few months of the war were very strange ones for Agnes.

"I miss Ted so much," she confided to her friend over the road, "and when he's on leave it's lovely to have him at home with us all the time." Mrs Harrison looked keenly at the younger woman's face and marvelled, not for the first time, how anyone with such a large family and years of coping with a man like Ted Winch could still look like someone without a care in the world.

For Agnes, Ted's absence was a mixed blessing. The relief from the constant worry over the long hours he had spent at the club and the timely renewal of the birth-control contraption, gave her such unexpected peace of mind that she found herself adapting to the onset of rationing with a dogged determination that reminded Emily of George in one of his more stubborn moods.

"Your father would have been proud of you," she smiled, as Agnes carefully measured out the baby's National Dried Milk ready for her morning bottle. And also appalled that his only child should have to work so hard, she thought to herself.

John, who was in his third year at the Boys' Modern School, now developed an all-consuming interest in the progress of the war and every night had his ear glued to the wireless to listen to war reports about somewhere called Dunkirk and the brave men of the British Expeditionary Force caught between the advancing German army and the sea.

Later in that year, a new, homemade map appeared on the back of the kitchen door on which John began to mark with little flags, battles won and lost by both sides. Early in that year of 1940, it was covered almost entirely with black swastikas, but as the Royal Air Force fought against all odds over the fields of Kent and the southern counties, gradually a few Union Jacks appeared and the new Prime Minister, Winston Churchill, told a fearful nation waiting for invasion that, "never was so much owed by so many to so few".

It was during those few, breathless weeks of the Battle of Britain that John's young imagination was fired by daily reports of heroic deeds of young fighter pilots not many years older than himself and he decided there and then where his future lay and at school worked harder than ever to achieve his ambition of entry into the R.A.F. as soon as possible.

"Don't worry, Agnes," comforted Emily when she listened to her daughter's fears for John's safety, "it'll all be over before he's old enough to join up."

But Agnes remembered the young men she'd known in the last war and how they had waved goodbye with a laugh and then were never seen again.

146

"I just hope you're right, Mum," she sighed and turned up the volume on the wireless to listen to the terrible news about the blitz on London and the bombing of Liverpool and Coventry.

"A Nightingale Sang In Berkeley Square" Vera Lynn, the forces' sweetheart, warbled and Agnes wondered sadly if there would soon be no Berkeley Square left for it to sing in.

In autumn of that year, Joyce started her secondary education at the Harpur Central School which backed on to the Boys Modern School in Horne Lane, where she would learn the practical things of life.

"We have domestic science and sewing, Mum!" she exclaimed at the end of her first day as she proudly displayed to Agnes the new school timetable. "And next term we start Pitman shorthand and typing. So I can get a secretarial job when I leave."

Agnes looked at her eldest daughter's bright little face and smiled at the optimism she saw there. Already, Joyce was like a second mother to the brood who came after her and no one was better at finding the shops where oranges or tomatoes and off-the-ration foods made their rare appearances but became scarcer with every week that passed.

It was Agnes's oldest daughter who had discovered the hall behind a house opposite Bedford Prison in St. Loyes, where the W.R.V.S. ran a clothing exchange scheme every Saturday morning throughout the war years.

"Look what I got this week," she said proudly to her smiling mother just before Christmas, as she unwrapped three or four good quality woollen vests and two hand-knitted jumpers for her younger sisters. "There's some lovely things there, Mum, and we always seem to have enough points for the exchanges. I'll look out for school shoes and some of the Vyella stuff next time!"

Later that year, clothes rationing was introduced in earnest and now Agnes put her dressmaking experience to ever more practical use as she unpicked and turned skirts, dresses and coats for her growing family and soon was earning much needed extra money as neighbours began to bring jumble-sale clothes to her to alter for their own children.

"It would be lovely to cut out and make up something new for a change, Mum!" she grumbled one day as the door closed behind yet another satisfied customer who had just paid Agnes five shillings for making her girl a school uniform from one of her own old pre-war skirts.

As the first year of war drew to a close and rationing was tightened up, Ted began to arrive home with mysterious bulges at the bottom of his kit-bag and that weekend the family dined well on a good roast dinner and there was a pound or two of cheese on the cold slab in the larder.

"The sergeant's a friend of mine," he confided to Emily one Friday night as he emptied the kit-bag yet again. Then he grinned at the expression on her face as he pulled out two woollen army blankets and handed them to Agnes.

"The kids need new coats this winter. Well — here they are!"

A month later two more grey blankets appeared and Agnes made up a warm winter coat for each of her three older girls.

The baby dresses continued to arrive cut-out and ready-to-sew from Clayton's and this was her regular work, for Agnes never started them until all the children were in bed and Emily fussed and worried that her daughter was working herself into an early grave.

"Sixpence a time, Mum," she reminded Emily. "And each one takes about thirty minutes, so I can easily earn five shillings a night."

The money was crucial to start with, for during Ted's first four months back in the army, Agnes, along with thousands of other army wives, failed to receive the small wives' allowance from the War Office. Each week she called at the post office only to be told that there was nothing for her but to remember that there was a war on and we mustn't grumble.

"Mustn't grumble be blowed!" she exploded to Ted when he came home on a forty-eight-hour pass one weekend. "How are we expected to live on nothing, may I ask? And what I make and Mum's ten shillings a week barely pays for the food. Look here," she took the rent book from her handbag to show him, "we are already twelve weeks in arrears and the rates haven't been paid since Easter!"

It was two days after Ted returned to his depot in Winchester that a knock came at the front door and

Emily opened it to find a burly, middle-aged man standing squarely on the doorstep.

"Mrs Winch at home?" he enquired, looking beyond Emily at the pram in the hallway.

With Beryl clinging to her skirt and Mary wailing for her breakfast behind her, Agnes was told that the man was a bailiff who had the power to put her and the children out on the street if the rates were not fully paid within two weeks.

It was the last awful straw and Agnes sat and cried with her two little ones and Emily tried her best to comfort her distraught daughter.

Opposite to the house in Castle Road was the one-man taxi firm whose big, old cab had twice taken Agnes to hospital, the first time in the final stages of labour when Ted was out and the second time when Joan was knocked flying by a car outside the bicycle repair shop in York Street and Mr Tye, the Co-op butcher across the road, picked her up and brought her in to the kitchen badly concussed.

"I really don't know what to do, Mrs Harrison," she whispered tearfully to the taxi-driver's wife who had seen Agnes's distress after the bailiff left that morning. "Where am I to find that money in two weeks?" And the tears started again as her friend poured a strong cup of tea and urged her weeping friend to drink it.

Then she reached for the telephone, still in working order since her husband joined the Navy and dialling "0" asked the operator to put her through to the Town Hall.

"Tell Mrs Winch to come in to see me as soon as possible," advised the local rating supervisor. "I'm sure we can arrange something."

Agnes was on the next bus into the town and an hour later sat before a big desk looking fearfully at the elderly, grey-haired man behind it. The tale of the late army allowance and the struggle to feed the children and pay the rent and the threats of the bailiff was heard in silence by the supervisor and when she had finished, the grim look on his face convinced Agnes that there was to be no mercy here and that soon they would be out on the street.

She was wrong on both counts however, for the elderly man, who should have retired to his country cottage in the year the war started but agreed reluctantly to stay on for the duration, merely gave a huge sigh and reassured her that no one would put her on the street and that furthermore, the bailiff, who had been an unpopular police sergeant on the local force had no right to frighten Mrs Winch like that and now perhaps, we can sort something out?

"He was so kind," Agnes told her mother later that day. "He's having a stern word with the awful man's office and promises we won't be bothered by him again. And," she added with a smile, which Emily was pleased to see after all the tears, "he says that if we can manage to pay just a shilling a week off the arrears he will be satisfied. Then, when the back pay comes through, pay the rest off in instalments."

On the same day that the bailiff knocked on Agnes's door, Lance-Corporal Ted Winch requested an interview with his colonel at his new posting in Winchester to ask him to use his influence to get his wife's money through.

"Good God, man!" exploded the colonel, who had a lot of respect for this old army man who knew the ropes and needed no square-bashing to turn him into a soldier again, "why didn't you come to me before this?"

Then turning to his desk-sergeant who sat taking notes behind him he barked, "Put me through to the War Office immediately!"

Five minutes later Ted was assured that Agnes's allowance book would be on its way to the local post office that very day and as he saluted smartly and turned on his heel to leave the office, the colonel shook his head in bewilderment at a Government in such disarray that it could allow something like this to happen. How could they expect loyalty from the men when their families were threatened with eviction?

Of course, the good colonel never knew about Ted's laden kitbags and three months later none of this really mattered, as Agnes's debts were paid and Ted was promoted to corporal then posted to a secret destination in Yorkshire after his transfer to the Intelligence Corps.

"Glad to have you, corporal," said the captain young enough to be Ted's son. "Your French will be very useful to us."

Agnes was never told exactly what her husband did in that secret place in the north of England for Ted had been sworn to secrecy by the Official Secrets Act.

"It must be something to do with France, Mum," she replied to Emily's questions about Ted's work. "Haven't you noticed that he's always singing old Maurice Chevalier songs these days when he's had a drop?"

It was true, for within a few months both Agnes and the older children had learned by heart some of the old Chevalier songs and a few pre-war Edith Piaf numbers too. When Ted came home on rare leaves, he spoke French so often that Agnes suspected he was using the language every day in his new army job.

Within six months Sgt. Ted Winch was posted again, this time to Sierra Leone and Agnes began to receive heartwarming snapshots of her husband, looking thin and brown with small, black children on his knee and funny ones of him wearing baggy, khaki shorts and a pith-helmet standing beneath coconut palms on an exotic beach.

"It's not a bit like Hemsby, Agnes," he wrote on the back of one picture. "It's too bloody hot!"

There was a rising-sun flag on John's map the day the Japanese bombed Pearl Harbour and Agnes listened in wonder to the news of America's entry into the war and on Workers' Playtime on the B.B.C. Home Service, bluebirds flew over the white cliffs of Dover and Tommy Handley did his best to make everyone laugh when there didn't seem to be anything left to laugh about.

Agnes was certainly not laughing as she eyed the remaining small piece of Lifebuoy soap which must last the family until after the weekend.

"It's ridiculous, Mrs Harrison!" she exclaimed one afternoon as her friend stood waiting for her to finish altering one of her old dresses for her rapidly growing daughter. "My lot use all our soap ration in three days and after that it's a case of a handful of soda to soften the bath water. My girls hate it, but what can you do?"

"Have you tried boiling up the little pieces left at the end of the bar and then moulding them all together to make another small one?"

Agnes sighed as she waved goodbye to her friend and thought of all those lovely bars of scented soap she'd been given for pre-war Christmas presents and how they'd been put away and never used from one year's end to another. Oh! What she would give to have them now! And anyway she was sick of the carbolic smell of Lifebuoy soap which left your skin feeling so stretched and dry.

The four older children had just left for an afternoon at Newnham Swimming Baths, on the fifteen-shilling a year family season ticket when a ring at the doorbell brought Agnes's thoughts back from the past and glancing through the window she saw a harassed-looking woman wearing W.R.V.S. uniform standing on the front path surrounded by a small knot of children.

"Can you take any, madam?"

Agnes looked at her own healthy children and then at the little group standing so silently before her. The pale faces and lank hair told their own story and her heart went out to the mothers who had sent their children out of London away from the bombs and the sleepless nights to find shelter where they could in the care of those still willing to take in evacuees.

The children, some as young as four and the oldest no more than ten, each wore a label tied to a button or a lapel stating their name, age and address in London. The younger ones were snotty-nosed and red-eyed from crying all the way from St. Pancras Station and all of them had a gas-mask box slung across their thin shoulders.

"Poor little mites," murmured Agnes to the anxious woman on the doorstep, who had to billet the evacuees before the next train-load arrived in the morning. "But I have seven of my own," she explained, as the woman smiled tiredly and crossed off the number of the house from the list in her hand.

"You should have seen them, Mum," Agnes sighed as she opened another bundle of baby clothes that evening and prepared to settle down for the night's work at her old sewing machine. "They looked as if they'd not had a square meal in months. And their clothes! Well, my lot would never go out dressed like that, I can tell you!"

And Emily remembered her own poor childhood in Liverpool and all her brothers and sisters who wore hand-me-downs and were glad to get them when their breeches were in tatters and how no one in the family ever wore the right sized boots.

A month later, and despite protests from her mother, Agnes took in a family from Southend who had been bombed out twice. The father had found work at the Britannia Iron and Steel Works in Bedford and there was a small boy and judging by the size of his mother's belly, another baby due any day now.

"You can have the front bedroom, Mrs Hackett," smiled Agnes as her mother stayed disapprovingly out of sight. "And the use of the bathroom and kitchen. It will be a bit squashed but my children are nearly all at school now, although they do come home for their dinner."

It was early in May that Agnes opened the door yet again to find a young woman, also heavily pregnant, standing on the doorstep and asking for accommodation just for a few weeks.

"My husband's in the army, missus and I've knocked on every door in the road," she said and then burst into tears as Agnes drew her into the hallway with promises that she would see what could be done.

Upstairs, Emily tried to reason with her stubborn daughter.

"You know perfectly well that we've no space left, child!"

And a good job too, thought Agnes, as she remembered the dark days of last summer when she and thousands of others like her were preparing for the threatened invasion after the tragedy of Dunkirk. How she had cried over the ironing board at the thought of losing her first four children as evacuees to Canada rather than risk them living under the Nazis in a defeated Britain. And how they were due to leave on the next Red Cross ship out of Southampton and the terrible shock at the news of the sinking of the last one with thousands drowned and more tears of overwhelming relief when the scheme was abandoned by a very shocked Admiralty Office.

"And I already have to bake the bread at night for I can't get near the stove any more in the daytime," complained Emily as Agnes looked around her mother's little back bedroom and the older woman's heart sank as she saw the unasked question on her soft-hearted daughter's face.

"It won't be for long, Mum. She's just a girl and the baby's due within a month. Only until the husband's posted anyway."

So Emily moved into the tiny room next to the larder on the ground floor, which was already occupied by two of the girls in the family. And upstairs, the young mother-to-be settled into Emily's old room and her husband came on weekend leaves and in the small, walled garden, six criss-crossed clothes lines were never enough to take all the washing and Agnes asked Mrs North, next door, if she could use hers whenever they could be spared.

The neighbour on the other side, an elderly widow who was rarely seen behind stiff, lace curtains, took two lads of thirteen from the next batch of evacuees but refused to have any mothers and babies in the house.

"I can't stand the noise, Mrs Thomas and that's a fact," she confided to Emily one day over the garden wall. "Albert and I never had any of our own, you know."

Within two months the boys had returned to London and for the next two years, Agnes's house was bursting at the seams and next door an old woman lived alone in a four-bedroomed house.

The young wife stayed for eighteen months and left at the end of that time with another baby on the way and the news that her man was a prisoner of war in Germany.

"Keep in touch, my dear," Agnes told her as Mrs Harrison stowed the battered suitcase on the luggage rack at the back of her husband's old taxi and prepared to drive the girl down to the railway station.

"How's she going to explain that?" asked Emily as they waved goodbye and thought of the brave man who had been a P.O.W. for over a year now.

The Hacketts occupied the front bedroom for another six months after the young woman left until Agnes told them that they must find other accommodation because Ted was being invalided out of the army with blackwater fever contracted in Sierra Leone.

"We'll Meet Again", sang Vera Lynn on the wireless and Agnes sang along with her as she read the letter from the War Office about Ted's imminent medical discharge and made plans to re-decorate their bedroom before he returned.

The day after the Southend family left, she stood in the centre of her once beautiful bedroom, staring in dismay at the accumulated filth of two years' occupation by the slovenly woman to whom she had given shelter.

The room stank of urine and unwashed bodies and her once-lovely rugs were unrecognisable beneath a thick coating of dropped food and baby's faeces inadequately wiped up.

Emily came into the room as Agnes walked slowly over to the corner by the window where a flap of faded wallpaper hung down to the floor.

"Phew! For goodness sake open the window and let some of this awful smell out!" her mother pleaded. But Agnes did not reply for she was sniffing and wrinkling her nose in disgust as another, unfamiliar odour came up to meet her from the flapping, stained wallpaper.

Reaching out to take a corner of the paper, Agnes tugged sharply downwards and then screamed aloud as the reason for the smell was exposed on its back.

The room was alive with bugs. Fat, blood-filled bugs swarmed behind the wallpaper as Emily and Agnes pulled it frantically from the dirty walls and bore it away in great armfuls to be burned in the back garden. But it seemed that the more they killed as the bloated things scuttled for their lives, the more emerged from the skirting boards and the sickening stench was overpowering whenever one was squashed underfoot.

"There's only one way to get rid of them, Mrs Winch."

The hastily summoned Pest Control officer from the Town Hall was sympathetic to Agnes's plight but he had seen all this many times in his job and it was just routine for him to seal up the windows and then the door from the outside after fumigating the room with a vile-smelling spray.

"You can't go in there again for at least a week, my dear," he advised as Agnes followed him down the stairs and realised to her dismay that the Pest Control van was parked right outside the house.

"Whatever will people think, Mum?" she agonised as she watched the van move away from the kerb and saw that the old woman next door was watching from behind her stiff, lace curtains.

It was over a month later, when the bedroom was clean and the walls coated with fresh, cream distemper and the dingy paintwork covered with Woolworth's best white paint that Agnes welcomed her Ted home.

He was a very different man from the one who had left England so cheerfully only the year before, for the illness had left him thin and hollow-cheeked and his poor hands shook uncontrollably as he tried to hold his cup still on the saucer.

"You'll Never Know Just How Much I Love You", crooned Bing Crosby on the wireless and Agnes cried over her sewing at the sentimental words and then for the next few weeks nursed Ted through recurring and frightening bouts of malaria when the whole bed shook as she tried to administer the quinine prescribed by Dr Chillingworth.

When he was at his worst and unable to get to the lavatory, it was as much as the two women could manage between them, to lift him out of bed onto the chamberpot and Agnes wept again as he filled it up with evil-smelling black urine and afterwards was so weak that he begged them to leave him on the floor until the sweating and nausea passed.

Gradually, as his strength began to return and his meagre appetite improved, Ted was able to tell Agnes about the big fever hospital in Sierra Leone and the terrible night he just wanted to die.

"I'll never forget that old battle-axe of a sister," he whispered hoarsely, for the fever had affected his vocal chords and a lifetime of smoking meant that it would take him far longer to recover. "A Queen Alexandra nurse, she was," Ted continued as Agnes bent nearer to catch the words. "She just wouldn't let me die! Kept on talking about home and you and the children. All through the night she talked, until the fever broke and I was out of danger. Great old girl. A proper Florence Nightingale!"

Ted's honourable discharge on medical grounds came through before the summer was over and with it the problem of how to earn a living, for the army pension was so small that, as Agnes complained to Mrs Harrison, "It won't be enough to keep him in cigarettes."

It was in 1943 that John, inspired more than ever by the exploits of the crews on the Dam Busters raids, announced that when he was sixteen in December, he was applying for an apprenticeship in the R.A.F.

"When I'm eighteen," he assured his stunned mother, "I can try for flying training and if the war lasts long enough," he grinned, "I'll be flying Spitfires!"

Just before the fifth Christmas of the war, Agnes's first-born left the family home to realise his dream and his mother sat in the boy's bedroom the next morning looking up at the dozens of model airplanes suspended from the ceiling. The large war-map had long ago been transferred to the wall in John's room and now Union

Jacks were stuck in all along the north coast of Africa and halfway up the leg of Italy. On the small chest by the window was John's carefully displayed collection of twisted pieces of shrapnel and the remains of a fire-damaged flying boot which had once kept a German pilot's left foot warm before his Heinkel was shot down and the local boys beat the Civil Defence Corps to the site for coveted souvenirs.

"Little monsters," Emily muttered later as she surveyed the grisly trophies when she came up to strip the narrow bed. But Agnes knew it was John's way of participating in the struggle going on in the skies above Britain and North Africa and Italy and she prayed that her son would not die in an airplane like that unknown, young German boy.

A few months after John left home, Joyce was ready to leave school at fourteen competent in Pitman shorthand and typing at sixty words a minute. Two weeks later she started work in the office of Harry Hills Gents Outfitters, opposite Braggins & Sons, school uniform suppliers to the town in Silver Street, Bedford.

"They say I'll get a rise when I've been there six months," she assured her mother as she handed over the wage-packet at the end of her first week with the firm. Agnes smiled as she returned a pound of it to the girl for pocket-money, kept a pound towards the housekeeping and later quietly put ten shillings of that into the new National Savings account she'd opened for her daughter.

The old town these days seemed to be full of servicemen, for there were several airfields within a bus ride of the dance halls and pubs of Bedford.

Joyce's best friend Mary was walking out with a G.I. and Agnes knew it would not be long before her daughter started jitterbugging at the Corn Exchange with one of those smooth-talking young men who were looked on with suspicion and envy by the British Army lads. Not least, she suspected, because as Mr Punch put it, they were, "overpaid, oversexed and over here".

With the rest of the children now at school and Shela and Joan passing the scholarship to the Bedford Girls' Modern School, Agnes continued to work far into the night to earn enough money to keep the family out of debt but this year of the war continued as grey and dismal as the previous ones had been, for Ted's health was slow to improve and by Christmas he was still not in work.

The new year was one week old and Agnes was settling down to a day's work at her sewing while Emily washed up after breakfast. The ring at the front door bell took Agnes by surprise for it was not rent day until Friday and she was not expecting any customers.

"Hallo, sweetheart. And how's my favourite girl doing these days?"

Agnes knew the voice but the face of the man who had been so obnoxious to her all those years ago had changed beyond recognition. Alf Perkins had spent the war in Devon away from the air-raids, making a good living out of "surplus stock," he told a surprised Ted. But the shelling of the Royal Naval Dockyards in

Plymouth, early in the war, had put him in hospital in Exeter.

Agnes looked at the black patch over one of the man's eyes and shuddered at the sight of a livid, red scar from his forehead down to his jawline.

"I really copped it that night, Ted," he grimaced over a glass of whisky as the two old friends shared their experiences in the bar of the club that evening. "But this lot is coming to an end soon, mark my words, old son. And when it does there will be good pickings for those with their wits about them."

"Alf's back in Bedford now, Agnes," Ted informed her the next morning, "and he wants me to go into business with him. Something to do with army surplus stock. I told him I'd think about it but he won't wait for too long for me to make up my mind. Says there's big money out there just waiting to be picked up by the smart ones."

All that week, Agnes worked and worried about Ted. She no more trusted Alf now than she had in the old days and even then she suspected Ted only tolerated him because of their club membership and the perks it brought to the family.

The man's daughter-in-law had remarried a year or two after the R101 disaster and given up the little cafe in Tavistock Street. Agnes often saw her in the town where they were both registered at Sainsbury's in Midland Road for bacon and butter. On the next ration day she made up her mind to speak to her about Alf.

"If you take my advice, Agnes," the woman spoke quietly to her friend as they waited for the shop

164

assistant to weigh up her butter ration with the wooden butter-pats, "you'll tell your Ted not to have anything to do with him. God knows what he's been up to these last few years but it can't have been anything legal because we've had the police round to us twice asking about him."

Over supper that night, Agnes repeated what her friend had said about Alf and Ted shook his head and called the man a rogue and that was the end of any idea of going into business with him.

"Anyway, Agnes," Ted laughed shortly, "he wanted me to invest five hundred pounds and we just don't have it!"

It was several weeks later that Ted secured a job at the American Red Cross G.I. Club in Bromham Road in Bedford.

"It's only storeman's work," he sighed as he prepared for his first day. Then the ghost of the old familiar grin appeared as he added, "But it's good money and you can bet there'll be perks attached. Those Yanks seem to have everything!"

Ted was right for soon the family began to make meals of tinned frankfurters and enjoyed treats of American candy and popcorn when these things were unobtainable in wartime Britain.

"Those boys are very generous now they know I have kids at home," Ted informed Emily as she surveyed the strange tinned sausages and wondered how to cook them. But they made a nice change from stew and dumplings, she had to admit. Although she didn't hold much truck with this foreign food, the children seemed to like them and that was good enough for Emily.

For George, Agnes's good-natured second son, the road to a better education presented no challenges and he was the one who effortlessly passed the scholarship with flying colours to win a place at Bedford Public School.

"The next best after Stowe, I was told, Ted!" enthused Agnes after meeting George's new headmaster on parents' day.

Now, the struggle to provide proper school uniforms intensified as each of her children claimed their place at secondary schools through their own efforts. For there was no question of paying the fees demanded by these good schools and Agnes worked harder than ever to give her children the opportunities they deserved.

Soon after Ted started work at the G.I. Club, Agnes applied for the position of tailoress at the big American Red Cross Officers' Club on the corner of Kimbolton Road and Goldington Road.

The interview with the nice American lady went without a hitch and Agnes arrived home full of the details about her new job.

"Will you be alright, Mum?" she asked anxiously after breakfast on her first day. "I'll be home by six so that's only two hours you have to keep your eye on the children."

Emily was now over seventy and although she still pulled her weight in the household, Agnes knew her mother could no longer cope for too long with the noise of the big family and that more and more she

166

sought peace and quiet in her little room at the back of the house.

"Don't worry, child," Emily smiled at the worried look on Agnes's face. "Joyce and Shela will help with the little ones and in the school holidays I'll send them all down to the park!"

When America came into the war and the G.I.s came into Bedford, the local girls made the most of these well-dressed, well-paid young men who knew how to treat a girl and what if your best friend was stupid enough to get in the family way, it wouldn't happen to you!

Agnes knew that Joyce, like most of her friends, had an American boyfriend but she made sure that her daughter brought him home rather than get into trouble in the meadows by the river, where many a young girl was seduced by the exciting American accent and false promises of a better life "back home".

Within a year, two of Joyce's old school friends were left stranded with big bellies only to find that their G.I.s were hastily posted elsewhere when the girls' plight was revealed to the Commanding Officer at Twinwoods or Thurleigh, a few miles out of Bedford.

"It's the way of all soldiers abroad," stated Ted as another girl in the street was taken to the old double-fronted house at the top of Queen Street in the Black Tom area of the town to give birth to her little American baby. "They live for the day — or the night as the case may be. They might not live to see another one."

It was a worrying time for Agnes, who kept a sharp eye on Joyce's comings and goings and Ted often waited at the front gate when she was not home by ten o'clock. More than once he went looking for her if she was only a few minutes late and Emily told and retold the story of Lily, Agnes's old friend who got into trouble when she was young.

"She's getting old now, Joyce," Agnes explained to her oldest daughter who had listened yet again to her grandmother's story. "You must make allowances for her. Old people sometimes live in the past for they imagine it was better than the present. I can tell you that it wasn't. Even with this war on!"

And Joyce took up a cup of tea and some of the drop-scones the old lady had made that afternoon and stayed to talk to her for much longer than usual.

Emily still made all the bread the family needed and the old, green and gold cake-tin that had been full of "Fairy Toffees" when it was new one Christmas long ago, was always now filled with ginger parkin and great slabs of bread pudding to feed the hungry children when they came in from school.

"Why can't we have iced buns like Mabel has next door?" asked Shela one day as she licked the mixing bowl clean after one of Gang-Gang's big baking sessions.

"Because those shop buns are full of bicarbonate of soda. That's why!" Emily retorted as she stooped painfully to open the oven door to place a tray of apple turnovers carefully on the middle shelf. But the next Sunday, the children had pink-iced fairy cakes for tea and after that there always seemed to be a thick crust of homemade bread spread with beef dripping from the weekend roast waiting for Shela on the larder shelf when she got home first from school.

Shela was fourteen before she tasted shop buns and when she did she was sadly disappointed.

"Not as good as Gang-Gang's, Mum," she confided to her mother, who nodded and smiled as she thought about the long years when Emily did all the cooking and how well the children looked on it.

Emily was slowing down at last and now rested every afternoon on the old, brass bedstead in her little room; but she was there for the children when Agnes was at work. Although the old lady did less in the kitchen, the two oldest girls had to pull their weight in the house, although Shela would much rather sit with her nose in a book than look after those noisy kids all afternoon. And Agnes was able to spend longer hours in the sewing-room at the Officers' Club. Longer hours meant more money.

Agnes had been working in her new job for just a few weeks when the sewing-room door opened one day to admit a smiling, balding man who wanted to know if she could alter his smart, grey suit for him.

"I need it by tomorrow evening, Ma'am, if you could oblige me!"

And Bing Crosby smiled again as Agnes recognised him and replied that it would be ready for him by the morning.

A month later, Bob Hope poked his turned-up nose round the door to ask Agnes to sew on some shirt buttons for him and this time she remembered to get his autograph before he left to perform with Bing at a big concert on the air-base at R.A.F. Duxford.

The polite, young men who knocked quietly at the resident tailoress's door and called her Ma'am, paid well for their alterations and Agnes was able to charge two shillings and sixpence for turning up "pink pants" and one pound ten shillings for altering the dark green uniform jackets into battle blouses which the aircrew preferred for flying duties.

There were heartbreaking times when one of the young officers slipped quietly into the room to collect something one of his buddies had left for alteration.

"I'm afraid he didn't make it this time, Ma'am," they explained gravely. And Agnes knew that another boy not much older than John had been in one of the Flying Fortresses that crossed the town every day now in their hundreds on daylight raids on some German city. And had not returned.

"We have to send everything back to his family, Ma'am," they explained as Agnes listened sadly and remembered the fresh-faced boy who would never wear the garment she'd altered so carefully. "But the captain says to make sure your bill is settled in full." And although Agnes protested, the money was always left discreetly on the table, sometimes with a couple of Hershey bars or a bag of jelly-beans for the cute kids of the nice lady in the sewing-room.

In June of that year came the long-awaited response to demands painted on every available blank wall space all over Britain.

"Open The Second Front Now"

In her workroom at the American Officers' Club on that day, Agnes heard the sounds of music coming from the barber's shop across the corridor.

"The Boogie Woogie Bugle Boy Of Company B", chanted the Andrews Sisters defiantly. The rest of the building was eerily silent, for all the aircrews were on standby waiting for orders to begin the invasion of Europe.

"I wonder how many of them we'll see here again, Mr Morris," she commented as the elderly man who had a son serving in the Royal Air Force rearranged a pile of hot towels for the third time that morning and offered the nice little tailoress who worked so hard a cup of tea before she went back to her workroom.

The D-Day landings were the topic of every conversation in the local shops and on street corners and when John came home on weekend leaves, American and Canadian flags joined the Union Jacks all along the Normandy coastline on his big war-map.

"General Eisenhower is in charge now," he enthused as she watched him move the flags steadily eastwards across France and Belgium and, when Paris was liberated, Ted came home after a night out at the British Legion Club singing a song he'd last heard twenty-five years earlier in a nightclub in Montmartre sung by Mistinguette, the famous French cabaret star.

It was just before Christmas of 1944 that Agnes received a surprise invitation for all the children to come to the party that the young officers were holding for the British staff and their families in the big canteen at the club.

"Will Glenn Miller really be there, Mum?" Joyce kept asking as she helped Agnes get the younger ones ready for the treat.

"Well, I know he's staying at the club this week," smiled her mother. "Mr Morris tells me he's bound to be there along with some of the boys in his band. There's even a rumour that Bing Crosby will look in at some time and his old pal Bob Hope is passing through. So if you're lucky you'll see him as well!"

The hundred or so children at the party had not seen food like it for over five years and they made the most of it. A long table at the end of the room was piled high with doughnuts, jellies, ice-creams and every kind of fancy cake you could imagine and the three-tiered Christmas cake, festooned with red and green ribbon, was a wonder to behold.

"Come on, kids. Help yourselves!" The quiet voice of the tall man in the smart dark-green officer's jacket and beige trousers, the uniform of the U.S.A.A.F., urged the children towards the table as his famous band began to play carols and Major Glenn Miller smiled as he showed Agnes a photograph of his wife and children safe at home in America.

Later, there were games organised by two young "lootenants" as Joyce had learned to call them and later still, as more refreshments appeared, the same balding man whose suit Agnes had altered in time for his stage performance earlier that year, appeared on the stage and took the microphone to sing, "I'm Dreaming Of A

172

White Christmas", and told jokes with the funny man with a turned-up nose and a big smile. Bing and Bob did their bit at that party and then went on to another one at a secret airfield somewhere in Norfolk and before the Bedford children went home they were each handed a parcel of candy and chewing gum by their generous American hosts.

With just a few days left before Christmas, Agnes was hard at work in the sewing-room trying to get all her work up to date with the help of her eldest daughter who was almost as skilled with the needle as her mother had been at her age.

"If you can get those trousers turned up for me, Joyce," she said, "I can get on with this battlejacket for the Major. He's flying over to Paris in the morning and he particularly asked me to get it finished in time tonight."

An hour later, the door opened and the tall, quiet man Joyce remembered from the party slipped into the room to try on his new jacket.

"Thanks a million, Ma'am," he smiled as Agnes handed it to him and then, carefully placing a little envelope on the table, turned to Joyce and asked if she'd like to walk with him to his jeep waiting outside to take him out to the airfield.

It was cold and foggy in the car park and Joyce shivered in her thin blouse and skirt as Major Glenn Miller climbed on board and his driver handed her a large bag of oranges to take home for the family. Then he waved and smiled as the jeep moved away into the fog and Joyce went running back into the warm workroom to show her mother the oranges that she hardly remembered and little Beryl didn't remember at all.

The next evening, as the children tucked in to the oranges, the six o'clock news bulletin on the Home Service reported that the light aircraft carrying Major Glenn Miller and his manager had never reached its destination and it was believed that it had gone down in the English Channel.

"Oh, those poor men," sighed Agnes, thinking of the quiet-voiced major who had shown her his family snapshots at the Christmas party. "And what a sad Christmas it will be for their wives and children."

"Mairzy Doats And Dozey Doats", sang Jo Stafford on the wireless and Agnes laughed at the silly song then listened with sadness to the news about more buzz-bombs falling on London.

"The Jerries are getting desperate now," a subdued Ted told her one evening in March as he sat smoking his Player's Full Strength by the fire in the kitchen. And the cough which had begun in the trenches all those years before, caught at his weakened chest as he struggled for breath.

The terror of the V2 rockets in a last, all-out attempt by the enemy to demoralise London even as the allied armies crossed the Rhine into Germany itself, was shown to silent customers at the Granada cinema in St. Peter's Street and Agnes and Ted went down to R.A.F. Halton in Buckinghamshire for John's passing-out parade.

174

"They've accepted me for flying training," their suddenly very grown-up son told his parents that evening as Agnes kissed him goodbye. "It takes about six months and then I'll be flying the new jets!"

Agnes's heart sank as she watched her first-born walk confidently away from her back to the barracks and she knew that she had finally lost him to his dream of flying and tried hard to feel glad for him.

"It'll all be over before he completes the course," comforted Ted on the way home in an echo of the very words her mother had used when John first announced his intention of learning to fly. And now it was only six months away and this awful war ground relentlessly on, waiting to take him away from her for good.

CHAPTER
TWELVE

"Just come to look at it!"

Agnes was sitting with her feet up after a long day at the club and she still had to iron the children's uniforms for school in the morning.

"Don't you think we are doing well enough, Ted, without taking on all that hard work?"

Ted was full of enthusiasm for the idea that had slowly been forming in his mind ever since he'd seen the premises to let at the end of Castle Road.

"It's ideal for a cafe," he stated, as Agnes plugged the electric iron into the double light socket above and the bulb began to sway as she started the ironing. "Not anything very elaborate," he continued as she did not reply. "Just teas and snacks to start with and I can run it easily with Joyce's help. The Yanks are going home soon, Agnes. Then we'll both be out of a job."

The small, double-fronted shop had been a coal-order office for C.A.E.C. or "Cacky" Howard as he was known locally, the coal merchant. With a reasonable rent of four pounds a week it was indeed, as Ted had said, ideally situated in a busy area in Castle Hill just round the corner from the old house in Newnham Street. It was surrounded by workshops and garages, small clothing factories and all manner of enterprises employing hundreds of workers.

Directly opposite the shop, on the other side of a huge static water tank, installed there at the beginning of the war in case of air raids, stood George Ford & Son, Upholsterer and Mattress Maker. Across the road in Castle Works, H. H. Bennet manufactured ladies' clothing while in Castle Lane, just around the corner, T. C. Ginn, the removal firm, ran a thriving business. Near the entrance to Castle Mound and almost opposite St. Cuthbert's Church, Mr Keech owned a Billiard Hall and Bacchus, the electrical goods shop, and Wells, the furniture shop, both had workshops in Castle Lane. Gent's Mineral Waters factory in Castle Hill backed onto John Bull the jewellers at the entrance to John Bull Passage leading out into the High Street.

"And they'll all need their tea-breaks!"

Agnes looked searchingly at Ted's animated face and realised with a pang that the man who could outsell every salesman in his old firm was desperate to be his own man again. He would never again drive around the Home Counties persuading small grocers to buy his goods but the old spark was still there. No one knew better than his wife how degrading it had been for Ted to work as a storeman and how hard he had tried to make up for the lack of all the good things they'd had before the war when money was plentiful and they were the only family in the street to own a car.

As Ted went on to tell Agnes that an old friend from the Conservative Club who now worked at the

Ministry of Food office in the Town Hall would help with food allocation forms and the necessary catering licence, she knew that any opposition from her would be to no avail. Ted had found the outlet for his business talents at last and was really happy for the first time since he'd come home from the war.

In the old days, Agnes told her mother a few days later, she'd often grumbled about Ted's time spent with his cronies at the club but now those acquaintanceships were paying off as first one then another was contacted and work on the shop began and furniture and equipment produced magically from long-closed stores was dusted off and installed.

Castle Hill Cafe was ready and open for business within six weeks of signing the lease with Mr Filby, the landlord and the proprietor of Castle Hill Garage just behind the new shop.

"What a day to open," commented Emily as she helped her daughter unpack the thick, white cups and saucers and polished the bell-jars for the counter where sandwiches would be displayed for sale. "April the first! I just hope your Ted knows what he's doing, that's all!"

It had been decided that Agnes would keep on her job at the Officers' Club until business picked up in the cafe and then she would give in her notice to work in the family firm.

It had been hard work to persuade Joyce to leave her job at Harry Hills the gents' outfitters in Silver Street, for she was now sixteen with a regular boyfriend and she enjoyed her evenings out.

178

"It will only be for a few months," Ted assured his sceptical oldest daughter. "Then your mother will take over."

As things turned out, Joyce lasted only two of those months working for her father for she was a strong-willed girl who not only objected to washing up for a living but positively rebelled against working a fifteen-hour day with only one afternoon off a week.

It was two weeks after V.E. Day and the cafe was still festooned with bunting from the celebrations and Ted's old radio played "We'll Gather Lilacs" to appreciative customers when Joyce decided she'd had enough. No amount of reassurance that things would get better if only she had patience prevented the girl from stating at midnight one Saturday, when her feet were aching fit to fall off, that she'd be looking for another job on Monday morning.

"I've not been to the pictures in over two months, Mum!" she protested as she pulled on her coat and then flounced out of the door leaving her mother to cope with an angry Ted in the little cafe.

"No one can blame her," sighed a harassed Agnes as they prepared to leave the shop half-an-hour later. "She's young and wants to live a bit before settling down. She'll never do that working in the cafe."

Since the business opened, Shela, the second daughter, had spent every available moment in the cosy, little shop, working in the evenings and at weekends learning how to keep the books and the rationing records for the Food Office. Within three months she was capable of simple book-keeping and banking, ordering goods and paying accounts until, as her father said, she understood the business as well as he did himself.

"She wants to leave school, you know, Agnes," he told his wife yet again. And again Agnes would not hear of it, for the girl was in the fourth year at her secondary school and her mother wanted her to gain the School Certificate and then matriculate and go on to college.

"When you employ staff, your troubles begin!" the manager of John Bull's the jewellers warned Ted more than once as the family struggled to get the little business off the ground and although it was growing slowly, they knew that sooner or later they would need more help.

When Shela went back to school in September she did not move up to the next year with her friends.

"Her work has fallen behind, Mrs Winch," explained the young form teacher after Shela had tearfully told her mother how awful it was to be in the same class as last year's third-year kids, and all a year younger.

Agnes blamed herself for not putting her foot down hard enough over the girl's homework and the long hours her daughter spent in the shop and she made her promise to try her best at school at least until Christmas when there might be a chance to be re-installed with her old friends in the fifth year.

On the first day of the next term, Shela refused flatly to go to school and Agnes made an appointment with the headmistress to tell her that her daughter was very unhappy and that she was needed in the business. The next day, Shela started her working life at fourteen years and five months and school was left behind as she worked hard in the shop and kept her father happy.

The war was over but food rationing remained and Ted used every means possible to boost trade in the little business. Every Thursday, the pig-swill man called to take away the overflowing bin and replace it with an empty one. Inside the bin were six dozen eggs supplied quite illegally and in blatant contravention of the strict rationing laws but for Ted they represented the draw he'd been looking for and soon the little cafe became known as the place you could always get a fried egg. And business boomed.

The two distinguished-looking men who came in for coffee every morning at eleven o'clock precisely, were soon followed by a score or so more who found the cafe a convenient and friendly place for a short break from rehearsals.

"That's Sir Adrian Boult," whispered Shela as the taller of the two men paid for his coffee and smiled as he spooned three spoonfuls of sugar into his cup. "He says that the rehearsal rooms are unheated and the poor chaps in the orchestra have to keep their coats on!"

Ted was delighted that the B.B.C. Symphony Orchestra had chosen Bunyan Meeting Hall, just around the corner in Mill Street, for their rehearsal rooms for it meant a big boost in snack sales.

All during the previous year, the orchestra, unable to work or perform in London, where first the buzz-bombs and then V-2 rockets kept audiences at home, had come to Bedford to rehearse and perform.

Their concerts, with Sir Adrian and Sir John Barbirolli conducting, were regularly broadcast from the Corn Exchange in St. Paul's Square and just as regularly, the gentlemen of the string section left complimentary tickets for the nice café proprietor's wife and her daughter.

"My taste's more Glenn Miller than Mozart, Mum!" protested Shela as they took their seats for the first concert. But two hours later she had changed her mind as they left the hall with all that glorious music still ringing in her head.

"It was lovely, Dad," she told him later as she washed up the last few cups. "I want to go again."

Ted remembered that conversation when he bought the girl's fifteenth birthday present later that year. A wind-up gramophone was now perched on Shela's bedside table together with a set of 75rpm records. Her favourite music was the Rachmaninov Piano Concerto, for she'd recently seen it played by Ann Todd in *The Seventh Veil* at the Granada and afterwards she saved to buy the records for herself.

With the increase in sales, food allocations grew and Ted was talking about converting the first floor into a restaurant.

"He's not been near the club since we opened, Mum." Agnes was slicing a quartern loaf on the big slicing machine in the corner of the kitchen for cheese and tomato sandwiches. Emily nodded in agreement as she buttered the bread and grated cheese and silently thanked God that business was keeping her son-in-law sober and Agnes happy.

182

Joyce had found another job in a rival gents' outfitters and as she was the only female on the premises, was thoroughly spoiled by the three elderly men who walked about the shop with tape measures round their necks and were all old enough to be her grandfather.

"They'll be retired when the youngsters are demobbed," Ted warned his eldest daughter, then added with a knowing look and a wink, "then you'll have to watch out for yourself, my girl. Those boys have been away for a long time."

But Joyce was happy enough as she turned seventeen and went to the pictures twice a week and dancing on Saturdays at the Dujon Ballroom in the High Street. Sometimes she felt quite sorry for Shela, working until eleven every night and running the snack counter on her own on Sunday afternoons. Now and again she dropped in with her friends to give a hand.

"You're mad to do it, Shela!" she protested one Sunday evening as her sister locked the door behind her and began the weary trudge back to the house nearly a mile down the road.

"But I like it!" retorted Shela. Then she added with a big grin, "It's better than school, anyway. And you never did get on with Dad, Joyce. You're too much like him. I know how to handle him, that's all."

It was true, for Shela had discovered early on in her short life that if you stood up to Dad he respected you. But that didn't mean he let you get all your own way — far from it. He expected you to work as hard as he did himself and then he could be very generous and every few months there would be a big, white five-pound note extra in her little wage packet to spend on clothes or new shoes. Although, she thought ruefully, there never seemed to be much of an opportunity to wear them.

Catering wages in 1946 were very poor and the two girls now employed by Ted relied on tips to make their earnings worthwhile. But the girls who would do this kind of work were, with the exception of the one reliable girl who stayed for three years, intent on moving on from one cafe to another in the Bedford area. Most of them were waiting for their men to be demobbed and then good staff would be hard to find, for like the girls in service after the Great War, they would demand much better pay and the Trades Unions would make sure they got it.

With a Labour Government now in power and Clement Attlee at the helm, wage structures were being reviewed constantly and never again would the folk who did all the hard work of industry and commerce be content with a bare living wage.

"Those days are over," announced Alf Parker as he reached over the counter to pick up the betting slips that Ted had collected for him. "And a good thing too. The boys will spend more money with me that way."

Then he grinned as he openly looked Agnes's trim figure up and down appreciatively and winked at her as she came down the stairs with a fresh batch of sandwiches for the bell-jars.

"I can't think why you do that for him, Ted!" she protested later as she bent over the counter trying to hide the embarrassed flush that odious man always brought to her face and neck. "You both know it's illegal."

"Oh, old Alf's all right, Agnes. We all have to make a living," replied Ted. But he failed to tell his wife of the little business venture he and old Alf had hatched up just before she came down the stairs.

The fruit machine was installed in the cafe a few days later and within a week it had taken enough money in sixpences to pay the rent on the shop for a month. But there were complications to this satisfactory state of affairs for as Ted found out later, this was another of Alf's dodgy enterprises. The pinball machine, now taking up another corner of the cafe and taking only pennies, was viewed with a tolerant eye by the local constabulary but a one-armed bandit was an entirely different matter.

"My boy put his entire wages in that thing!"

The short, red-faced woman leaned over the counter, glaring at a startled Shela who was alone in the shop on a quiet afternoon before the evening rush started.

"And I want it back! He'd not even had time to pay me his board and lodging. So you tell your boss that I'll be back tonight with my old man. And he's a lot bigger than me!"

"She means it, Dad," Shela told her father when he got back to work after his afternoon forty winks. "Four pounds, ten shillings, she said. Or she'll get the police onto you."

Later that evening, Ted took the woman's husband for a quiet pint and even more quietly, handed back his son's wages.

"There you are. Five pounds, I think you said?"

In the cafe, Shela plied the unpleasant woman with coffee and jam puffs until the men came back and hoped that the whole thing would be hushed up.

She was wrong and so was Ted for thinking he could bribe the boy's father with an extra ten shillings. For just after opening time on Saturday morning, when Bing was giving out with "A Gal In Calico", and Shela was busy in the back sugaring and jamming doughnuts, and the coffee machine was beginning to gurgle on the counter, young Albert Filby from the garage next door came in and whispered something urgently to her father. A huge police sergeant, accompanied by two young constables were, even as he spoke, approaching the cafe on foot with the sole purpose of taking possession of Ted's goldmine in the corner.

"Quick, Mr Winch!" the boy urged. "They're nearly here. Come on. I'll give you a hand to shift it out of the way."

Shela watched open-mouthed as the heavy, lead-based machine was lifted bodily from its shelf before the struggle to carry it up two flights of stairs and finally to hide it safely out of sight behind the flour-sacks in the kitchen.

Down below in the snack-bar, she just had time to place the new Granada advert on the vacated shelf before the door opened to admit the three policemen. When a breathless Ted reached the bottom of the stairs again, she was spooning extra sugar into the constables' teas as Sgt. Kirby looked carefully around the room.

186

"Just checking, sir," he informed Ted as he opened the door of the big fridge near the back door. "We have to act on information received."

Later, as they drained their cups and prepared to leave, the sergeant told Ted that they'd be calling in again sometime. "I hope for your sake, sir, that we won't be finding what we'll be looking for. Nothing illegal that is!"

Then they were gone and Ted lit up a Player's cigarette, sighing with relief that old Kirby had failed to spot all those eggs in the fridge and then thanked Albert for his help before handing him a free jug of tea for his trouble.

The one-armed bandit, which Ted had found out nearly too late was illegal to operate in a public place, disappeared the next day and Shela never did enquire of its whereabouts. She only knew that her father would have emptied it first.

Agnes was glad to see the back of the thing for it had caused a lot of bad feeling and she knew they had lost regular customers over it.

The upstairs restaurant opened in the new year and Agnes gave in her notice at the Officers' Club, which was beginning to wind down its activities as the American boys went home, to begin an even longer working day than when she'd had her own little dressmaking business in Hitchin.

As staff came and went with depressing regularity and trade continued to expand, Ted increased the hourly wage rate until it was well over the minimum catering wages level.

"It's the only way to get good staff, Agnes," he assured his exhausted wife as he cashed up the takings late one Saturday night.

Shela sat on one of the stools against the counter with her head resting on her folded arms. She was fast asleep for it had been a fifteen-hour day and once again one of the girls had failed to show up.

Thursdays were so busy and in the evenings everyone was rushed off their feet for it was Land Army girl night. The first time it happened, Ted was caught unawares as the hungry girls invaded the shop to buy up every cake and bun on the premises.

"We can't get into town again before next Thursday, Mr Winch," they laughed as they demanded good-naturedly to be served all at once. "These will keep us going over the weekend."

By the next Thursday extra stock had been bought in to satisfy their needs but, wily businessman that he was, Ted never put out fresh cakes until all the stale ones had gone.

"Tell them it's a halfpenny off each when they buy six or more," he urged Shela, "and charge a penny for the bag."

"Well, Ted," warned Agnes that night as they wearily climbed the stairs to bed, "if you don't get more staff in soon and permanently, I'm quitting and I'll see Shela does the same. What's the use of making good money and not having a minute to call your own?"

Later, as Ted reached for her, Agnes turned her back on her husband for the first time in all the years of their marriage. On Monday morning he was down at the Bedford Labour Exchange offering a pound over the odds for three reliable girls and a week later they were installed as a waitress, a cook and a snack-bar attendant and Agnes and Shela both had time off on quiet days.

At home, Emily kept the rest of the family going as best she could and, with the Yanks gone home, Joyce began to write to a young English soldier on duty in Egypt.

Mary and Beryl, the two youngest of the family were both now in the local secondary school and Agnes fretted that she was unable to spend enough time with them as she'd done with the older children.

"It's OK, Mum," protested Mary who was almost twelve and secretly enjoying a situation that gave her far more freedom than her friends. Emily was there for when she and Beryl came in from school but her grandmother was now well over seventy and no match for two lively girls fast approaching adolescence.

"Maybe It's Because I'm A Londoner", sang Bud Flanagan on the B.B.C. Home Service one warm Sunday afternoon in August of 1947 and Agnes smiled to herself at the words and glanced across to where Ted was sleeping off his dinner in the old chair by the fireside. How she would love to go back to the city for the day to stand in the crowds along the route of the royal wedding and cheer as the young princess and her handsome sailor rode by in the gold coach.

But Ted could never stand there for hours at a stretch and Agnes would not go without him. Ah well, perhaps they'd get that television set installed before the big day in November and then they would see it all in comfort.

She was just starting on the hem of Joyce's "New Look" skirt when she heard a shout from Mary somewhere upstairs. Then the girl rushed headlong into the kitchen to say that Gang-Gang had gone to sleep with her eyes open and her face looked all funny.

Ted, who had woken with a start at the sudden commotion, looked quickly at Agnes and then at the scared face of Mary before telling his daughter to stay where she was and keep Beryl quiet. Then, with a churning stomach and a sudden horrible, dry taste in her mouth, Agnes beat him to the door and rushed headlong up to her mother's room.

"Mum! Mum!" She shook Emily's shoulder as the old mouth fell open and her mother's faded, blue eyes tried to focus on the white face of her daughter.

"She's had a stroke, Agnes," said Ted quietly as he helped to make his mother-in-law more comfortable and laid her glasses carefully down on the bedside table.

The next few hours were full of horror for Agnes, who remembered the old woman she'd found dead one morning in the village so long ago. Oh, God! Please don't let my mother go like this, she prayed, as Dr Chillingworth told her gently that there was nothing he could do for Emily but she would need careful nursing if she was to stay at home.

"What are we to do, Ted?" Agnes was beside herself with anxiety. "She wouldn't last long in hospital. I just

190

know. She needs me here all day and we can't expect the youngsters to see to her."

By the time Shela arrived back from the cafe that evening, plans had been made for looking after her grandmother.

"I'll be here until teatime every day," explained Agnes, looking keenly at her three youngest daughters. "After that, I think between you, you can manage to look after Gang-Gang in the evenings."

For Joan, now nearly fourteen, looking after her grandmother was a real challenge, for she harboured ambitions to become a nurse at the local hospital. The training could not be started until she was seventeen and Joan was anxious to get in some practice. Already she belonged to the Junior Red Cross and was forever trying out first-aid techniques on her younger sisters who had no patience to sit still for hours being bandaged and splinted, artificially respirated and the like.

For Ted, the sight of Emily lying helpless in the old, brass-knobbed bed was more disturbing than he cared to admit. All through his marriage, begun when he was in his thirties and too old to change his ways, Ted and his mother-in-law had maintained a more or less friendly relationship, spiced now and then with a few choice words on both sides as to the effects of drink on his children and on his wife in particular. More than once and usually when his hangovers were bad, Ted asked Agnes, in her mother's hearing, why the old faggot didn't go back to Liverpool where she'd come from?

191

And Emily, in her turn, normally a quietly-spoken woman and not one to provoke rows, always had her say. Afterwards, Ted usually bought her a small present or flowers to be left quietly on her dressing table and Emily baked him a special cake or made sure that he got the best cut from the Sunday roast. There was never an actual apology made or a word of remorse passed between them and the uneasy truce would hold until the next clash when everything would start all over again.

The knowledge that Emily's presence had made his early married years unusual to say the least, left Ted with mixed feelings for his mother-in-law and to see her now, old and helpless, did nothing to assuage his conscience.

The arrangements for Emily's welfare worked well for the next few months for Ted managed to find a young man recently demobbed from the services, who had been a cook at one of the big R.A.F. stations in Norfolk and who now needed a steady job in civvy street.

"He's a bit of a twerp, Agnes," Ted informed his relieved wife, "but he has good references and his missus will give a hand if necessary."

So Cecil started work at the cafe and Agnes heaved another sigh of relief as her workload was halved.

It was just before Christmas, when John was due home on leave and Joyce was about to announce her engagement to her soldier, when Emily had another stroke and this time there was no question of nursing her at home for she was unable to do anything for herself at all.

"It's for the best, Mrs Winch," Dr Chillingworth assured a distraught Agnes. "She needs expert nursing now." Then he added gently, "But don't expect too much, my dear."

Emily lived on for another two months and towards the end drifted into a coma so that neither Agnes nor the caring nurses were able to communicate with her at all. When she died, a small, shrunken shadow of the robust woman she'd been in her youth, Agnes found it hard to cry for the old woman in the cold, hospital bed but she broke her heart for the caring, selfless mother who had loved and supported her all her life.

CHAPTER
THIRTEEN

"Will this be suitable, Mrs Winch?"

Nineteen-forty-eight, three years after the end of the war and still clothing and fabrics were rationed and Agnes was desperate to find a length of decent, black material for a skirt.

Emily's funeral was at the end of the week and Mrs Baylis, the kindly woman who, with her husband, ran the ladies' and gents' outfitters shop on the corner of York Street and Castle Road, had searched all her shelves and cupboards before coming up with the last two yards of gents' black, pin-striped suiting from a long-forgotten roll of pre-war stock.

Aunty Nancy was coming down from Liverpool for a few days and Ted had instructions to meet her at Midland Road station at four-fifteen the next day.

"I hope she doesn't mind sleeping in Mum's old bed, Ted." There's nowhere else, Agnes thought wearily as she shook Emily's old patchwork quilt out of the window and replaced it deftly on the big, brass bedstead.

The funeral service in the "tin tabernacle", Christ Church in Denmark Street, and afterwards the cremation in the old Victorian crematorium beside

Bedford Park were very quiet and subdued and as Agnes sang "Abide With Me" and looked around at the half-dozen or so faces in the little chapel before the plain coffin disappeared through the velvet curtains, she suddenly remembered her mother's voice at her father's funeral.

"Nice and quiet, child. That's the way I want to go."

The girls at the cafe were waiting for the small funeral party and upstairs in the restaurant room, closed for the afternoon, they had prepared a tasty ham salad. Afterwards there would be a trifle and talk of the old days and Nancy would get tipsy on three small glasses of Ted's best sherry.

Then it was over and muted goodbyes said and at last Agnes could snatch a few minutes' rest before she was due back at the shop.

"I told Mum to take the night off, Shela." Joyce's concerned face appeared round the corner of the big fridge in the cafe kitchen. "We'll manage without her tonight."

Ted's wireless was playing "Slow Boat To China" as Shela watched her older sister disappear up the stairs to start the preparations for the night's customers and she wondered what Joyce's fiancé, Johnny had to say about yet another postponement of their wedding. The first had been when he was taken ill and spent what should have been his wedding day in hospital having his appendix out. And now the funeral. For they could not, as her mother told them, in all decency, hold the wedding for at least another month. The vicar was very understanding but even he needed some prior notice of the third attempt. Agnes sat with her feet up on the sofa in her pretty front room and thought about her mother who had so looked forward to Joyce's wedding.

"She's very young," Emily had sighed. "But she'll make a good wife. You've taught her well, Agnes."

The wedding dress hung in Agnes's big wardrobe and the long veil secured with an orange-blossom headdress was still in its box carefully folded in tissue paper. Agnes had made them both, sitting through the night at her sewing machine when everyone else was in bed.

The dress was made from yards of beautiful, white parachute silk that John had brought home unexpectedly on one of his infrequent leaves and the veil from a cherished length of white lace bought before the war for an evening dress and never used because Agnes was pregnant.

That must have been Joyce, she thought, as her mind went back to the past and the early years of her marriage. It was strange, Agnes mused, how her mother had so quickly become part of the family. It had suited Ted alright for her to be there. Help with the children. Company for his wife. And freedom for himself.

Then Agnes remembered the little flare-ups between her husband and her mother and how she was always the peacemaker afterwards. Divided loyalties always. Had she been wrong to want her mother with her all these years? Had Ted really approved or just given up on the situation long ago? Perhaps that accounted for the nightly absences from home when he should have been with her and the children.

Agnes sighed aloud, then as if speaking to her mother said quietly, "We'll never know now, Mum. But at least I know you were well cared for."

Over the next few weeks Ted was unusually solicitous for Agnes's well-being and she was again reminded of the early days of their marriage when nothing was too good for her and he was full of good humour and intent on making her laugh.

Once only did he talk about Emily after the funeral and that was to tell Agnes that he'd arranged for a tablet to be placed on the wall of the cemetery in her memory. "She was a good 'un, if ever there was one," was praise indeed from Ted and Agnes was comforted by that short remark from a man who she now realised had suffered from the tensions in a household shared with two women.

By the end of the summer and two months after Joyce's hastily rearranged wedding, when the newly-weds were happily installed in the front bedroom converted into a bed-sitting-room, a good offer was made for Castle Hill Cafe, now a thriving business but one which had taken up almost every minute of the last five years of Agnes's life.

"We can't turn it down," explained Ted. Then he added with a grin, "And I think we've all had enough. Our Shela's getting restless and you are always tired out."

"But what will we live on, Ted?"

Agnes knew that her husband was too old to go back on the road and she also knew that his health was failing. The long years of heavy smoking and drinking

197

were finally taking their toll and now Ted sometimes found it hard to breathe properly and even harder to cope with the cold of winter.

So the good offer was accepted and Ted set about finding a smaller, less demanding business that he and Shela could run between them. The little tobacco and confectionery shop in Bromham Road on the other side of the town appeared to be the answer and it was not until they had been the owners for some three months that Ted realised he'd bought a pig in a poke.

For the shop was one of a pair owned by the same man, who, as the solicitor found out too late to save Ted's investment, had at the last minute transferred more than half the confectionery allocation for the smaller shop to his remaining bigger one. What was left was not enough to live on and no amount of explanations and appeals to the Food Office produced a larger allocation. Sweets and chocolates, still rationed in 1948, had to be supplemented by something else and Ted, always a trier, opened a small tea-room behind the shop.

"We'll get the students from the college in The Crescent in for their coffees, Agnes, and there will be plenty of passing trade. You'll see!"

At first, Shela managed to run the two little businesses on her own and after a few weeks Ted brought in an assistant to help in the shop and give a hand in the tea-room when necessary. They all worked hard to build up trade, even opening from ten to three on Sundays, something almost unheard of at that time but by the end of the year, Ted knew he was backing a loser and the shop went on the market for far less than the purchase price.

"We'll just have to cut our losses, Agnes," he told her grimly. For Ted's pride had suffered as much as his pocket in his latest business venture and he kept well away from his friends at the Conservative Club.

The failure of the business was not the only thing worrying Ted as he finally handed over the keys to the eager, young couple glad to start on their own at so low a cost.

Agnes had her suspicions by the end of September and when October came and went, she was sure.

"We'll be having our babies about the same time," she announced to an incredulous Joyce whose retchings every morning in the bathroom made her mother feel queasy in sympathy although she'd never been prone to morning sickness, after the first month or two, with any of the other children.

"Oh, Mum!" wept poor Joyce one morning as Doris Day warbled "Buttons And Bows" on the wireless. Then she rushed to the bathroom yet again as another violent bout of sickness overcame her. "How long will this go on? I feel so ill all the time." Then she burst into tears as Agnes tried to comfort her and they both ended up laughing and crying at the same time.

On John's next leave and the first time he brought his girlfriend to the house, he was confronted by his mother and his sister both blossoming in pregnancy and he marvelled that the old man could still manage it at his age.

"But he's only fifty-four, John!" Agnes protested as he looked disbelievingly at her swollen stomach and remarked coldly that his father was old enough to know better.

Beryl, the youngest of the family, was nearly ten when her little brother Robert was born after a difficult pregnancy and a long and painful labour. For Agnes was now forty-five and this last effort took its toll on her health as toxemia set in and the doctor ordered complete bed-rest for the last eight weeks of it.

Joyce's first son, born four weeks before Robert, had already settled into the routine of all new babies by the time Agnes brought her new child home. The little flat, which was Joyce's first married home, now consisted of her mother's old bedroom turned into a bedsit and George's old room, little more than a boxroom, where Agnes had a sink and cooker installed soon after the wedding the year before.

"Go away and have another baby," the lady in the Housing Department at the Town Hall advised Joyce and Johnny when they presented their son's birth certificate at the little window in the dreary old office. "Then you'll have enough points for a council flat."

"Perhaps I'll get my own room back then," complained George who had been relegated to the tiny room behind the kitchen on the ground floor. At almost fifteen, Agnes's second son was doing well at Bedford School and had his sights firmly set on university and a law degree to follow.

"He's the brains of this family, Ted," Agnes often reminded her husband who privately considered the boy should leave school next year and start helping with the household bills. Then she reminded him of Shela, whose education was cut short for family reasons and he learned to keep his thoughts to himself.

For the first few months of little Robert's life, Agnes chose not to think so far ahead as to what George's future might be and while the life of her large family went on around her as usual, she found herself revelling in motherhood once again.

For the fair-haired, sweet-natured child who had arrived so unexpectedly at the very end of her child-bearing years was a constant joy to her and as her strength returned and her figure quickly reverted to its trim, former shape, Agnes delighted in sewing all the boy's clothes just as she'd done all those years before for John and the others. And she and Joyce spent many hours together that summer pushing their prams in Russell Park and watching portly gentlemen in panama hats solemnly bowling their way up and down the perfect green in the corner of it.

"That's what Dad should be doing, Mum," declared Joyce one day as they stopped at the bowling green on the way home from feeding the swans on the river. "It would get him out in the fresh air if nothing else."

But Agnes did not reply, for she was watching intently as an elderly man leaned forward to take aim at the jack and she knew that her Ted would never cope even with that gentle exercise. How could he when it was all he could do now to climb the stairs to bed at night?

Mother and daughter were on a rare visit to the Granada to see *South Pacific* at the end of that year, when Joyce began again to show the first symptoms of pregnancy. But this time, the sickness was more of a boon than a trial for she knew there would be a new home at the end of it.

All through that next summer, as Robert sat up in his pram to watch the bowlers and Agnes looked after both the babies when Joyce was sick, the two mothers wheeled their sons across the park and out to the new estate on the other side of it where Joyce had watched the building of a new row of council flats with great excitement.

With the birth of her second son, the promise made by the lady in the Housing Department was kept and as the keys to a brand new flat in the little estate of Hereford Road were handed over to her daughter and her husband, Agnes knew that the happy days with their new babies in the old house were nearly over. And soon the little family began to pack up ready to move out to a new life on their own.

"I'll miss our cream buns," were Joyce's last words to her smiling mother as the furniture van pulled away from the kerb and Johnny handed the new baby to her in Mr Harrison's taxi.

Agnes knew that she really meant she'd miss the old home but as she reasoned with Ted that evening, "They all have to fly the nest sooner or later."

There was no answer, for Ted was concentrating on rolling a cigarette and not until it was lit and smoking away in his tobacco-stained fingers did he say, with some humour, "Can't be soon enough for me, Agnes. Perhaps we'll get a bit of peace in our old age at last!"

Life for Ted, who for so many years had been first the well-dressed man about town and later the successful business man, was now a much slower affair. The only one of his old cronies at the club to keep in contact was Alf, who still turned up on the doorstep at Christmas and holidays with a bottle of Johnny Walker and the two old friends would sit and talk over old times until it was empty and Agnes had to guide Ted up to bed around midnight.

"Silly old devil!" she laughed to her own friend across the road, "he thinks he's still twenty-one!"

But now Agnes was more than concerned for Ted's health as he tried to hold down one job after another and in the end gave up altogether as she applied Thermogene ointment and wadding to his back and the cough which had troubled him for many years became progressively worse.

"Emphysema, Mrs Winch," murmured young Dr Eyears who had taken over after old Dr Chillingworth retired. "Probably damage of the liver as well. He won't make old bones I'm afraid but let him have his cigarettes. They can't do any more harm now."

So Ted sat in his comfortable, old office chair by the kitchen fire and kept an eye on Robert as best he could as Agnes once again installed her sewing machine in the front room and a notice in the window stating that she was open for dressmaking and alterations of all kinds.

As her father had predicted all those years before, his lass was once more making her living with the needle.

CHAPTER
FOURTEEN

By the time Robert started school, Ted was more of a father to the little boy than he'd ever been to the others and in good weather, it was a proud man who met the child every afternoon at the school back gate in York Street. On his good days, when the coughing was not too troublesome, he pulled Robert up onto the crossbar of his old bike and together they explored Russell Park and the river bank, feeding the swans and eating Walls ice-cream on the bench near the suspension bridge.

As the months went by and Ted's failing health brought desperate measures in winter to ease the pain in his chest, it seemed to Agnes that her husband was changing before her eyes. Never had she seen him so patient or so concerned for the older children as he was for Robert. Was he, she asked herself often, trying in his own way to make up for those early years as an absent father? Or had age and illness softened the hard exterior at last and allowed the frightened man beneath to show love to his last child?

As others flew the nest, when first John married, and the next year it was Shela's turn, wearing her sister-in-law's beautiful wedding dress made by Agnes and the next year Joan married her childhood sweetheart and clever George won his place at London University, suddenly the house seemed too quiet during the day.

Agnes was very surprised when, after a year in London, George followed his older brother into the Air Force on a university commission to do his National Service and when that came to an end wrote to say he'd decided to make a career in the service.

A few weeks later, Agnes found herself gazing at the usual obligatory photograph of her second son in his smart, officer's uniform and knew she was also looking at a younger version of Ted as he must have been before they met. And her heart ached for the man who sat breathlessly hunched over the fire, while her head told her not to dwell on the past. For the realities of the present were far more pressing.

At least George is doing more with his life than his father was able to do, she consoled herself and when the boy was posted to Cyprus and within a year met and married Irene, a pretty Irish girl, Agnes smiled at the wedding photograph and knew another of her children was settled and happy.

With Robert at school and his father to mind him in the holidays, Agnes worked harder than ever at her old treadle sewing-machine for there were still three children to provide for and Ted's sick pay was pitifully small.

"If the rent goes up again, Mary," she sighed to her young daughter, "I'll have to get a regular job."

The dark-haired girl, now the oldest of the family still at home, was in her sixteenth year and couldn't wait to leave school. Already she'd been interviewed for a job as telephonist at the G.P.O. and knew that her best friend from school would be with her during her training.

"It'll be great, Mum," she enthused as she hemmed up her new skirt for the dance that night. And Agnes looked on and smiled and thought of herself at that age with all of life in front of her and hoped with all her heart that it would be easier for this eager girl.

Already, family life in the old house was much more comfortable for the remaining members than it had ever been for the older children. For a start, there was more room, although on the days when Joyce and Shela brought their children to visit and then Joan arrived with her rapidly expanding brood, Agnes was reminded of the old days when bedrooms were shared and living-rooms turned into extra bedrooms and no one had any privacy at all.

"How did you manage it, Mum?" asked Mary as six little ones played in the back garden and Agnes bounced Shela's latest on her knee.

"The same way that you will, one day, I expect," replied her mother, frowning a little at the slightly sharp edge to Mary's voice.

As she had feared, three months later the rent of the house increased to three pounds a week and Agnes began to scour the job vacancy columns in the local newspaper.

"Home dressmaking is mostly alterations these days, Ted," she told him as she rubbed more Elliman's embrocation on his sore back. "And some folk won't pay much for it, I can tell you." Then she added wistfully, "It's been months since I actually cut out and made anything. Times are hard for everyone, including us and I have to do something about it."

The "something" made its appearance in *The Bedfordshire Times* the next Friday and on Monday morning, Agnes presented herself at North Wing Hospital in Kimbolton Road for an interview with the sewing-room supervisor for a position as a seamstress.

"It's mostly making up nurses' aprons, Mrs Winch," explained Miss Brown, the elderly spinster who had worked in the same place for most of her adult life. "And repairs of course," she added. "Sheets and pillowslips. Curtains. That sort of thing."

"It'll probably drive me potty within a month, Ted," Agnes confided as she dished out the supper that night. "But the money's reasonable and more importantly, regular. Do you want any more of this macaroni cheese?"

The first few weeks at the heavy, old industrial sewing machine were the most boring in Agnes's sewing life. How can anyone, she thought, as she sat down to work every morning, simulate any kind of enthusiasm for endless yards of white sheeting and great piles of pillowcases all waiting to be hemmed or repaired?

And Agnes was so tired. Perhaps it was the boredom of the work but more likely it was the result of working late into the night on her own sewing jobs that made her eyes strain to keep open at the machine and on her trips to the lavatory along the corridor made her nod off more than once as sleep overcame her by late afternoon.

It was nearly going-home time on one dark, January day and Agnes was wearily thinking what she could cook for supper when, halfway along a sheet hem, the machine whirred to a sudden stop as with a great *thunk*, the thick needle passed right through her forefinger and impaled it to the metal plate beneath.

Agnes sat looking at the finger for a few seconds and felt no pain at all as she reached over to switch off the current and called out to the woman next to her that she'd had an accident and could she help?

Then the room swam before her and she fainted where she sat and after that, people were running and a man in a white coat stood over her as the supervisor eased the sewing foot slowly upwards to release the needle still attached to Agnes's finger.

"I didn't feel a thing until they pulled the wretched thing out!" Agnes assured an anxious Mary who had been called to the hospital Casualty Department to take her mother home. "But then it really hurt!"

Over the weekend, both Mary and Beryl fussed over their mother and all the cooking and washing up was done for her as the finger throbbed and the nail blackened and on Monday morning, a small hole was drilled into it to release the blood and ease the pain.

By Tuesday Agnes was back at work but a surprise awaited her as she took off her coat and settled down again to the sheets and a new needle on her machine.

"Matron's coming in today," announced the supervisor in an excited voice. "She wants three uniform dresses made up by the end of the week. You've had dressmaking experience, haven't you, Mrs Winch?"

Thank God for Matron, thought Agnes later that day as she measured the stout figure of the kindly woman who would be a real friend to her long after she retired several years later.

Within a few days, the dresses were ready for fitting and with Matron Ball's approval Agnes was promoted to dressmaker, responsible for all the ward sisters' dresses and aprons and her wage packet was heavier by two pounds a week.

So the money situation at home was eased, as first Mary started work at the Telephone Exchange and then Beryl landed a job as a counter assistant at Linford's the grocer's shop on the corner of Castle Road and Denmark Street.

"It's handy for getting home for dinner, Mum," explained Agnes's pretty youngest daughter, "but when I'm sixteen, I'm applying for a hairdressing apprenticeship."

"There's no money in that, Mrs Winch," old Miss Linford assured Agnes when she called in for Robert's Wagon Wheels for his school lunchbox. "She'd do better to stay on with us to learn the grocery trade."

"Learn the grocery trade!" laughed Beryl as she thought of the endless weighing out and filling blue paper bags with two pounds of sugar apiece and the ancient bacon-slicing machine which tried to slice off your finger if you were not careful. And the old, ginger cat asleep in the sun behind the fly-blown windows and the scuttling of rats in the warehouse behind the shop and how her first task every morning was sweeping up their droppings before customers saw them on the counter.

"Not me, Mum!" declared Beryl as she prepared for work the next day. "Anyway," she continued with a confidence in her voice that reminded Agnes of herself at that age, "I'll have my own business one day. And it won't be in the grocery trade!"

Robert sat quietly in the corner of the kitchen reading his *Eagle* comic and Ted's old wireless was playing "Singing In The Rain", as Agnes finished the ironing that evening and wearily gathered up the clothes to take them upstairs to the airing cupboard in Emily's old bedroom at the back of the house.

What would her mother have made of it all? she thought as she laid the boy's fresh underwear carefully on the slatted shelf and hung his school shirt from a coathanger on a hook behind the door. And as she looked round the room that had been Emily's, she heard again the wise voice that had counselled and comforted her so often over the years. "Everything comes out right in the end, child." Then Agnes smiled and shook her head at her own fancies and leaving her memories behind in that quiet room, went quickly back downstairs to the people who needed her in the present.

Agnes's days at the hospital were now much more fulfilling and although she was always tired by the end of them, she still continued with her own dressmaking business and often still worked late into the night to finish something for a customer.

At weekends, neighbours and passers-by became familiar with the sight of Agnes's dark head bent over her sewing machine in the bay window looking out onto Castle Road. As she worked, Agnes's thoughts were often with her children and grandchildren for all was not well with two of her girls.

Only the week before, Shela had arrived unexpectedly with her three little ones and a white, worried face showing signs of recent bruising. Joan was the same for they had both made bad marriages to inadequate men who thought nothing of beating them and neglecting the children.

"I wish you could come here, Shela," sighed Agnes as the girl wiped more tears away from her eyes, "but your father is so ill now. And then I have your sisters to consider and young Robert."

It was the same story with Joan who now had five children in as many years and a husband who worked only intermittently and Agnes knew that often her girls went hungry so the children could have enough to eat.

"It's no good, Joan," Shela advised her younger sister one day as they both left the house together to walk back to their own homes on the other side of the town. "Mum would help us if she could, but Mary and Beryl don't want us there."

It was true, for the two youngest girls, now eighteen and sixteen and contributing to the family budget, were enjoying their young years in a house free at last from babies and countless nappies drying by the fire and all the paraphernalia and bustle of a big family.

"You are right," replied Joan shortly as she tucked the shawl more tightly round her new baby, "but just you wait until they've got kids of their own. They won't be so high and mighty then, I'll be bound!"

On her eighteenth birthday, Mary became engaged to her first and only boyfriend and a grand wedding was planned for the next summer.

"You can take over Joyce's little flat," promised Agnes, whose loyalties were constantly divided between her older and younger daughters.

They all needed help and she was always there to give it when she could but she knew that feelings were running high between her girls and words exchanged that would eventually be forgiven but never entirely forgotten as they all grew older and their burdens lessened.

"We don't want someone else's kids here!" Mary announced as Shela departed after one of her frequent and prolonged visits. "And anyway, why should Beryl and I work to keep them, may I ask? They've both got husbands. Let them do it!"

There it was again, thought Agnes. That sharp note in Mary's voice and she urged her daughter to have some compassion for her sisters who were going through hard times.

"Have you forgotten, my girl, how hard Shela worked in the cafe when you and Beryl were still at school? She had no fun in her young years and no chance of a decent education either. Just you remember that when you get ready for your next dance in your own bedroom — not one shared with two others and nowhere decent to hang your new dress!"

But Ted did warn both Shela and Joan about the men they were so set on marrying, thought Agnes. And he was right about both of them. Or was it that the girls were self-willed like their father? And now they were paying for it.

For Beryl, just starting the hairdressing apprenticeship which was the first step in her plans for the future, life in the family home was second only in importance to her ambitions to be independent and self-sufficient in as short a time as possible.

"Take no notice of her, Mum," she remarked after one of Mary's frequent outbursts. "It's probably pre-wedding nerves. She'll get over it."

But the exchange of harsh words and the bad feeling in the house continued to worry Agnes, who was by now having to nurse Ted through a long, cold winter. Worse, he was no longer able to keep an eye on Robert when the boy came in from school.

After a particularly bad week, when Ted could hardly draw one breath after another and no amount of back rubbing or Thermogene padding eased his pain, Agnes knew the time had come for her to be with him constantly.

"He won't get any better, Mrs Winch," the caring, young doctor murmured after Ted needed oxygen for the third time that week. "It's just a matter now of trying to keep him comfortable. Perhaps you should consider letting the hospital do the work for a few days," he added, looking with concern at Agnes's drawn face. "You look as if you could do with the rest."

So Ted was admitted to the big ward in the Chest Department of the same hospital where Agnes worked and she visited every evening and fretted about him every day.

"Is Dad going to die, Mum?" Robert wanted to know as his mother gave him his supper and told him to be a good boy for Beryl who would see him off to bed.

"We all have to die sometime, Robert," was the only thing she could think of to say in answer and then blinked back her own tears as she saw those in her little son's eyes before she said goodbye and wheeled her old bike out of the shed for the short journey to the chest ward.

By the end of the month, Agnes had worked out her notice at the sewing-room and Ted was back from hospital and installed once again in his old office chair by the kitchen fire.

Mary's wedding was two months away and Agnes was sitting up half the night trying to fit in all her sewing jobs as well as the wedding dress and four bridesmaids' dresses. She loved the work for it meant she could design and create the garments from start to finish — something she had sorely missed over the years of endless alterations and making and mending.

As she worked, Agnes could hear Ted's cough getting progressively worse and every night, as she helped him to bed it seemed to her that the flesh on his already thin frame was simply falling away until now he looked little more than a dried-up old man with hollow cheeks and so stooped that he seemed to have shrunk almost down to her own height.

Robert spent a lot of time with his father, although the sick man could no longer take the boy on the outings he'd come to love.

"It's all right, Agnes," Ted wheezed every day when Robert was due home from school. "I'll make his tea. You get on with your work. It won't be long now."

Did he mean the wedding or his own end? thought Agnes distractedly as she stoked the fire and helped him on with his warm cardigan before closing the door and walking purposefully along the hallway to her workroom at the front of the house. She knew Robert was quite capable of getting his own tea ready but he would pretend that he needed Ted's help in the kitchen and she wondered how so young a child knew instinctively that his father's pride must be kept intact for as long as possible?

On the other side of the road, just in front of Mr Harrison's taxi office, two women stood gossiping and Agnes recognised one of them as an old customer. The woman had come to her some two years ago to have a skirt turned and then introduced a friend who wanted similar work done by the clever little dressmaker eager to earn enough money and who had a sick husband unable to work.

It was in the Gas Company office in the Broadway, where the woman worked and a few weeks later, that Agnes heard herself and her home being discussed behind the glass partition at the back of the room. She was paying an overdue gas bill when she heard her name mentioned and then stood transfixed as the unseen voice described Agnes's plain, little workroom and the sound of Ted's coughing from the next room.

"Disgusting it was, I can tell you!" The sharp tones of the woman came clearly to Agnes as she picked up her receipt and put it carefully away in her handbag. "There was no heating in that room and none in the rest of the house I should imagine. And no proper changing-room, either. Why, I had to get undressed and have my fitting right there in full view of anyone passing by in the street. Still, she's cheap enough. I expect I'll use her again."

For a moment, as Agnes tried desperately to control her breathing and shock turned to anger, she contemplated walking right round behind the counter and confronting the vicious-tongued woman face-to-face. Then, as the door in the partition opened and the woman came through into the shop, Agnes heard herself asking quietly to speak to the manager, to whom she related what she'd just heard. Within a few minutes, she was politely asked to come through to his office and Agnes's customer was sent for.

It was a red-faced woman who later apologised to Agnes but then tried to convince her that it was not her she'd been discussing at all but some other dressmaker she'd been to for alterations.

"It was me, Mrs Keating." Agnes spoke quietly but with some satisfaction at the sight of the woman's embarrassment. "And it was my home you were running down after taking advantage of the reasonable

216

rates for the work I did for you. Please do not bring me any more. I am far too busy to bother with your little alterations!"

As she rose to leave the office, Agnes knew the woman would be reprimanded although, as she said later to Ted, "Her kind won't be deterred by a simple ticking-off. She's a nasty piece of work intent on making mischief."

As Agnes watched through the front window, the two women moved on further down the road, heads bent together in conversation and Agnes wondered who else Mrs Keating was tearing to bits with her tongue. Then she turned back to her work and was soon concentrating on that nice Mrs Sloane's blue costume that she'd promised to finish for her for Easter.

Easter! she thought with sudden panic. It would be here within weeks and all that work to finish!

Two weeks later, George applied for compassionate leave from his R.A.F. station in Cyprus and John took an overnight flight home from his new civilian job with West Indian Airlines in response to the urgent telegrams sent to them by Mary from her G.P.O. switchboard. They read:

"RETURN HOME SOONEST. FATHER DIED
EARLY TODAY." SIGNED: MOTHER

PART FOUR

1957 to 1971

CHAPTER
FIFTEEN

The small cortège of funeral cars headed by the high, shiny hearse made its way up Foster Hill Road to the cemetery on a cold, windy day in early April.

The service in the "tin tabernacle", Christ Church, round the corner in Denmark Street had been adequate but brief and as Agnes watched Ted's coffin being carried through the doors past the building-fund board shaped like a giant thermometer with its red pointer at £12,000, the sense of disturbing unreality which had threatened to overwhelm her for the last three days, finally took hold.

It was her Ted inside that long box beneath the wreaths and sprays of spring flowers arranged so carefully on its top and propped at angles along its length, just like, she thought in a curiously detached way, an overdone display in a florist's window.

Suddenly, Agnes remembered the sheaf of arum lilies she'd carried at their quiet wedding and in this new state of detachment from reality, wondered why no one had chosen those beautiful white flowers for Ted's funeral.

Opposite to her in the first following car, John and his wife sat with concerned eyes, while, beside her,

Robert stared out of the window as his older brothers and sisters climbed silently into other cars and the procession began to move away from the church.

The kindly vicar who would marry Mary and Roy later that month, stood by the graveside speaking the solemn words Agnes had last heard at her mother's funeral and a cold wind caught at his cassock as the earth was cast into the grave and Beryl, elegant in black, stood calmly alone at the head of it to say goodbye to a father who was already old when she was born.

Robert clung to his mother and stood with downcast eyes as the coffin was finally lowered and Agnes's wreath of daffodils and tulips disappeared with it into the ground.

"What a waste," murmured George not knowing whether he meant the flowers or the man. Agnes looked across to where he stood with his new wife and for an instant saw again the face of Ted as he had been in his youth.

On the journey home, as she sat, still dry-eyed, beside Joyce who was already beginning to fuss over her mother, Agnes had the odd thought that Ted would be wondering where she'd got to and hoped he was coping on his own all this time.

Then the house was suddenly full of people and she had no time to wonder what had happened to Ted's old chair, quietly removed by one of the boys and heaved up through the trap-door into the attic.

Later, oh much later, when the house was quiet again and Robert was in bed, Agnes wandered around the rooms looking for the chair, for she wanted to sit in it and rest her arms in the same place where for so many years Ted had rested his.

"Come on, Mum, why don't you go to bed now?"

Joyce was worried for her mother, who had gone through these last awful days in an unnatural calm that had unnerved Ted's oldest daughter until Joan suggested that their mother was still in shock and would need careful watching in the days ahead.

How could Agnes tell them that the overwhelming relief she'd felt when Ted finally gasped his last terrible breath and the stiff hospital sheet was pulled up over the gaunt face was far more disturbing than the grief she wanted and expected to feel? But somehow couldn't.

On an afternoon of bright spring sunshine, Mary and Roy were married just a few feet away from the place where Ted's coffin had stood on its trestle only three weeks earlier. Agnes smiled her way through the day and agreed how beautiful the bride looked and said thank you to people who said how brave she was and how proud Ted would have been today.

Shela's youngest and one of Joyce's little boys were bridesmaid and pageboy to their Aunty Mary who went off on honeymoon to Babbacombe with her new husband, secure in the knowledge that Joyce's old flat would be waiting for them on their return.

Life in the old house returned to somewhere near normal in the two weeks they were away and although Robert often cried himself to sleep, refusing to be comforted, Agnes still shed no tears but, instead, plunged into her work with an energy born not only of a persistent feeling of guilty freedom but also out of sheer necessity. For Ted's meagre invalid allowance died with him and the widowed mother's pension Agnes collected weekly was barely enough to pay the rent.

"How often did I try to persuade your father to buy this house?" she sighed one day to Joyce who had come to tea with her children and was seriously concerned about her mother's appearance.

Agnes had lost weight and Joyce knew she was up half the night at her sewing, for Robert had told her he often heard his mother moving about in the small hours and once she'd not been to bed at all when he came down for his breakfast.

"But he wouldn't hear of it," Agnes continued, as she turned away from her daughter's keen gaze to pour herself another cup of tea. "Always cautious, was your father. Didn't want to hang a millstone round his neck, so he said."

"Well, he must have had his reasons," replied Joyce gently, as she saw the worry on her mother's drawn face. "But if only he'd done as you suggested then, you'd own this place now."

"No good thinking of 'if onlys', dear," sighed Agnes. "It's now I'm concerned with." And she handed Joyce a letter from the National Assistance Office and watched quietly as the girl read that her widowed mother had been awarded only an extra sixpence a week because she was still of working age and able to make a living for herself and her son.

224

"If it wasn't so humiliating, it would be funny!" Agnes said with a small smile and then put a warning finger to her lips as Robert came in from the garden with Joyce's oldest boy. "We'll manage somehow, won't we, Robert?" she said brightly as she opened the old Fairy Toffee tin now containing biscuits and passed it across to him. No Wagon Wheels this week, she thought sadly.

With Mary and Roy installed in the two-roomed flat upstairs and paying Agnes a small rent, finances were temporarily eased but as Joyce pointed out, what they paid their mother for the rooms was used up in the extra cost of electricity as Agnes found herself feeding the shilling meter in the cupboard under the stairs at almost double the rate of before.

By September of that year, the newly-weds had found their own home with a mortgage arranged and Mary continued in her job at the G.P.O. Once again the house was quiet with Robert at school and Beryl just finishing the last few weeks of her hairdressing apprenticeship at Ruth Browning's Hairdressers, opposite Bedford Prison in St. Loyes.

This youngest daughter, still full of ambition and drive, constantly reminded Agnes of herself at nineteen, for Beryl wanted to start her own business and had already been to look at several small shops to let, before her father died.

"You are still under age, Beryl," he'd said, urging caution as she began to plan the layout of the most suitable one near to where Shela lived in the old part of the town. But almost the last thing he did before he

225

died was give his approval of the premises on the basis that the toilet was clean and in working order.

"It'll have to be in your name until I'm twenty-one, Mum."

Agnes and Beryl stood in the middle of the empty shop in Foster Hill Road, where a previous owner had gone out of business the year before. "But I know I can make a go of it and then things will be easier for you at home."

So Beryl ordered the new basins and hairdryers from the hairdressers' suppliers and Agnes bought two dozen pink, fluffy towels on her Provident cheque and ran up pretty curtains for the shop window.

At first, Beryl was on her own in the shop but as business increased, an old friend from her apprentice-ship days came in to help and by the first Christmas the appointment book was full and a young school-leaver was brought in to shampoo and make tea for the customers.

A year later, all the initial debts were paid off and Beryl began to make a clear profit.

"Your father would have been so proud of you!"

Agnes smiled at her young, pretty daughter as the girl brushed her blonde hair up into a fashionable French pleat and secured it carefully with pins before slipping a circular skirt over her slim hips and several layers of net petticoat beneath.

"I'm off to the Dujon tonight, Mum," she declared, as she flapped her hands to dry her newly-varnished nails more quickly. "I'm meeting Geoff there."

226

Geoffrey was Beryl's first serious boyfriend and Agnes liked the quietly-spoken, well-mannered young man who had helped her daughter with the shop alterations and was there on dark evenings to see the girl safely home with the day's takings.

Agnes knew that Beryl was not ready to settle down yet but she couldn't help thinking that her daughter could do a lot worse than a steady chap like this for a husband. And then she smiled as she remembered her father saying exactly the same thing about herself and Bernie, the A.A. man, all those years ago.

A few days later, the letter that arrived from John, in Trinidad, gave his mother other things to think about.

"We'll be home at the end of the month and while we're there we want to look for a good site to build a house. As an investment. You and Beryl and Robert can live there until we decide to come home for good but that won't be until the children are ready for secondary school. So it will be some time yet."

"Good for John!" laughed Beryl as she read the letter through that evening. "It'll do us all good to get away from here to a nice, modern place." And she looked up at the ceiling which was badly in need of a coat of paint and then down towards the Ideal boiler surrounded still by Agnes's old, brass-topped fireguard. How many years had that stood there? she thought. And how many nappies had hung there to dry over the course of them?

Agnes's youngest girl, now a businesswoman in her own right, had more than once contemplated finding her own flat but each time a suitable one came up, she delayed making the decision for she knew she was still needed in her mother's home. Agnes's only income was from her pension and what she made from her sewing and that meant toiling far into the night and making economies in her small budget.

"You have to live your own life, Beryl," she'd protested to her daughter many times. But the plain fact was that Agnes depended on the girl's generous contribution in order to make ends meet in a house that was suddenly and inexplicably too big for the three of them.

Beryl did not tell her mother until many years later that she had written to her brother suggesting the move and offering to furnish wherever he chose.

"Mum is wearing herself out, John," she'd stated in her letter. "And since that bad flu last winter she's never really picked up. It's a good idea to get her and Robert away from here."

It was true that Agnes often felt ill and tired and she knew that Robert's growing defiance was the result of the boy missing his father. But she missed him too, she thought sadly, for since Ted died, she had driven herself harder than ever to try to be both mother and father to the boy in an effort to rid herself of that dreadful feeling of relief and the uneasy guilt which had haunted her ever since. She had never discussed this feeling with anyone and it was now, more than ever, that she wished with all her heart that her mother was still here to talk to and to give wise counsel.

The new house on the corner of Berry Drive in Bromham, some three miles north of Bedford, was started three months later and by the next summer

228

Beryl and Agnes were choosing carpets and furniture and wonderful modern fittings for the spacious kitchen in their sparkling new home.

By August, everything was ready for the move and Agnes's married girls took what they wanted of the old furniture and the rest was dispatched to Peacock's sale yards in Newnham Street.

On the last day in the old house, Agnes stood quietly in the front room where all the years of her sewing had been done, watching as the few things she wanted to take with her were loaded into the van at the kerbside.

Robert was carrying a big stack of his books and comics down the stairs as Beryl closed and bolted the back door and Shela, who had come over to help, took a last look around the suddenly dark, little kitchen then joined her mother in the front room.

"Come on, Mum. Let's get away now." She spoke quietly but firmly to Agnes and watched with concern as her mother squared her frail shoulders then, lifting her greying head high, walked out of the last home she'd shared with Ted into the sunshine and smiled at her friend Mrs Harrison across the road before climbing into Beryl's new mini-car for the short journey to their new home.

High above on that sunny morning, a young Russian cosmonaut began the first ever space orbit of the earth and the nation that put him there began to build a wall in Berlin.

CHAPTER
SIXTEEN

During the year that had passed since Agnes and her two youngest children moved into their bright modern home, Robert seemed to have settled well at Robert Bruce School in Kempston and Beryl was about to open another shop.

"There's only one problem, Mum," she said, as she combed out Agnes's hair one evening. "The meeting with the Housing Department is scheduled for the very day I'm boarding the ship at Southampton."

For many weeks, Beryl had been undecided about Geoffrey's proposal of marriage until finally she'd written to her older brother asking to stay with his family for a few weeks to give her time and space to make up her mind.

Geoffrey Millman, whom Beryl had first met while dancing at the Dujon, was a popular and up-and-coming young wicket-keeper for Notts County Cricket Club and this winter season he had been selected to play for England in India.

"It's a great honour, Mum. And well deserved too. But it means he will be away at the same time as me. That gives us both time to think things through."

Beryl had set her heart on the idea of owning at least three hairdressing shops before she was twenty-five and here she was at twenty-one and well on the way to realising that ambition. Was she really prepared to let this relationship stand in the way?

"I have to get away, Mum!" she declared after yet another sleepless night. "I owe it to myself and to Geoff, who is being very patient, I must say."

So the travel arrangements were made, a manageress found for the shop in Foster Hill Road and Agnes was left to handle the tenancy of the new one in Brickhill Drive on an estate north of the town.

"Goodbye, Robert. Look after Mum for me."

They were at the railway station to see Beryl off and as Agnes hugged her daughter goodbye and waved until the train disappeared round the bend she hoped with all her heart that her girl would make the right decision.

It was three days after Agnes signed the lease for the new shop on Beryl's behalf that the phone rang in the hall and the school secretary asked to speak to Robert Winch's mother.

"Robert missed school on two days last week, Mrs Winch and he's not in again today. Is he unwell?"

For a moment, Agnes did not know what to say, for every morning, without fail, she'd seen Robert climb onto the bus which would drop him near the school and in the past, Beryl often gave him a lift to the end of Hillgrounds just down the road from the school entrance.

"He has a bad cough," she heard herself answer, as her mind raced and the old, familiar feeling of unreality left her breathless and shaking. "He'll be at school tomorrow if he's better. Thank you for calling. Goodbye," she managed faintly as she hung up and tried desperately to think where he could be.

Agnes knew that Robert still cried sometimes at night and several times she'd comforted him and sat on his bed until he fell asleep. At nearly thirteen, her youngest son was fast approaching adolescence and missing his father even more than when Ted died.

The boy's bedroom was the usual untidy jumble of books, comics and football gear and as Agnes looked around searching for some clue as to his whereabouts, she suddenly spotted a new pack of fishing hooks propped against the desk light. Fishing! That's where he'd be! Probably with that new boy who had moved in along the Stagsden Road a couple of months ago.

It had started to rain when Agnes first saw the two boys crouched beneath a big, green umbrella beyond the bridge about a mile upstream from the village. It was pouring as she opened the gate and pushed Robert, still protesting, up the front path and into the hall where they both stood dripping water onto the new rug.

"Get those wet things off, my lad. Then we'll have a hot drink and you can explain."

Half-an-hour later, as she turned the gas fire up to full and Robert sat shamefaced in dry clothes opposite her on the sofa, Agnes wanted more than anything to hug the boy and believe everything he told her. But she knew this would be weakness and although she could see he was not far from tears again, she also knew that she must be strong for both of them.

So she listened quietly as he told her of his increasing misery at the school and how he couldn't cope with his lessons. She also heard how he had lain awake night after night and never wanted to get up in the morning and how he'd even contemplated running away with his new friend.

"His dad left home last year, Mum, and he hates school. Just like me."

Then the tears came as Robert cried for his father and himself. The rain had stopped and the sun was glistening on the forsythia bush near the gate as Agnes covered her son with Beryl's car rug and the boy fell into an exhausted sleep that lasted well into the afternoon.

The next day, Agnes was on the bus with Robert and while he was in assembly she had a long talk with his headmaster who had not known about the boy's home life until now.

"We'll keep an eye on him, Mrs Winch," the tired-faced man assured Agnes. "Now that we know, I'm sure we can help."

He was as good as his word for when Beryl returned from Trinidad, suntanned and full of plans for her engagement to Geoff next month, Robert was sleeping well again and his teacher reported a renewed interest in his lessons.

"Poor kid," remarked Geoffrey, who had become a regular visitor at Agnes's house over the previous year. "It's tough to lose your father at that young age."

It was from that time on that Geoffrey, who was busy with his cricket career as the new captain of Nottinghamshire, and working in his father's jewellery business, began to give time to Robert. And the quiet relationship lasted until the boy was grown up and better able to deal with the grief that had overwhelmed him as a child.

During the school summer holidays that year, Agnes began to take her youngest son to London on the cheap day return tickets now available on the trains. As they wandered through the drab streets of her childhood and she pointed out her old home in Gray's Inn Road and the little school in Acton Street, still standing after all the wartime bombing, and together they found the green squares and gardens she'd first discovered for herself so long ago with Uncle Joe, it seemed to Agnes as if her old companion walked with them and she even fancied she could smell the pungent smoke from the tobacco in his floppy, rolled cigarette.

"Who was he, Mum?"

Robert was curious about this man from his mother's distant past, who had shown her all the things she now wanted him to see.

"Look, Robert! This is Carnaby Street. Let's look in the shop windows." Agnes smiled at the boy's delighted face. "Perhaps we'll buy something while we're here."

During the next hour or two, Robert and his mother browsed through this old part of London which had seen an unexpected revival with the hippie movement and the "Swinging Sixties" demanding such colourful clothes for both men and women in reaction to the drab and conservative Forties and Fifties.

The Beatles sang their songs, "From Me To You" and "Please, Please Me", over and over in the little boutique near Mary Quant's first shop, Bazaar, where Robert tried on the brightly-coloured waistcoat that cost more than Agnes could easily afford. But the boy's expression as they made the purchase more than justified the price for his mother.

"Would Uncle Joe have liked it, Mum?"

Robert's question on the way back to St. Pancras station made Agnes laugh for anything less likely to please Uncle Joe would be hard to imagine.

"No, Robert! Not quite his style."

Then, as the train pulled out of the big, echoing station and began to roll past countless, small back yards all through the suburbs and eventually out into the green countryside, still with all those cows, observed Agnes with a smile, she told her young son about Uncle Joe with his cloth cap and shabby clothes and his fondness for a glass of beer and those perpetual, droopy cigarettes he rolled as he walked along with his little niece.

"He took me everywhere when I was your age, Robert. Next time we come to London, we'll go to the Victoria and Albert Museum. And after that we could go up to Horse Guards for the Trooping of the Colour. You'll love that. And then there's the Tower and we could go for a trip up the river. And St. Paul's and Westminster Abbey. We'll see them all!"

So the plans were made and although there was never enough time to see everything they'd wanted to, by the end of the summer Agnes and Robert had visited all those wonderful places of the city that she'd remembered from her childhood. And it seemed to Agnes, in those few months, that she fancied she was young again with all of life before her and choices to be made which would be very different from the reality of her hardworking life.

Looking now at Robert's fair hair and blue eyes, so different from Ted's dark features, Agnes had the odd notion that Joe had come back again to brighten her days as the boy slowly changed from a child to a young man with a mind of his own and a quirky sense of humour so like her long-dead uncle's.

Robert was watching Cassius Clay knock out Sonny Liston to become World Heavyweight Boxing Champion as Agnes began to work on Beryl's wedding dress and once again, the skills she'd learned as a girl came into their own.

The beautiful dress, of cream slipper satin and the four bridesmaids' dresses of turquoise, moire silk were completed by the end of February the next year. And then Agnes turned her hand to making her own outfit of a blue silk suit with matching blouse which she planned to wear with the smart hat and bag Beryl had bought for her for Christmas.

"It's like being back at Spurrs," she laughed one day as Beryl stood before the cheval mirror in her wedding dress and turned slowly round before her mother's admiring gaze.

"You look lovely, dear. What a glamorous sister you have, Robert!"

Easter Saturday that year was so cold that the smaller bridesmaids wore woollen cloaks over their dresses outside the church until the photographer was ready for them and Beryl shivered in the chill wind blowing up from the river and catching at her long train and in the end, Geoffrey had to put his foot on it to prevent it flying away altogether.

That's the last of my girls married and gone, thought Agnes, as people began to drift away and a procession of cars wound its way into the town and the welcoming warmth of the Bridge Hotel in St. Mary's Street.

As she danced later, first with George, who had looked resplendent in church in his best dress uniform complete with long sword down the left leg as he gave the bride away, then with Mary's steady, young husband, Agnes tried to bring her thoughts back from her other girls who were all in difficulties in their marriages.

Joyce, now with four children, was having a hard time making ends meet and was not happy living in Plymouth, so far away from the rest of the family.

"It's a case of going where the work is," she sighed, as her mother helped her pack for the move. "Johnny works as much overtime as he can get but there never seems to be enough money to go round."

Agnes knew that her oldest daughter was a careful housekeeper and her home was always bright and clean, despite four boys with muddy football boots and the family dog whose main aim in life appeared to be getting in pup as often as possible.

The first telephone call from a distraught Joyce, some months previously, had worried Agnes more than she would admit and it came when Beryl was away in Trinidad, so she had no one to talk to about its disturbing contents.

"It's the electricity bill, Mum. We just can't pay it and they're threatening to cut off the supply if it's not settled by next Monday."

Joyce was in tears as her mother told her to calm down and then asked her how much they owed and promised to send a Postal Order first thing in the morning.

The second call was taken by Beryl who listened in silence to the tale of woe and then told her sister she'd send a cheque to cover the amount.

"How long has this been going on, Mum?" she wanted to know when she talked to her mother that evening.

So Agnes told her how she'd paid the first bill herself out of her savings account and assured Beryl that Joyce was starting an evening job soon to earn the extra the family needed.

"Good Lord, Mum. What a life!" exclaimed Beryl. "Kids all day and work every night. I'll watch I never get into that situation!"

Agnes smiled to herself at her daughter's outburst, then gently reminded her about her own struggle when she had seven little ones around her and an elderly mother to care for until she died.

238

"But Dad always provided well for us, didn't he, Mum?" Beryl queried and Agnes told her that was true but she'd never have managed in the later years without the dressmaking she'd worked at late into the night.

"He never took out much insurance, as you know, Beryl. The little bit he did have just about covered the funeral costs. No," Agnes sighed heavily and then continued quietly, "your father never planned too much ahead, I'm afraid."

And Beryl looked with a new respect at her mother, who had endured so much in her own marriage that she seemed to be able to take on board the troubles of her children as each one tried to cope.

It was in the spring of the next year with Agnes recovering from another bout of flu that left her debilitated and constantly tired, when a second invitation from John arrived.

"Look, Robert!" she exclaimed. "They want me to go over for a long visit. John will send the air tickets when he knows I'm ready to leave."

Robert made hardly any comment about the forthcoming trip, only to say that his mother could swim in the sea and get nice and brown and not to forget to bring him back some shells from the seashore. Secretly, the boy was upset at the thought of his mother being away for two or even three months and he only cheered up when Geoff and Beryl insisted that he came to stay with them in their bright little flat above the new shop.

"We'll go fishing, Robert, and I've just bought my new binoculars so we'll be able to do a lot of birdwatching in the summer holidays."

Geoffrey, who was an only child, enjoyed the company of the quiet, good-natured boy who was something of an afterthought in his parents' marriage and so missed the hurly-burly of a big family enjoyed by most but endured by some of his older brothers and sisters.

The preparations for Agnes's trip were completed by the end of June and when the B.O.A.C. tickets arrived two weeks later, she knew she would be spending her fifty-ninth birthday in John's home in Trinidad.

"Can I come to the airport to see you off, Mum?"

Robert was anxious to be with his mother for as long as possible and looking at her youngest son's pleading face, Agnes relented and told him he could take the day off school.

"But it's back on Monday, Robert. Understand?" And the boy knew she was thinking of the days when he played truant and was worried that it would happen again.

"Don't worry," Beryl urged her mother as they both kissed her goodbye. "Geoff will take Robert to school every day. He can come home on the bus."

Then she watched with a smile as Agnes checked her luggage in and with a final wave of her hand, disappeared into the departure lounge to await the call to board the huge plane waiting on the runway just beyond the windows.

240

Agnes's eldest son had piloted planes since he was nineteen years old but she had never flown before and this first time was an experience she would never forget.

As the great plane taxied past the spectators' balcony, Agnes tried to find Robert's face among the crowd but quite suddenly, the aircraft gathered speed and then they were on the runway itself, before incredibly, the airport buildings were falling away below until they looked like a child's toys scattered untidily on a green field.

"The Captain's compliments, Mrs Winch. He hopes you enjoy the flight."

A young air-hostess stood in the gangway near Agnes's seat smiling at her and holding out a glass of something in which hundreds of bubbles rose to the surface and was a pale, yellow colour.

"Why, thank you, but . . .?" Agnes was at a loss for words until the girl explained that John had trained with the Captain and he was aware that his old friend's mother was a passenger on her first flight.

"Let me know if you need anything, Mrs Winch."

The girl smiled again and moved quickly away as Agnes sipped the champagne and wondered what Ted would have made of it all.

Eight hours later, as the plane touched down at Idlewild Airport in New York, the newspaper headlines read, "Great Train Robbery In England", and three disembarking passengers, all American, asked if she knew the little town of Linslade where it took place?

241

The girl who waited for Agnes at the barrier holding up a large card reading "Mrs Agnes Winch", in large letters, was a West Indian Airlines hostess overnighting in New York. And yes, she was more than happy to guide Captain Winch's mom into a yellow cab and then into the elevator at the Sheraton Hotel and finally leave her in her room on the fifty-first floor overlooking the great, bustling city where cars crawled along like ants so far below and the windows were sealed tight and there was air-conditioning so that your skin felt dry and it was difficult to get to sleep.

But when Agnes awoke the next morning with a whole day to spend in New York, the friendly girl was there to walk her along Fifth Avenue and into Sachs, the great department store and then on to Times Square to see the world headlines flash across the New York Times building.

"Some robbery, ma'am!" her companion exclaimed as Agnes took in the enormity of what had happened in England on the day she left.

All too soon they were on their way back to the airport where her companion was working on another flight and her charge was handed over to another friendly girl who ushered Agnes smoothly through all the paraphernalia of departure and then she was airborne once again as the plane seemed to skim over the tops of those incredible skyscrapers as it turned south to make its way down the East Coast towards the warmth of the Caribbean and John's friendly wife waiting for her in Port-of-Spain.

242

CHAPTER
SEVENTEEN

"Dad was always against me marrying him."

Shela and Joan, now living near to each other on the same estate at Goldington, met frequently for tea and sympathy as their marriages went from bad to worse.

"And Mum never had a good word for mine!"

Joan sighed and called to her youngest to stop making such a racket or the neighbours would complain again.

The two sisters, who had both fallen for men who were, in Agnes's private opinion, "no better than they should be", could barely make ends meet as their husbands drifted intermittently from one poorly-paid job to the next and the children wore hand-me-downs from Joyce and sympathetic neighbours and both women tried to hide their bruises from Mary and Beryl whenever their younger sisters visited them.

But with Agnes still away in Trinidad and Mary now pregnant with her first child, it was Beryl who made it her business to call more often on the older girls.

How could she fail to notice the almost empty cupboards and the patched and darned clothing neatly laid out ready for school the next day? And how could she miss the drawn faces of the pair of them as they both made the effort to appear normal when their smartly-dressed sister arrived and the two husbands kept well out of the way as if too ashamed to face up to their inadequacies when she was there?

"Now don't fuss, Shela. I have the wherewithal and you don't, that's all." And Beryl put a bundle of new bedding on each of the three little beds and kissed her sister gently on the cheek before leaving to deliver the same to Joan down the road.

"Stop going on about it, Shela," advised Joan later that day. "She can afford it and we can't. So, we'll both be grateful, eh?"

The older girl looked up quickly at Joan's sharp tone but she made no comment for she knew that if anything, her sister's plight was worse than her own. Joan was pregnant yet again and her man was out of work once more.

Although Agnes was far away from all this as she enjoyed the sunshine and a slower pace of life in Trinidad, her thoughts were often with the family she'd left behind in England.

John's three blonde-haired girls were tanned and healthy and content for life in the Caribbean to go on like this for ever but their parents knew the time was fast approaching when an English schooling meant they'd have to leave the beautiful white house at Bay Shore to go back to a normal one in the old country.

"We'll stay at Bromham with you and Robert for a few weeks, Mum," explained John, who had tendered his contractual three months' notice to the airline the week before Agnes arrived. "Then Margaret and I will

244

look for a place near the new job at Speke Airport in Liverpool."

So Agnes's holiday began to slide past as she regained her health and spirits and Beryl wrote to say Robert was well and going willingly to school and that he and Geoff were having a high old time bird-watching but that everyone would be glad to see her home again.

"But stay where you are as long as you want, Mum," added Beryl in her chatty letter. "I know how lovely it is there and the long break will do you good."

After two months of lazy days on white beaches and swimming in the warm sea and sipping iced mango juice at midnight beneath a tropical sky where the stars were so big that they seemed to be just above the red-tiled rooftop and meals were always eaten outside, Agnes had put on weight and looked better, remarked John, than he'd ever seen her before.

"Time for me to go home, then."

Agnes made up her mind quickly. Suddenly, she knew that she was homesick for the familiar faces and places of the old town where the rest of the family lived. And besides, there remained the question of finding herself a job. For during the long days in Trinidad, she had come to a firm decision. She would no longer rely completely on Beryl's continuing generosity but would be almost independent and earn her own and Robert's keep as best she could.

Although she was now almost sixty, Agnes was quite determined to keep going as long as her youngest was still at school and even then until he was well established in his own job, whatever that might be.

The long flight home, made comfortable by John's quiet arrangements with the airline, was full of anticipation for Agnes, who could not wait to see her young son again and tell him about all the wonderful things she'd seen at Bay Shore. And how John's girls, the two oldest not much younger than himself, were looking forward to their own homecoming in the next few weeks.

Agnes had been home for only a few days when a tearful Shela arrived on the doorstep just after nine one morning to announce that she'd finally had enough and that she'd thrown her husband out.

"Thrown him out, Shela?"

"Well — locked him out is nearer the mark, Mum."

The beating the girl had taken three nights before proved to be just one too many and suddenly, the spirit that had cowered beneath the blows for so long broke through the fear and pain and Shela took charge of her own life again.

"The Housing Department has transferred the tenancy to me and changed the locks, back and front. I'm suing for a divorce on cruelty grounds. They say it will take three years to come through."

Agnes looked with concern at her daughter's drawn face and wondered for the thousandth time why her girl had put up with the bad treatment for so long.

"I've got my job safe and that will keep us going," said Shela, visibly calming down now that she'd told her mother of her decision. "Next year, perhaps I can get Deborah out of the hospital and home where she belongs."

Shela's youngest, suffering from coeliac disease and chronic asthma, had been looked after in a residential hospital school at Arkley near Barnet since she was six years old and now she was nearly ten. And Agnes knew Shela blamed herself for the long absence, but how could she stay at home to care for this child when she needed to earn money to support her family?

When she left that afternoon, after a long talk with her mother, Shela was more optimistic about the future than she'd been for years. At least now she would no longer have to wait fearfully every night for her violent husband's return and be too scared to turn her back on him when he was in one of his rages. For, as she told Agnes, she'd rather see the blow coming for there was more chance of dodging it that way.

"I'll go over to see her at the weekend," Beryl assured her worried mother as they talked over the day's events later on the telephone. "Don't worry," she continued, "Shela will survive and now he's gone she'll pick up the pieces and get on with her life at last."

As Agnes prepared for bed that night, her thoughts were not only with Shela. For Joan, now with six children, had recently moved to a house twenty-five miles away near Kettering and Agnes regularly took phone calls from her, complaining about her husband's ill-treatment and neglect of the children. "I'm getting away as soon as I can," she told her mother on one of these calls. "You'll see. I'll find a way."

And Agnes knew she meant it, for there was an inner core of hardness in Joan's nature that reminded her mother of Ted when he was a young man. Perhaps the privations of his youth had made him that way and now the same thing was happening to her long-suffering fourth child.

That night, Agnes's dreams were of her own mother and the long years they'd spent together as the family grew up and the sensible advice she'd always taken for granted through her own hard times. And Emily's image was still vivid in her mind next day as she walked down to Berry Stores just along the road and noticed a small card in the window advertising for a part-time assistant.

Half-an-hour later, the job was hers and her mother's voice came to her again as she turned the key in the front door lock to let herself into her bright, welcoming home. "God helps those who help themselves, Agnes."

Over the next few years, she knew her mother had been right. For the new job brought her many new friends, some of whom, when they realised she was an accomplished dressmaker, introduced her to the local amateur operatic society, the Bromham Independent Players.

"You are just the lady we've been looking for, Mrs Winch."

The big man with a beard and a commanding manner shook Agnes warmly by the hand and then introduced her as the new wardrobe mistress who would solve all their costume problems in the future.

"Are you sure you'll manage it, Mum?"

Robert, now almost seventeen and in his first job learning to be a cabinet-maker at Stanley Woods & Son in Olney, had become very protective of his mother, who, in his private opinion, should not be working at her age but sitting with her feet up in retirement.

"But I enjoy the job, Robert," Agnes told him yet again. "And the work for the society is fun."

She didn't add that without her small wage packet, even with the help of Robert's board and lodging, they'd have a lean time of it even though Beryl, now with three shops to run and two small children of her own, still somehow found time to visit her mother regularly and always there was a gift of either a cheque or a bag full of groceries on the table before she left. Usually in a tearing hurry to get back to her busy life.

"How are the girls?" was the question Beryl asked each time she rang to say she'd be over to see her mother. And now Agnes was able to answer cheerfully that they seemed to be coping.

Shela, who was about to obtain her long-awaited divorce, had already met a widower some years older than herself, who wanted to take care of her and the children and to the girl's overwhelming relief, enable her to bring Deborah home from the hospital.

"He wants me to marry him, Mum," she confided to Agnes. "And I probably will when I'm free."

And Agnes understood and approved silently of her daughter's decision although she was, as she admitted only to herself, uneasy about her new son-in-law's drinking which Shela excused too easily and blamed on his early years in the navy.

Joan had been as good as her word and left her useless husband as soon as the youngest child started school. After her divorce, the Housing Department found her a big, old house in Ashburnham Road near the railway station. It was also not too far away from the hospital on the Kempston Road, where she resumed the nursing career abandoned years before on the birth of her first baby. Somehow, Joan coped as the children grew up with no help from their father and now she was seeing a hardworking man who needed a wife after years of bachelorhood and living alone.

And now it was nearly Christmas again, the tenth since leaving the old house in Castle Road and for Agnes, hanging the last ornament on the tree in the corner of the sitting-room, it would be the very first she'd woken up to on her own.

To everyone's surprise, Robert had announced his intention early in the summer that he and his petite and good-natured girlfriend, the only one he'd had since leaving school, would be getting married at the end of it.

"Why don't you wait a bit, Robert? You're not even twenty-one yet!" Agnes remonstrated with her youngest son as he enthused over his plans for the future but in the end his mother gave her consent and the young couple had a pretty wedding with a reception afterwards out at Beryl and Geoff's house at Pavenham and were soon settled into a small flat in the town centre.

The news that Robert's wife was already pregnant after just a few months of marriage brought a rueful smile to Agnes's face.

"He'll grow up in a hurry now," she confided to Joyce, who was back in Bedford once more as her

250

husband changed jobs again and who was making up for lost time as she made sure to visit her mother every week.

Joyce's years in Plymouth had ended with the longed-for baby girl after four strapping sons and as Agnes watched the child playing on the patch of lawn outside her sitting-room, she wondered if her eldest girl would go on to have more children as she herself had done, seemingly so effortlessly all those years ago.

"No, Mum! That's the last. Five is more than enough and kids today expect so much more than we did at their age. Johnny's always singing that song from *Fiddler On the Roof*. You know, that one about "If I Were A Rich Man". If he thinks we're having any more he has another think coming!" And Joyce laughed at her mother's expression as she went out to the garden to bring the little girl in for tea.

Would I have said that about Ted? Agnes wondered later as she finished the last costume for the society's new show. *The Boyfriend* was full of catchy numbers and Twenties-style dresses and Agnes was in her element as she made each one up to hang on the rail in her bedroom. Probably not. Her thoughts were back in the time of these pretty clothes as for a few seconds she felt again the excitement of meeting Ted and the wonderful way he always had, in those early days, of making her feel beautiful and quite special.

"He was a real charmer, alright."

Agnes spoke aloud to her reflection in the mirror as she turned sideways on to look at her still trim figure in the new, silk dress she'd made for the opening night of the show. Ted would have liked it, she thought. Then with a sigh and a little shake of the head at her own foolishness, she slipped quickly out of the dress to hang it with the others on the costume rail.

As she lay in bed that night and reckoned up the years, Agnes could hardly believe that she was already four years older than Ted had been when he died and she remembered George's remark at his father's funeral: "What a waste!"

And now she knew he had meant the man and not his mother's flowers.

CHAPTER
EIGHTEEN

"We'll be down to see you tomorrow. In time for lunch."

John's voice on the other end of the telephone line suddenly took on a serious note as he added, "There's something we want to talk over with you, Mum."

All through the morning, as she prepared the meal, Agnes wondered what it could be that would bring John and the family all the way down from Liverpool just for the weekend. It was usually Agnes herself who made the effort to visit them in their rambling Victorian house on the outskirts of the city. She had been several times now and always John sent the rail-tickets in good time, for he knew it was a big expense for his mother, now living on her pension and the part-time job at the shop.

As she laid the table for lunch, Agnes looked across with pride at her new electric sewing machine in the corner of the sitting-room. It had been a present from George last Christmas and now she no longer had to push away at the Singer treadle machine which, although it was like an old friend, had definitely seen better days and increasingly made her knees ache after two or three hours of sewing.

"What a blessing it is, George," she wrote in her monthly letter to her second son, now a newly-promoted Wing Commander in the R.A.F. and based permanently in Brussels.

This was the son Agnes saw the least, for his steady rise from Flying Officer at twenty to his present rank meant, as he explained from time to time, he was always on the move and service life left little time to visit relations in England and even less to get to know all the nieces and nephews who had appeared with relentless regularity since he first left home to go to university.

George had two children of his own now and while Agnes regretted that she saw them so infrequently, she always reminded herself that her son was making a success of his life entirely due to his own efforts and despite some of the drawbacks which being part of a large family inevitably entails.

She had no more time for thoughts of the past however, for just as Agnes was laughing at that silly Benny Hill going on about "Ernie, The Fastest Milkman In The West", John and his family arrived as promised at twelve-thirty. As Margaret helped her mother-in-law in the kitchen and the girls exclaimed over the society's latest costumes for *Gigi*, the reason for the hasty visit at last became clear.

"We've found a house near High Wycombe, Mum," John stated with a big smile on his face. Then he added quickly, before Agnes could interrupt him, "And we want you to come with us when we move."

Later, in the car on the way to see the new house, Margaret sat beside Agnes on the back seat and told her about John's new job with Britannia Airways and the need to move nearer to Luton Airport.

Agnes knew that British Eagle Airlines, where John had been working since coming home from the West Indies, had recently gone bust and all the pilots had been applying for new flying jobs ever since.

"He's been looking around for quite some time now," Margaret said quietly as John turned the car off the main road near Aylesbury and it began to climb through miles of beech woods *en route* to the village of Speen perched high in the Chilterns.

Halfway along Studridge Lane, John brought the car to a stop in the drive of Applegate House.

"And this will be your new home!"

Agnes looked with interest at the big house standing in its own extensive grounds and then at the small one beside it.

"Applegate Cottage, Mum. It was built as an artist's studio," John explained, indicating the square half-timbered house some thirty yards from the main building, "but I've had plans drawn up to convert it into a bungalow for you."

It was a beautiful spot in the middle of a quiet, remote village with one small shop-cum-post office and just a few miles from High Wycombe and Princes Risborough. It was also a long way from Bedford.

"Of course, we'll have to sell the house at Bromham before the bungalow is finished," John stated in his matter-of-fact way. "And that means living in with us for the first few months." Then he added cheerfully, "Take your time, Mum. Think about it before you decide. And if you don't want to leave the old town, we'll find something else for you. A nice flat maybe. Somewhere near to the girls."

But Agnes knew John was keen to get her away from the trials and tribulations of the rest of the family and she also knew that he was offering her security for the rest of her life. How to balance one with the other, that was the issue.

At sixty-seven, Agnes was still active and alert but her sensible oldest son could see that she had slowed down over the last few years and now that young Robert was out of her hair, he considered the best thing for his mother was to move her some miles away from the source of most of her worries, to live out her life in the peace and quiet only he could offer.

It was three months later that Agnes said goodbye to her colleagues in the shop and the operatic society to prepare for her new life in the Chilterns with John and his family.

"You should be moved in by Easter," he assured his mother as she settled down for the journey in his BMW and they began the long climb up through the beech-woods now glorious with autumn colours and half-an-hour later turned into the wide drive of his new home.

The pieces of furniture Agnes chose to take with her into this new life had arrived earlier that day and the rest, as after her previous move from the old house, had been distributed amongst the family in Bedford.

256

As she had packed her belongings over the last few days and various children and in-laws called to collect their designated bits and pieces, Agnes wondered again what had happened to the remnants from the house where her children were brought up and if the good, old stuff had since been replaced by the tasteless, modern furniture so popular with the young homemakers of today.

And her thoughts went back again, as they seemed to do more and more frequently, to that wonderful day when she and Ted chose a houseful of good furniture at Maples in London and there was no limit to the amount she could spend on their first home together.

The only piece left from that memorable day was the drop-leafed dining table with barley-twist legs, which first Emily and then Agnes had polished so lovingly over the years. And here it stood, bearing all the marks and knocks of family life as the number of children outgrew the space available on its stained and scratched surface.

"We can get that renovated, Mum." Margaret's kind voice broke into Agnes's thoughts as her furniture was stacked into John's second garage until such time as the bungalow would be ready. "It's a good piece and should come up really well."

Agnes smiled and nodded at her sensible daughter-in-law as the up-and-over doors swung down on the remnants of her past but she knew she would never have the old table smartened up to match the furniture John was planning to buy for his mother's new home. For it represented all that had gone before and so was almost as precious to her as the babies who had spilled their milk and banged little spoons on its once pristine surface over the years.

John was as good as his word about the bungalow, for just after Easter the next year, Agnes stood in her new sitting-room looking proudly around at all the new furnishings bought piece by careful piece since she'd left Bedford and the elegant curtains and swags she'd made up herself on the new sewing machine.

In her hands was a bowl of purple hyacinths given to her that morning by John's youngest child to welcome her to her new home and Agnes knew exactly where she could place it.

The old table, in pride of place by the window, somehow looked just right in the room as she spread a creamy, lace cloth over its dents and scratches then carefully positioned the hyacinths in the centre where they would catch the afternoon sun.

In the small kitchen, where fresh blue and white check curtains hung at the window and the new cooker sparkled beside the first fridge-freezer Agnes had ever owned, the young voice singing softly on the new transistor radio implored, "Take Me Home, Country Roads".

"I am home," Agnes murmured to herself. "Another home and another life and I must make the best of what's left."

PART FIVE

1971 to 1982

CHAPTER
NINETEEN

The first night of the show was only a month away and still Agnes was busy on alterations to the ladies' costumes. *The Pirates of Penzance* was the third yearly production for the Wycombe Savoy Opera Company, in which Agnes served as wardrobe mistress with ex-Prime Minister Harold Wilson's wife Mary as President. She had found such pleasure and interest in the work that there was no time to worry too much about the goings-on in Bedford. John had been right about that, she thought with a small smile as she turned back to her sewing machine.

Within three months of settling into the new bungalow, Margaret introduced her mother-in-law to one of the members of the society and after that, just as she had before, Agnes became quickly involved. Soon she was making her name as the woman who could make fantastic costumes out of old, charity-shop clothes and what's more, make them look as good as those from the hire companies the society paid out to before she arrived.

And Agnes enjoyed the work so much for it reminded her of the time when Flora Robson had suggested that she make her future in the theatre and the old notebooks and files on theatrical design she had so carefully gathered over the years now came once again into full use and the new wardrobe mistress loved every minute of it.

Margaret, the quiet and easy-going young woman who had welcomed Agnes into her home as if she was her own mother, encouraged and supported her in this new venture.

"It's given her a new interest in life," she stated, as John raised more than one eyebrow at the amount of work involved.

"After all," he had protested more than once, when his mother's sitting-room light was still burning long after they had turned theirs off at midnight, "Mum is almost seventy now and it's time she slowed down."

But Agnes would not listen to that kind of talk, however kindly meant and shooed her son away from her small room now almost permanently covered with brightly coloured costumes of all shapes and sizes in various stages of completion.

Sometimes, when Margaret was at her new part-time job, selling and modelling exclusive fashions for Country Casuals shop in High Wycombe and John was on standby for the airline, he would amble over to his mother's home with a couple of rashers of bacon draped over a forefinger, an egg in one pocket and a tomato in the other.

"Get the frying-pan out, Mum. Do me a fry-up!" he laughed and mother and son sat together to eat their breakfast and Agnes remembered she'd not done this for him since he left home at sixteen to join the R.A.F.

262

"It's your birthday soon, Mum," he announced one bright July morning while they listened to John Denver singing "Annie's Song" over their shared breakfast. "Your seventieth, isn't it?"

"That's right, John," Agnes replied with a laugh as she splashed hot dripping deftly over the egg in the old frying-pan. " 'Three score years and ten' as the Bible has it. I'm nearly there!"

"And Margaret and I would like to take you out for a meal to celebrate. That is," he added hastily, as his mother handed him another slice of toast, "if you've not made any other arrangements."

Agnes was hoping that the occasion would only be noted in a quiet way, so she was more than thankful for John's suggestion of a good dinner at one of the little local restaurants he knew well.

"You look very smart," Margaret smiled as she helped Agnes into the car a few days later and John caught his mother's eye in the mirror and winked at her before turning out of the drive to head through the village towards High Wycombe.

It was three-quarters of an hour later when Agnes realised that they were not, after all, going anywhere local and she wondered aloud where John could be taking them.

"You'll see," was his casual reply. Then he added with one of his quiet chuckles, "But I'm sure you'll like it."

Then to Agnes's astonishment, they were on the outskirts of Bedford and John was explaining that they had to make a slight detour first to see Mary and Roy who would be joining them later.

"She's doing something in the church hall," he confided as he brought the car to a stop in the big car park next to St. Andrew's Church in Kimbolton Road. "Arrangements about the harvest festival, I think she said. Why don't you bring Mum in to wait?" he suggested to Margaret as he opened the car door. "I'll only be a few minutes."

So John went ahead to warn nearly fifty family members that Agnes was on her way and when she walked into the darkened hall with Margaret, not a sound could be heard from one of them.

Then, as Agnes's heart jumped in her chest and she held tight to Margaret's reassuring hand, the lights went up to reveal long, trestle tables set out for a meal and "Happy Birthday" rang out as she stood speechless just inside the doorway.

They were all there. Every one of them. There were John's three girls and Joyce with Johnny and their five children. And there was Shela with her three and Joan with her six. At the next table sat George, grinning broadly, with his wife and two children and next to him Mary and Roy with their pigeon pair. And over there sat Beryl and Geoffrey with their two girls and the little boy, now nearly three years old.

"Come on, Mum, you're sitting next to me." It was Robert who led his mother into the room to her seat between him and his young wife and their baby boy smiled at Agnes as she patted his dark head and exclaimed at how big he had grown.

Then the band struck up with a song that Agnes had heard only yesterday on her transistor radio.

"You Are The Sunshine Of My Life", the young voice sang into the microphone and as Agnes got her breath back after the surprise sprung on her by the family, she realised how much she missed them all.

"Come on, Agnes. Let's do this one together."

It was Shela's second husband who held out his hand to his mother-in-law and they managed it twice round the dance-floor before Agnes said she'd had enough and George was also out of breath as he led her back to her seat.

"He's not well," Shela confided later as her mother noted George's high colour and the higher number of whiskies he put away during the evening. And her thoughts turned, unbidden, to Ted all those years ago before the doctor's advice to let him have his cigarettes for it was now too late to prevent further damage to his poor lungs.

"He's a good man," Shela spoke quietly as she watched her mother's expression of concern. "But I met him too late to do anything about the drinking and smoking. I just let him enjoy himself now."

Joan's new husband, Tony, claimed the next dance with Agnes and she listened as he told her all about the new house they'd just moved to and how the children were settling down in a more stable lifestyle than they'd ever known before.

"It's what all kids need," he said with a smile. "And women too for that matter."

Agnes could see that Joan was happy but she found herself wondering how long her restless daughter would stick to this good but rather staid man who was helping her to bring up her children.

"As long as it takes," was Joan's response to her mother's tentative enquiry about the marriage. "And longer if I'm lucky," she added with a laugh.

Later, Agnes sat quietly beside John as one by one, her children came to say goodbye as the little ones fell asleep on their mothers' laps and the older grandchildren became over-excited and quarrelsome towards the end of the evening.

She tried to count the number of her grandchildren as each one kissed their Gang-Gang goodbye. Was it twenty-six or twenty-seven? And now there were two great-grandchildren as well!

"I wonder what your father would have made of all this?" she laughed as John held open the car door for his tired mother and Margaret tucked the rug carefully around her aching legs.

Agnes dozed a little on the way home but just once, half awake, she heard John talking quietly to Margaret.

"I promised the old man I'd look after her." He spoke the words quietly but there was a trace of bitterness in the way he said them and Agnes remembered her eldest son's early disapproval of his father's ways and his impatience with the sick man's later dependence on his mother and then, worst of all, the boy's barely concealed contempt when he learned of her last pregnancy.

As she switched off the bedside lamp that night, Agnes's thoughts were once more with Ted and even after all this time, she grieved. Not for his loss but for the waste of a quick mind that had never realised its full potential.

CHAPTER
TWENTY

It was October 1975 and the Society was putting on *Merrie England* again this year.

Agnes glanced at the clock on the mantelpiece and saw that it was already after midnight as she switched off the sewing machine and wearily stretched aching arms above her head.

She had been hard at work on the costumes for over a month now and everyone said that they were the best yet.

"Whatever shall we do when you retire, Mrs Winch?" The producer stood beside his excellent wardrobe mistress admiring the stunning costumes she'd made at minimal cost to the Society's budget.

"You can worry about that when the time comes," replied Agnes. Then she added mischievously, "And that probably won't be before you!"

Although she was often tired, the work had given Agnes a new lease of life, for after the big birthday party in Bedford and the quiet months that followed in her little house, she found she was often restless with so little to do and all day to do it in.

But John's three girls, and lately Beryl's two, sometimes needed sewing jobs done for them and as she worked away on dance dresses or outfits for weddings and parties, Agnes remembered her own stylish clothes of so long ago for tennis club socials and later, the Licensed Victuallers' Association evenings, dancing with those young men who looked like Rudolph Valentino. And through her sewing, she lived her young dancing years all over again as each granddaughter swirled in front of Gang-Gang's big mirror to show off her new dress.

The ties with the family in Bedford had loosened a little now that Agnes was living away from them all but she still got the occasional telephone call from one or the other of them and a weekend visit to see their mother was a real treat for those with a car and the others somehow managed it twice or three times during the summer months.

Each time she waved another little family goodbye after a happy day's visit, Agnes thanked whoever was responsible for such matters that her girls were settled and happy at last.

The boy who came so late in her marriage now had two growing sons of his own and ran a small taxi business from home.

"It's long hours and hard work, Mum," Robert said, when Agnes worried over the amount of time spent away from his family, "but I'm independent this way and Denise understands."

I hope she does, thought his mother, for Robert's wife was young and pretty and deserved more attention than her overworked husband had time to give her. More than once, Agnes had heard the suppressed resentment in the girl's voice when she rang her mother-in-law about Robert being out all night and sleeping for much of the day.

"Then he wakes up with a sore head and accuses me of not trying to keep the children quiet while he sleeps!"

"He's asking for trouble, John," Agnes confided to her oldest son on one of their frequent breakfast-sharing mornings. "She won't put up with that for very long."

John grinned and reminded his mother of his own long absences from home on long-haul flights to far destinations and the way Margaret always seemed to cope with them and him when he arrived home tired and in need of pampering and rest.

Agnes carefully refrained from telling him that although his easy-going wife missed him when he was away, she had often confessed it was sometimes a relief to see John's flight bag loaded into the car before waving goodbye as he drove off and knowing he wouldn't be back for at least five days and sometimes even longer if he was flying a plane to Australia.

"He's such a perfectionist, Mum," Margaret sighed wearily as she joined Agnes for coffee one morning after seeing her husband off. "And so critical if everything is not just right."

And Agnes sipped her coffee and remembered the countless hours John had spent in his cramped bedroom in the old house, sandpapering and painting the balsa-wood model aircraft which hung from every available spare inch of the tiny ceiling. And how he always knew if anything had been moved or even touched while he was at school. And the rows he had with the younger children if anything was missing from his cherished possessions.

"Well, dear, I don't suppose he'll change now, do you?" Agnes sympathised with Margaret but she knew John had chosen the right girl, for she was that one in a million who could tolerate her son's criticisms and the occasional sarcasms which reminded his mother so much of Ted in his younger days.

The Wycombe Savoy Operatic Company's presentation in that year of 1975 was the best ever and as Agnes came on stage to receive her bouquet on the last night, she was overwhelmed by the standing ovation which lasted well over two minutes.

"The costumes are marvellous, Agnes!" enthused the leading lady, who looked truly stunning in a blue and gold creation made from a brocade curtain which Agnes had unearthed at the back of a charity shop in High Wycombe. On the girl's head was a crown fashioned from the wire skeleton of a small lampshade covered in red velvet rescued from an old cocktail dress about to be discarded by a neighbour. The jewelled cross on its top had been created from an assortment of Rowntree's fruit gums surrounding a magnificent "pearl" oval mint, courtesy of the same company.

As she looked around her at the bustle and excitement of the cast greeting friends and relatives at the party they put on at the end of each run, Agnes felt a quiet pride in the skills she had learned so long ago and she smiled to herself as she crossed the room to speak to the producer.

"I've made up my mind, John. I would like to go on for another year or two."

"Good for you, Mrs Winch! You would have been sorely missed, I can assure you. And next year it's to be *The Pirates of Penzance* again!"

"And all those wonderful costumes to make," laughed Agnes. In her mind she was already planning the sumptuous creations for the next show.

Later, as John drove the three of them home in the small hours and his tired mother dozed beside her, Margaret looked with concern at the older woman's drawn face and afterwards made her promise to have a long rest now that it was all over for another year.

"Time enough to start again in the spring, Mum," was her advice as they shared their coffee a few days later.

But the new year was to bring fresh concerns to Agnes. One cold day in late February, Shela rang to say that her husband, George, had now just a few weeks to live and that she was at her wits' end trying to nurse him and keep going on the teacher-training course she'd taken up to save her sanity some three years earlier. And as the month drew to a close, the good man who had helped her raise her family gave up the fight against the dreadful effects of alcohol and cigarettes and died a painful and distressing death in hospital as his wife held his hand and prayed that his agony would last no longer.

CHAPTER
TWENTY-ONE

"Stay in bed, dear. I'll bring you a cup of tea."

Shela had been staying with her mother for three days now and since the night she'd turned up on Agnes's doorstep, white-faced and exhausted, she'd done nothing else but sleep.

"Let her, Mum," advised Margaret. "She's tired out and the rest will do her good."

As they drank their tea together with Agnes sitting on the end of her sofa-bed, Shela began to talk to her mother for the first time about George's illness and his terrible, slow death.

"It was so awful, Mum. And I couldn't do anything at all to help him at the end."

Agnes watched quietly as the tears came again and she remembered Ted's gaunt face as he gasped for breath in the very same hospital ward where Shela's husband had died.

History had repeated itself in the worst possible way but Agnes knew that once the shock and grieving had passed, Shela would feel the same overwhelming relief that she herself had experienced when Ted died. She also knew that this would be the time her daughter would need the most help for with relief would come a guilt so hard to bear.

Shela slept again for most of that day but as the evening drew in and mother and daughter sat together outside on the square of lawn behind the little house, there was a new calmness about Shela and Agnes hoped that the worst was over.

"Time to go back to work," were Shela's reassuring words as she kissed her mother goodbye a few days later and turned her little car towards home and her new job at a school in Luton.

"She'll be alright now," John spoke quietly as they waved goodbye to his sister. "She's a survivor. Just like her mother."

But as the cold spring turned into a blazing summer and the longest heatwave since the war began to take its toll on her energy and spirits, Agnes grudgingly admitted to herself for the first time in her life that she was tired.

Not of life. No — never that. Physically tired, so that getting out of bed in the mornings became so difficult and at night, bedtimes could not come soon enough.

"Anaemia, Mrs Winch."

The young woman behind the desk smiled kindly at her elderly patient as she wrote out the prescription and then looked puzzled as Agnes told her about that horrible Parrish's Food she'd taken as a girl for the very same ailment that was troubling her now.

"I think we can offer something a little better than that today," the doctor laughed as she saw Agnes out and reminded her to come back in a month's time. "Just for a check-up, Mrs Winch."

A week later, Agnes fainted in Margaret's kitchen as she tried to fight that old, familiar, frightening feeling of unreality which had slowly grown worse for the last few days.

Then the tests began, as Margaret hovered and Joyce, called overnight to the hospital in High Wycombe, bustled and John talked quietly to the doctor behind the glass panel of the closed door.

"It seems that you have a tired heart, Mum."

Joyce spoke softly to her suddenly aged mother who seemed inexplicably to have shrunk so that it was, somehow, the small frame of a child who sat propped up against the big, white hospital pillow looking calmly out at all the fuss going on around her.

What were they talking about? A tired heart indeed! She couldn't have a tired anything with all that work waiting to be done for the Society and anyway, Joyce always fussed too much.

Agnes sighed and closed her eyes. Perhaps if she pretended to be asleep they would all go away and let her rest. Then she'd be able to get out of this bed and go home where she belonged.

When she awoke, it was dark and only the dim glow from the lamp on the night-sister's desk and the soft snores of the other patients around her told her that it must be the middle of the night.

A ridiculously young nurse padded softly over to Agnes's bed to enquire if she would like a cup of tea.

"Please. But the bedpan first, nurse."

Later, as she sat poised on the cold, metal thing, Agnes reflected with a small giggle that this was the first time, apart from the lying-in periods after her babies and the one they thought had been growing in her fallopian tube that time and of course that awful miscarriage, that she'd ever been confined to bed for more than two or three days at a stretch.

Perhaps she was getting old, as John had stated earlier to Margaret, thinking his mother was still asleep and would not hear him. But in her mind, Agnes did not feel old. In her mind she was still the confident, eighteen-year-old girl who had embarked on life full of hope and optimism on the day she finished her dressmaking apprenticeship.

Well, she'd show them, she thought, as she thankfully drank the hot tea and the little nurse prepared to settle the nice, old lady down once again in the crisp, hospital bed and offered her a sleeping pill.

"No thank you, nurse. I'll be able to sleep now and tomorrow I'll be better," answered Agnes sleepily as the girl smoothed the sheet yet again and tucked it expertly in tightly across the thin, old shoulders.

Before she slept, Agnes pulled it out again. And before the week was over she went home with a supply of phenobarbitone tablets which she was told she must take for the rest of her life.

The heatwave lasted until well into September and by that time, Agnes was at work again on the new season's costumes for the Society.

"Perhaps next year, Margaret," she reassured her anxious daughter-in-law when she asked about Agnes's

276

promised retirement. In fact, it was to be several years and many more productions later before she left the Society and handed over somewhat reluctantly to her successor.

But the reason for that was not ill-health or age or any of those other tiresome things the family kept talking about.

It was on a beautiful day in early autumn when the beeches at the end of the garden were blazing with colour and Agnes's chrysanthemums were at their best, when John called out to his mother to come across to the big house for a cup of tea and a chat.

When she thought about it later, Agnes realised that she should have suspected that something was going on, for the signs had been there for several months. John's unexplained visits to his oldest daughter, now settled in America with her own family. And Margaret's sudden departure only the month before to join him there and their delayed return so that Agnes was asked to feed the cat and keep an eye on the house and the youngest girl for an extra week or so.

"We have an idea to put to you, Mum. But don't make up your mind right away. There's plenty of time."

John's careful voice and the carefully-concealed concern on Margaret's face made Agnes's heart leap painfully in her chest as for a few seconds, the table swayed away from her grasp and she was thankful that her chair, pressed hard against the back of her knees, supported her suddenly wobbly legs.

"Margaret and I have decided to live in America when I retire, Mum."

So that was it, thought Agnes, as she sipped her tea and smiled brightly at this son who had given her such a good home for the last twenty years and who now wanted to live near his own family in retirement.

"That doesn't mean you have to leave your little house, you know."

Margaret spoke gently to the older woman she had come to love like her own mother over the years and Agnes knew it was not easy for them to tell her that they were going away. For good.

So she listened to the plans for their new home and heard all about the ideal site they had already bought in pine woods just a few miles from their daughter's house on the north-west coast of America near Seattle. Thousands of miles away from me, thought Agnes bleakly but the smile never left her face as John told how he'd been offered early retirement and that the house in the States would be ready for them this time next year.

"So you see, Mum, there's plenty of time. We'll sell this house, of course, but you can stay on in yours as long as you want. We'll be able to stay with you on visits back to the old country."

For the next few weeks, all through the Society's latest production of *Merrie England* with its endless rehearsals and costume fittings and late nights spent at her sewing machine, listening to her Gilbert and Sullivan records from previous shows, Agnes turned the news of the impending departure over and over in her mind.

How could she think of giving up her snug, little home? But as the weeks went by and friends from the Society called less often and Christmas came and went and she knew it would be John's last one in the big house next door, Agnes began to nudge round the unthinkable.

By Easter the next year, when the Society met for its Annual General Meeting, she knew what she must do.

The small room at the back of St. Mark's church, with its illuminated cross overlooking High Wycombe, was suddenly hushed as the short, elderly lady, who was the best wardrobe mistress they'd ever had, rose to face the committee with a smile on her face and sadness in her heart.

"So it is with great regret that I tender my resignation and wish the best of luck to my successor," Agnes announced quietly.

"They made me an honorary life member, Margaret," Agnes sighed, looking wistfully at the handsome carriage clock handed to her by the smiling president of the Society as a leaving present. "That will look very well on my new mantelpiece. Wherever it might be."

CHAPTER
TWENTY-TWO

Two days after Prince Charles and Lady Diana Spencer were married, Agnes began her preparations for yet another move.

"You are coming to us, Mum. For as long as you like."

Beryl and Geoff's old farmhouse home in the Bedfordshire countryside near Felmersham was roomy and welcoming as Agnes settled into their little bed-sitting-room overlooking the duck pond and the view down the hill to the village.

Now it was September and still no suitable place had been found for her and Agnes began to think and feel like one of those stateless people at the end of the war who drifted about Europe waiting for a government somewhere to let them in.

"It's not that I feel unwanted, Joyce," she assured her oldest daughter who had invited her mother to her own crowded home in Putnoe for the weekend. "But I do hope we find somewhere for me soon."

Agnes needed her own place to care for and she did not like this feeling of uncertainty and the necessity of always blending in with Beryl's family plans. For with three boisterous children in the house, a seventy-seven-year-old grandmother sometimes found the noise and chaos too much to bear.

Joyce looked with concern at the worry on her mother's face and gently suggested that she should go up to her room to try to rest for a while.

It was as Joyce's three youngest sat down for their tea and Shela, who had arrived unexpectedly to see her mother, sat drinking hers, that the sound of breaking glass came from the room directly above followed by a loud thump and then silence.

Joyce was up the stairs first with Johnny close behind her and as Shela hastily put down her teacup and told the children to stay where they were, she also climbed the stairs two at a time to her mother's bedroom.

Agnes was lying flat out on the floor beside the shattered remnants of the glass of water she'd just carried from the bathroom. She was still unconscious as Johnny rang for an ambulance.

"It's another of your attacks, I'm afraid, Mrs Winch." The tired-faced young doctor on duty in Casualty took Agnes's pulse again and listened to his patient's recent medical history from her worried daughter. "We'll get you up to the ward and then do some tests."

Joyce held her mother's hand and watched anxiously as the nurse inserted the cannula in the back of the other one for the drip hanging above the narrow hospital bed.

"This can't go on, Shela!" The older sister spoke sharply to the younger woman although she knew that none of what had happened was her fault. "Why ever didn't John see her settled before making his plans for the States? That's what I'd like to know!"

Why indeed, thought Shela as they kissed their mother goodbye and promised to visit the next afternoon and the ward sister told them that Mrs Winch would probably be kept in for three or four days until she was stabilised.

"Then she'll need care and plenty of rest."

On the way back to Joyce's home, Shela gave voice to her opinion that John had cared for their mother for the past twenty years and that he probably thought it was time someone else took over.

"But that's what he wanted, Shela!" protested Joyce as she backed the car into the garage. "And," she added with a sigh, "that's what he promised Dad he would do. And now it appears that it's up to us."

For Agnes, lying once again in a strange, hard bed, the night was full of dreams of Ted and her mother both smiling at her and telling her not to worry for everything would be all right.

But early the next morning, as she tried to eat the lukewarm porridge brought by a smiling Indian ward-orderly, Agnes reflected that everything was not all right. Here she was, in her late seventies, homeless and sick and altogether feeling very sorry for herself as she tried to smile and assure the same young doctor she'd seen last night, now looking even more tired, that she was feeling better and asking when could she go home?

"Not just yet, Mrs Winch. You must rest and try not to worry. In a few days perhaps."

By the end of the week it was decided that Agnes should go to Shela's home when she was discharged.

"You'll get some peace and quiet here, Mum," said her second daughter softly as they pulled up outside the isolated farm cottage to which she had moved with a new partner some eighteen months after George died. "I'm only doing supply teaching this year so I can choose when to work and when to stay at home."

Agnes enjoyed the peace of the little cottage tucked away at the end of Wood Lane in Willington and as the warm, sunny days of late summer began to slide past and she regained her strength, Shela began to talk of her mother living with her permanently.

Agnes mulled over the idea all through the autumn as Shela took on more work and her mother sat again at her sewing machine making up new curtains and covers for the cosy little house which her daughter wanted her to look on as home.

But as the days shortened and Christmas came and went, the old longing for somewhere to call her own grew steadily stronger and Agnes told Shela that she wanted to look for somewhere in the New Year.

It was a month before Easter and Shela was settling in well at her new teaching post at a school in Luton, when her mother decided one morning not to get out of bed. For three months now, both Joyce and Shela and more recently Joan, had been looking anxiously in the local newspapers and visiting flats and rooms advertised at reasonable rents. None was suitable for an elderly woman who wanted to live alone.

"We'll get your name down on the list at the Housing Department, Mum," were Joan's words only last week as she drove away from visiting her mother. The Housing Department! That meant, as Agnes knew only too well, a small flat in a big block or one of those bungalows on a distant housing estate.

A dreadful feeling of helplessness overwhelmed her at Joan's words and this morning after Shela had brought her up a cup of tea and later called goodbye, Agnes just gave up hope.

"Where are you, Mum?"

Shela was back from work and the house was unusually quiet as she called up the stairs. Agnes was still in bed, apparently fast asleep with the curtains still drawn across the windows.

"I think you'd better come over, Joan. I don't like the look of her at all." Shela spoke quietly to her sister who was now a health visitor and would know how to cope with their mother. "She just lies there. Won't eat or speak. It's just not like her."

Upstairs, Agnes was not asleep. She heard the phone being replaced on its cradle and Shela coming up the stairs once more. Soft footsteps crossed the landing but before her daughter entered the room, Agnes pulled the eiderdown further over her head and lay quite still. She did not want to talk to anyone.

Later she dreamed of Ted, then awoke to find a soft light burning on her bedside table and slept again and

284

awoke once more to see bright morning filtering in through the curtains.

"Are you hungry, Mum?"

Shela's anxious face peeped round the door which had been left ajar so that she could listen out for her mother if she called out for her in the night.

Agnes knew that her daughter was worried and she was sorry for the girl who, over the years since George died, had had to contend with troubles of her own. For Agnes could see that Shela was far from happy in a relationship that had alienated her from her two sons who had not seen their mother now for nearly two years.

But Agnes had come to the end of the road. All she knew was that she would rather die here in this bed than go into one of those old people's homes she'd overheard being discussed one day in Joyce's house. She'd seen inside them more than once during her younger years working at the hospital. There they sat in those ugly, great chairs, either fast asleep or staring into space as if they were not there at all. Drugged, probably, she thought, shuddering at the memory. Drugged to keep them quiet most of the time.

Over the next few days, as Shela coaxed her mother into eating again and Beryl arrived unexpectedly one morning to wash and set Agnes's hair, the family held hasty meetings in each other's homes to discuss their mother's future.

"She's very fit for her age, Joyce."

Joan spoke with some authority for she'd had a word with her mother's doctor only the previous day.

285

"And quite capable of living alone. That's the problem. She needs her own place again."

So the talk went on and everyone tried to jolly Agnes along as she began to come slowly out of the depression that had overwhelmed her so suddenly on the day in spring when she didn't want to get out of bed. And now it was Easter and Shela was at home for the school holidays and Joyce was visiting for tea and telling her mother that she'd been on to the Housing Department again.

"You are well up on the waiting list so it shouldn't be too long now."

And what then? Agnes thought grimly. One of those flats in a tower block? Or a neglected bungalow like the one she'd reluctantly agreed to visit with Joan one day to see a lonely old woman whose husband had recently died? And miles away from everyone she knew and loved.

Agnes's mouth was suddenly very dry and she had difficulty swallowing the tea which Shela had put hopefully in front of her mother. Smile! Agnes thought desperately. Don't let them see you upset again. And her face ached with the effort as Joyce made her goodbyes and Shela switched on the television for the six o'clock news.

The screen was full of images of soldiers and tanks against a bleak background which the announcer said was the Falklands and Agnes remembered that Shela's girl was married to a soldier. It was as the war correspondent described the exploits of the young men

286

"yomping" across that faraway island that the phone rang and it was Joan with exciting news for her mother.

"What? Where is it? You never said!"

Joan had quietly answered an advertisement in *The Bedfordshire Times* for a small, two-bedroomed cottage to let in Cardington, only a short distance away from Shela's home.

"It belongs to a charitable trust, Mum. The Vicar says it's for retired people only. And it's empty! He says he'll be free tomorrow afternoon if you want to go along to see it."

Neither Agnes nor Shela slept much that night and both of them were up early the next day drinking tea and talking over the new turn of events.

"Don't be too disappointed if it isn't what you expected, Mum."

Shela could see that Agnes had changed almost from the very minute Joan had rung about the cottage and she prayed that this would be the turning point for her mother who had tried so bravely to contend with all the changes in her life and had so nearly broken under the strain of the last one.

Just after two o'clock they were knocking on the vicarage door and a smiling, elderly man picked up a bunch of keys from his hall table and led them a few yards down the road from St. Mary's Church to the third of a row of four small cottages on The Green.

"They are administered by The Cardington and Eastcotts Charitable Trust, Mrs Winch, as I explained to your other daughter yesterday," the Rev. Tubbs said as they walked around the little house and admired the well-kept communal garden behind. "But these days," he added ruefully, "we have to ask a realistic rent, I'm afraid."

Agnes fell in love with the cottage at first sight. Yes, it needed decorating and something would have to be done about that bedroom window which did not shut properly.

"When shall I know, Vicar?"

Later, they stood in the afternoon sunshine looking back at the porch and the old, leaded windows of the cottage as the good man assured them that it would only be a couple of days.

"I have to discuss things with the committee, you see, Mrs Winch." Then he added with a reassuring smile, "But leave it to me. I'll do my best for you."

The telephone rang, as promised, two days later and it was the vicar offering Agnes the tenancy of the cottage starting in one month's time and asking for two weeks' rent in advance.

"Ten pounds a week, Shela and that includes the television licence fee. I can manage that easily. Now I have to get going on curtains and covers again."

As she put the phone back on its rest, Agnes felt a great surge of thankfulness that the dark days were finally over and she smiled to herself as she remembered the little cottage of her girlhood. Yes, she would be as happy in this one as she had been there all those years ago.

It was two months before her seventy-eighth birthday when Beryl and Geoff unpacked Agnes's furniture which had been in storage in one of their barns on the

288

farm and the family moved their mother into her newly-decorated, snug little cottage by the green.

Across the fields, the great airship sheds of Cardington towered upwards and at the mooring-mast a new, modern airship swung lazily in a warm breeze. On its side was the word GOODYEAR and it seemed to Agnes, as she stood gazing at it, that it was a fitting description of the year when she came home once again.

the old notebooks and files, to the actual details she had
so carefully gathered over the years. Agnes would once
again find fulfilment and she never ceased to enjoy telling
everyone interested in it, that she was enjoying it enormously.

Margaret, the quiet and easy-going young woman
who had welcomed Agnes into her home as if she was
her own mother, encouraged and supported her in this
adventure.

"It's given her a new interest in life," she stated, and
only raised more than one eyebrow at the amount of
work involved.

"After all," he had protested more than once when
his mother's sitting-room light was still burning long
after they had turned theirs off at midnight, "Mum is
almost seventy now and it's time she slowed down."

But Agnes would not listen to that kind of talk,
however kindly meant and shoo-ed her son away from
her small room now almost permanently covered with
brightly coloured costumes of all shapes and sizes in
various stages of completion.

Sometimes, when Margaret was at her new part-time
job selling and modelling exclusive fashions for
Ledbury Casuals shop in their village and John was
on standby for the airline, he would amble over to his
mother's home with a couple of rashers of bacon
draped over a forefinger, an egg in one pocket and a
sausage in the other.

"Get the frying-pan out, Mum. Do me a fry-up!" he
laughed and mother and son sat together to eat their
breakfast and Agnes remembered she'd not done this
for him since he left home at sixteen to join the R.A.F.
yet.

PART SIX

1982 to 1996

CHAPTER
TWENTY-THREE

The big, walled garden shared by three of the row of four cottages on The Green was golden with daffodils and the first bluetits perched expectantly on the bird-boxes hanging from the big apple tree in the centre of the lawn.

Agnes stood for a few moments enjoying the spring sunshine after pegging out her small line of washing and noted with satisfaction that there would be a good show of wallflowers again this year.

Every November for the last four years, she had planted them out all along the old wall opposite her kitchen window and then waited for her reward the next spring.

"It's strange how a scent can remind you of years gone by," she remarked later to Joyce who had called in to take her mother for the weekly shopping they always did together.

By the end of May, the garden was filled again with the fragrance of the wallflowers and Agnes remembered the tiny cottage garden at Almshoe near Hitchin, where she'd picked gooseberries and blackcurrants as a girl. She thought with affection of the old woman always dressed in black and crocheted lace cap, who had cared for her and Lizzie so well on that summer holiday of long ago.

"She was only sixty-five when she died, Joyce. And they were always called gillyflowers in those days."

Agnes's thoughts were still in the past as she counted out six of those new pound coins to pay her daughter for the groceries she'd brought back for her from Sainsbury's at Kempston. Wretched things! "They make my handbag so heavy," she complained at regular intervals to a patient Joyce. "Why couldn't that Government have left well alone?"

Joyce smiled at her mother and observed how well she looked and how still, at eighty-one, she worked regularly on the old sewing machine that Johnny had serviced for her for the past twenty-odd years. It was in constant use as Agnes continued to sew for her grandchildren, and for each new bride in the family a beautifully designed and fitted wedding dress was created with pride and care for her big day.

Agnes had almost lost count of the number she'd made over the years but each one was made with love by the old lady who never forgot a birthday and was the first person to go to with both joyous news and heartaches and who always gave sound advice when asked.

The wallflowers were fading in the garden and Agnes was looking forward to watching a new programme that had recently started showing on the B.B.C. Shela had promised to call in after work to share a meal with her mother as she did regularly nearly every week.

The phone rang halfway through *Eastenders* and when Shela answered, the stunned look on her face told Agnes that something awful had happened.

"Sit down, Mum." Her daughter spoke very gently and then took the older woman's hand in her own and held on to it as she told her mother that the call was from Joyce and that she had some bad news to tell her.

"She'll be here soon, Mum. It's Mary's Roy. He had a heart attack at work this afternoon and he's just died in the hospital."

"He wouldn't have known much about it," Joyce assured her mother later after she had spoken to Roy's daughter, still at the hospital with Mary. "It was all over very quickly."

But Agnes could not understand why a good man like Roy should have to go before he was fifty and Shela explained that he had not been well for some time. "Mary kept him on a low-fat diet but she was always finding toffee papers in his pockets. Better than smoking, I suppose."

In the days that followed, as Mary prepared for the funeral and the family closed ranks around her, Agnes did her best to support her distraught daughter. Not with words but by just being there as she had always been for all of them.

"I'll have to go back to work full-time now, Mum."

It was a month after the funeral and Agnes was staying with Mary in her semi-detached house on the Hillyfields Estate in Bedford to help her sort out Roy's clothes ready to be taken to a charity shop.

Why is this always the most difficult thing to do? she thought sadly as she carefully folded a good, white shirt and placed it with half-a-dozen others in a Sainsbury's carrier bag.

"Will you manage now, child?"

Mary knew that her mother meant would she manage financially and she smiled wanly at the quietly voiced question for Roy had left her with a good pension and with his sudden death the mortgage was now fully paid up. So yes, she would manage, she assured her anxious mother. But behind the small smile, Agnes knew Mary would have given anything to have her good, kind husband back again. And she sighed as she finished packing Roy's things and then kissed her daughter goodbye with a promise to ring her before she went to bed.

Later, as she waited for the kettle to boil for her hot-water bottle, Agnes reflected on the unfairness of fate in taking her girl's husband so young. But she'll manage, she thought, as the kettle began to whistle. As we all do in the end.

Later still, as she settled down to sleep, Ted filled her mind again and Agnes knew what he would have said to his bereaved daughter.

"You can't change things, my girl. So you must make the best of it."

And Shela remembered her own dead husband and forgot the frictions of the past as she later phoned her younger sister to assure her that things would get better and to get on with her own life now that she was alone.

Just as she herself had done in the dark days after George died.

It was later in that same year, as autumn brought shorter afternoons to the old, walled garden and Agnes began to pull the curtains across the windows by teatime, when John came to visit unexpectedly one misty Sunday, to tell his mother that the plans to move permanently to America had been shelved.

Soon after Agnes had moved back to Bedford, John had just sold his big house in Speen when unexpected promotion had been offered by Britannia Airways to that of Senior Captain. And so his early retirement was postponed and the two of them moved into Agnes's little house next door and John flew over to Seattle regularly to supervise the building of the new home waiting for them up in the pine woods above Puget Sound.

"Margaret saw the specialist this week," he told his stunned mother as they settled down with a freshly-brewed pot of tea. "She has cancer."

Agnes looked with pity and concern at her son's drawn face and only guessed at the worry that John had been keeping to himself for the past few months.

"There's not much they can do for her now, Mum. Pain control and chemotherapy of course. But they don't hold out much hope."

Agnes handed him a strong cup of tea and wished, not for the first time, that her reticent son would speak what was in his heart. But she knew that he would keep it all bottled up and handle things in his own way, just as he'd always done. And she grieved for the kind, unassuming girl her oldest boy had married and who had asked for nothing more than a quiet family life and then retirement near her children in America.

Over the next few months, as Margaret began to fade and the lines of suffering on her face aged her so, Agnes waited quietly for John's phone calls and prayed hard every Sunday that the girl who had made her so welcome in her home when she needed it most, would, by some miracle, be spared.

The phone call she'd been dreading came early the next year and once again the family gathered to mourn another of its members and Agnes now had three children widowed prematurely.

When she looked in the mirror every morning now, it seemed the face that stared back at her was so like her mother's that Agnes had the strangest fancy she could talk to Emily as she had in the old days and somehow she was comforted by this odd thought.

The dark hair, of which her father had been so proud, was streaked with white and the trim waistline, which had returned to her so quickly after each baby was born, had begun to thicken a little. But still Agnes took pride in her appearance and so she made a new skirt and blouse for Margaret's funeral and re-trimmed the little, black hat she'd worn for the two others.

It was only later as she waved goodbye to John as he stood so alone on his doorstep, that Agnes knew she was right to grieve for the living, for no amount of grieving would bring back the dead.

"Poor man," she sighed aloud as Joyce turned the car for home after their short visit to John's quiet house. "He didn't deserve this."

And Joyce glanced at her mother's tired face and thought for the first time that at last the old lady was beginning to look her age.

"The funeral really took it out of her, Johnny," she told her husband later over supper. "I'll have to keep a special eye on her for a while."

It was a little over two years later that both Joyce and Johnny retired from their jobs and came to live in Cople, a mile down the road from Agnes's home. And the close relationship between mother and daughter that had begun in the first years of Joyce's marriage was renewed and each benefited from the other as their roles were gradually reversed without either realising what was happening.

But still the old sewing machine was kept busy as nearly every day Agnes climbed back up to her bedroom, where the light was better, to sit for a couple of hours doing the thing she enjoyed most.

"There! That's finished, Joyce." Agnes laughed as she snipped off the thread and switched off the machine. "And thank goodness, for I never thought I'd get it finished in time."

A little later, as Joyce went down to the kitchen to fill the kettle for tea, Agnes turned slowly from side to side in front of her cheval mirror to look critically at her new creation.

Yes, she thought with quiet satisfaction, blue always suited me. And then she smiled at the reflection of the small, white-haired woman in the old mirror in the sunny bedroom as Ted's oft-repeated words came back to her.

"Blue's the colour for you, my girl. Blue to match your eyes."

The moire silk dress and matching coat had been thought about and planned for the last six weeks for it was to be worn at a very special occasion.

George had taken the early retirement from the Royal Air Force that had been unexpectedly offered earlier in the year and at fifty-five was looking forward to a quiet life in the big house in Cambridge which he'd bought with that thought in mind.

Agnes knew that she would never forget that wonderful day at Buckingham Palace or her bursting pride as she watched her tall, second son bow before the Queen as the C.B.E. Medal was hung around his neck. Oh! He looked so smart in his R.A.F. uniform and then as he saluted and turned away to march quickly back to the ante-room once more, she seemed to hear Ted's voice in her head. "That's our boy, Agnes." And there was no mistaking that he was his father's son for he was exactly as Ted had been in his fifties.

The obligatory photograph was taken against the background of the black and gold palace gates and George's dark-haired Irish wife smiled broadly as he held the little medal-box wide open for the photographer to catch in the picture.

"He looked so handsome in his best uniform, Joyce."

Agnes's eldest daughter laughed as she enquired if her brother had managed the military bow to the Queen.

"Of course, dear. Irene says he's been practising it for weeks. I suppose when you get to be an Air-Commodore you should be used to wearing a uniform and standing tall!"

Later, Agnes lay in bed and tried to read her new library book but the words refused to make sense and at last she put it aside, switched off the light and tried to sleep.

At two in the morning, after she'd gone yet again throughout the whole family history, she gave up the attempt to sleep and let her thoughts wander at will.

John, now living in his big house on the beautiful west coast of America, was slowly rebuilding a new life for himself after a false start with a second wife. The marriage, entered into in haste and loneliness, lasted only a few years and then once again he was alone with his memories of Margaret and growing grandchildren living nearby to take up his time and energy.

Agnes wished she could see him more often. Perhaps next year she'd go over with Joyce to visit her oldest boy's lovely home in the pinewoods overlooking the ocean.

Thoughts of her caring first girl came unbidden and Agnes reflected that Joyce was one of the world's workers. Her children were her life but she always found time for her elderly mother, now fast approaching ninety.

Then there was Shela, back in Bedford once more after a third, hasty marriage had ended disastrously and a near mental breakdown which was endured so far away from those who could have helped her through it. The family had rallied round this daughter who in recent years had chosen a life so isolated from them all. Ah well. She was settled now into that cosy flat in Newnham Street and so odd that she should choose to live almost next door to the old house in the town.

Agnes sighed and turned over again, trying still to catch the sleep that would not come. Joyce would scold her if she overslept in the morning, for she'd think her mother had sat up half the night watching television again. Agnes chuckled to herself before her thoughts moved relentlessly on to her next girl, Joan.

What could she say about Joan? That she was headstrong and self-willed? Yes, both of those but most of all that she was, like her older sister, a soft-hearted but poor judge of men. Joan herself admitted that much and now she had given up on the lot of them and was getting on with her life and her job as a Health Visitor. Whatever she was, thought Agnes, punching the pillow into shape again, Joan was a survivor. And a home-builder. It would not be long before she settled down again in her own home. And all of her own making.

The operatic society carriage-clock present on the mantelpiece downstairs chimed three as Agnes threw off the covers, pulled on her dressing-gown and slipped her feet into the warm slippers Joyce and Johnny had given her for her birthday. Perhaps a cup of tea would get her off to sleep.

Sitting up in bed with the tea going cold in the cup, Agnes thought about Mary. Her girl who was widowed so young had pulled herself up by her bootlaces to secure a well-paid job with Eastern Electricity and was making her life work in the only way she knew how. Another survivor, thought Agnes and then wished with all her heart that Mary could find another good man like Roy.

And what about Beryl, the hardworking business-woman who had sold her three hairdressing shops to look after her family and in later years opened a high-class beauty salon in Bedford town centre above Geoff's jewellery shop and was looking forward to her first grandchild in the summer? The lovely house out at Felmersham which she'd furnished with such care and taste had been the elegant setting for so many family occasions over the years. But Agnes knew that her youngest girl was often so tired that whenever she came to visit her mother, she slept for an hour or more on the comfortable sofa in the little cottage.

She's like Joyce, Agnes smiled to herself. Doesn't know when to stop. But I wonder if she's truly happy, with all her achievements?

And then there's Robert. The bonny, fair-haired child who came to us so late and was Ted's friend and constant companion in the last, few, difficult years of his life. Not an easy time for her youngest, she thought sleepily. That first, young marriage failed and her boy was left with two small boys to rear. And now here he was, doing a job he loved on the ambulances. Always a carer, her Robert. And then a new, little wife and soon two small girls to make him a father of four! Another survivor, was Agnes's last thought as she finally found sleep.

And somewhere in her head, Emily reminded her daughter that she was the greatest survivor of them all.

CHAPTER
TWENTY-FOUR

"I managed to book a table at that new restaurant by the river. You know, the place that used to be Lightfoots near Russell Park. I'm told that the food is very good."

John smiled down at his short, white-haired mother as he helped her on with her smart, new jacket and settled her gently into the passenger seat of his hired car.

For many months, the entire family, orchestrated by George, had secretly planned Agnes's ninetieth birthday celebrations. Now, here she was, looking forward to a quiet meal out with John, who was over from the States to visit his middle daughter's family in Norfolk.

"We'll be meeting a few others here, Mum," he explained as he turned the car into the car park of Haynes Village Hall some miles from Agnes's cottage.

"What others?" exclaimed Agnes suspiciously as John, with a broad grin on his face, took her firmly by the elbow and led her towards the door.

"Don't tell me you've all done it again!" she gasped, remembering that other party of twenty years earlier.

"It's OK, Mum." John looked anxiously at his mother, who had now stopped abruptly in the middle of the car park and was beginning to look more than a little agitated.

At that moment, the door of the hall opened and there was Robert who had been looking out for their arrival and who knew that this time, if she was not given some kind of warning, the shock might be too much for his mother.

"Come on, Mum. We're all here, waiting to wish you a happy birthday."

Then he took Agnes's other arm as the oldest and the youngest of her children led her inside to be greeted by over eighty members of the family singing, "Happy Birthday, Gang-Gang." And she was cheered to her seat at the top table beside her other children and their various partners.

Agnes was glad to sit down and tried to regain her breath as she looked around the big room at all the smiling faces. Some she knew well and some, those grandchildren and their little ones she didn't see very often, she hardly recognised. How many was it now? Agnes tried to do sums in her head. She knew it had been twenty-eight at the last count and although each one received a card from Gang-Gang on their birthday, she was beginning to lose count of the great-grandchildren who arrived, it seemed, almost every year. There were, she knew, several great-great-grandchildren. Could they all be here?

The M.C. for the evening was as usual, George, who after the meal prepared earlier in the day by all the girls, got the proceedings off to a good start by reading all the cards and congratulatory messages from old friends, some of whom his mother had not seen for many years.

Just like a wedding reception, thought Agnes, as she tried to read the name tags hung around each child's neck, as they all came to kiss her and say, "Happy birthday, Gang-Gang!"

George had just finished reading aloud a poem from Shela about Agnes's long life, when suddenly, the door beside the stage was flung wide open and there was John, riding into the middle of the hall on a smart, blue mobile chair, bound round with ribbon and a huge pink bow and in its little basket balanced a great bouquet of red roses.

"Come on, Mum."

Joyce's calm voice and gentle hands helped Agnes from her chair and she was led over to the mobile where she sat smiling away as everyone in the room, it seemed, wanted to take photographs of her. And Agnes felt like a queen as she posed with one group after another and then with all the little ones sitting in a semicircle round the surprise present.

"This is my best birthday present ever, John." Agnes smiled as he helped her back to an easy chair drawn up near the stage and told her to expect another surprise any minute now.

As she sat there, waiting a little apprehensively for whatever they were about to spring on her next, Agnes looked round again at all those young faces and the sudden thought that she was responsible for all of them made her laugh aloud. And then she gasped in disbelief as the curtains parted and on stage were a dozen or so members of the Wycombe Savoy Operatic Society from her old home in Speen, launching into a fine rendition of songs from Gilbert and Sullivan.

Agnes recognised some of the costumes worn by the ladies as her own handiwork and felt again the pride she'd taken in making each one during her time as their wardrobe mistress. Yes, she decided, she'd made a good job of them. Flora would have been proud of her.

Later, as she waltzed slowly around the room with one of her strapping grandsons and the children played and chased each other round the tables, now set against the wall for friends and neighbours who had been invited to join the party later, Agnes's thoughts went back to the old Corn Exchange evenings and those two young men who looked and danced like Rudolph Valentino.

"What's making you giggle like that, Gang-Gang? Can't be my dancing, surely!"

Barry, one of Shela's boys, grinned down at his small grandmother and took a firmer hold of her waist as the music changed to a slow tango and they began to dance to "Jealousy". And for a few wonderful moments it seemed to Agnes that she was young again and somewhere Ted was smiling at her from his stool at the bar and she felt again the breathless wonder of falling in love.

By ten o'clock, when she had chatted and laughed with everyone at her party, by now well over a hundred people, Agnes knew that she'd nearly had enough.

"Must be that dancing, Joyce. I've not tangoed in years!"

And Joyce looked with concern at her mother as she guided her back to her chair and Agnes would have given anything to put her feet up on her own comfortable footstool at home.

"Are you all right, Mum?"

Her daughter's anxious voice cut into Agnes's tired thoughts and the smile that had briefly left her face as she eased off her shoes was instantly back as she reassured Joyce that no, she wasn't tired and yes, a nice cup of tea would be lovely if that was possible at this late hour.

It was well after midnight when John helped his mother out of the car and taking her hand firmly beneath his arm, led her back into the quiet cottage they'd left several hours earlier.

"Well, John!" Agnes exclaimed as the longed-for footstool was placed gently beneath her swollen ankles. "You properly fooled me, I must say! But I did enjoy it. Especially the dancing."

And she smiled as her young American great-granddaughter went into the kitchen to switch on the kettle for Gang-Gang's mug of bedtime Horlicks.

It was not until the next day, as more relatives visited and the local Round-Tablers called with a small cheque, "For your birthday, Mrs Winch, perhaps to help with the fuel bills this winter," that Agnes finally heard all about the secret negotiations being carried out ever since Easter.

"So that's why no one was ever at home every time I rang," Agnes laughed as John explained and Joyce smiled at her mother and told her how they'd all met in each other's homes in turn and how anxious she'd been when her mother had that bad turn only last week.

"Thank goodness you didn't do any damage when you fell on the lawn, Mum. You might have missed your own party!"

The ninetieth! thought Agnes to herself later that night as she plumped her pillow up behind her and prepared to read the next chapter in the book that George had given her for her birthday.

"The life of Flora Robson," began the blurb on the dust-cover, "has been a long and successful one." But not quite as long as mine apparently, Agnes murmured aloud as she turned the pages to find the last photograph of her old friend's sister.

The dark eyes of a middle-aged woman looked back at her from the page and as she read of all the achievements of the famous actress she'd known in her earliest days in the theatre, Agnes wondered how her own life would have been if she'd done as Flora suggested that day in the old workshop.

"You have a talent that is not given to many, Agnes. You would make a great success in theatre costume design."

Ah! Happy dreams, Agnes smiled to herself. But then there would have been no party yesterday with all those grandchildren and great-grandchildren there and would I have been so content as I feel tonight?

"Who knows?" She spoke aloud to her reflection in the old mirror at the foot of the bed as she put the book back on the bedside table and turned off the light. "Who knows?"

310

So the summer ended and the old walled garden was full of chrysanthemums and those Michaelmas daisies that Ted always liked and then so quickly, it seemed to Agnes, it was Christmas again and she rode to St. Mary's Church in style on her new mobile chair to attend the midnight service and Joyce collected her mother the next morning to spend the day with her family in the little bungalow in Cople.

The Easter weekend of the next year brought a lovely surprise for Agnes. For many months, she had been concerned for Shela's health as it deteriorated after her breakdown and now here she was, announcing her engagement, at sixty-three, to a good man who had been widowed the previous year.

"We'll be getting married in the summer," smiled Shela as she introduced Bill to her mother. "Then we'll be living just a few doors away from Joyce."

So her girl had finally found the happiness that seemed to have eluded her for most of her life. And Agnes smiled back at the look of content on Shela's face as she gave her congratulations and silently thanked the kindly fate that had brought these two lonely people together.

And now there were just Joan and Mary living out their lives alone. And John of course, Agnes reminded herself as she thought of her oldest son trying his best to make a life in that big, empty house on the other side of the world.

Shela's and Bill's wedding was a time filled with joy on an August day in one of the hottest summers on record. But it was cool inside the old church at Cople as they received the blessing and afterwards, as Agnes stood beneath the shade of ancient yews while photographs were taken, Emily's voice came to her as it so often seemed to recently. "You see, child. Everything comes out right in time."

It was in the first week of the new year when Robert came to visit his mother in her little cottage by the green, for he had some interesting news to tell her.

The day had been dull and wet and Agnes had kept her standard lamp switched on for most of it, for on days like this not much daylight came in through the small, leaded windows.

"I've got three weeks' leave due by the end of April," Robert explained as he handed his mother a fresh cup of tea. "And if I don't use it by then, I'll lose it altogether."

Agnes wondered what was coming next, for rarely had she seen her youngest son so animated or heard him speak so forcefully. She was not kept waiting long.

"I'm going over to see John again and I thought you'd like to come with me."

Agnes's heart raced painfully in her chest as she set her cup down carefully on the coffee table and tried to control the breathing that seemed to have suddenly grown so tiresome.

She had already made the long journey to Seattle, nearly five years ago now and she knew just how tiring it would be. Could she manage it again? Would the doctor give her the OK this time? But oh! how she longed to see her first-born child again. And Agnes thought with sadness of him living his lonely life, filling

312

in his time as best he could in that big house so far away.

She took a deep breath and steadied her unruly heart before giving her son an answer.

"When are we going, Robert?"

Joyce, of course, fussed and fidgeted around her mother in the weeks before the departure date. Making sure in her usual caring way that Agnes got the go-ahead from the doctor before any tickets were bought and that she had a sufficient supply of the pheno-barbitone tablets that kept her heart healthy and warm clothing for the cold weather she was sure to find on the other side of the world.

"Now, Mum," said Joyce for the hundredth time, "you must promise me that you won't overtire yourself at John's place. Don't try to do all the cooking this time. Let the men take their share."

And so on and so on until finally, Agnes held up her hand to stop her.

"I'm going to see John and I can think of no one better to look after me than Robert. He is a paramedic after all, Joyce!"

The flight out in early April was tiring but, as Agnes later related to John when he met them at Seattle airport, "I was too busy looking after Robert to worry about myself. Poor boy." She looked anxiously at her forty-seven-year-old younger son who had been stricken with a bout of food poisoning all the way across the Atlantic.

"I don't think it had anything to do with the airline, John," his mother added hastily at the sight of his raised eyebrows. "Probably something he ate the day before."

313

Nevertheless, it had been a worrying time for Agnes as she found herself trying to support Robert who kept fainting away and it was not until they changed flights in Chicago that the airline people got a doctor to see him and dosed him up enough to get him to their final destination.

A few days' rest in John's spacious house saw Robert making a full recovery and then Agnes was pleased to see him off playing golf with the brother who had been a distant figure to him ever since he could remember.

Agnes never did tell Robert what his older brother had said all those years ago when he found out that his mother was pregnant yet again and as he put it, "Far too old at forty-five."

So the days passed quickly as Agnes's first and last sons got to know each other better out on the golf course and John's girls visited with their husbands and their grandmother prepared tasty English meals for the two men in the evenings.

It was on their last day in the big, wooden house with its wide deck running along each side and overlooking the pine woods behind, that Agnes stood thoughtfully beside the open picture window watching her two boys in the garden below.

John stood in his old familiar stance, with one hand on his hip and the other pointing out to his brother all the changes he intended to make to the back of the house and garden in the next few months.

"The jacuzzi will be in that corner and the spare bedroom behind that and then I'll put in a new floor over the garage to make a studio flat so that visitors can stay there and —"

"But why are you doing all this, John?" Robert interrupted. "You're surely not intending to do it all yourself, are you?"

Watching from the window above, Agnes saw John's face redden suddenly and she could not hear his reply as he turned to walk back into the house. It was only later that Robert told his mother what John had answered.

"Of course I am! Why? Don't you think I'm capable at my great age?"

"And then," Robert continued, "he went on to tell me that he considered the house was his children's heritage and he was doing what he'd always promised to Margaret. To improve the property for their children while he still could."

And now, so quickly it seemed, it was time to leave and they were driving back to the airport in Seattle once more and Agnes, noticing uneasily that John was very quiet, felt impelled to make conversation with Robert as they left the pinewoods behind to pull out at last onto the freeway into bright sunshine.

Two hours later it was checking-in time and John hugged his brother and his mother in turn and said, a little sadly, thought Agnes afterwards, "I'll really miss you guys!"

She smiled at the unconscious Americanism and reached up to pat his cheek before they turned to go through to the departure lounge.

Her last sight of him stayed in her mind all the way across America and on the Atlantic leg she dreamed of her father and John together, although as she reasoned to herself later, they had never met.

Then she thought of how John walked now like an old man with bent back and a slow gait as she had watched him through the departure lounge doors and Robert had voiced aloud his mother's troubling thoughts.

"Thank God he's given up smoking!"

But later, as he tucked the light blanket around his mother's sleeping form, this youngest son, who had seen his father die with emphysema, knew that old John would go the same way. As he looked tenderly down at the worn face beside him, Robert hoped against all reason that it would not be too soon.

CHAPTER
TWENTY-FIVE

"Take a grip, Shela! Listen carefully."

It was a month after Agnes returned from America and George was telling his sister, with a note of incredulity in his voice, that he'd just had a phone call from a distraught niece in the States.

"John was found dead early this morning."

Then, as his sister stood speechless, holding the telephone tightly as if willing it to deny the monstrous truth, George's voice came again, calmer now and with a note of authority.

"Is Bill there, Shela? Get him to the phone if you can."

Shela felt sick and as the familiar pain in her chest sent her rushing for her inhalator, Agnes called from the patio where she'd been left alone watching the fish in Bill's pond darting backwards and forwards. Why had the others all gone inside the house so suddenly?

Then Joyce and Shela were beside her, helping their mother into the house and as she sat on the sofa, Shela was holding her hand and telling her that she had some bad news from America.

"Is it — John?"

The words were spoken quite calmly and as Shela nodded gravely and told her mother quietly that John had died suddenly but peacefully, and Joyce cried and put her arms around the old lady, it seemed to Agnes that her heart had completely frozen within her breast.

Then, somehow, Robert was there and there were more tears and Bill made countless pots of tea all through the long afternoon and evening. And still Agnes was calm and the numbness remained in her heart for many days as Joyce cared for her mother and persuaded her to stay with her for a while longer.

"I'm worried about her, Shela. And that's a fact."

Joyce's small face was pink with exertion after settling her mother down for the night.

"She's not shed a tear over John. It's not natural. She's so quiet and all she seems to do is sleep."

Agnes knew her girls were concerned for her and so she tried to be as normal as possible when she was with them but it seemed to her that she was dwelling in some small, quiet place of her own and that it was comfortable and safe in this place. Where no-one could reach her. Or hurt her as she'd been hurt on the day that call had come from George.

So she grieved in her own way for her boy, living over and over in her mind all the long years since Ted first balanced him as a baby on his big hand to be photographed and through all his triumphs and griefs and then suddenly, he was gone and oh, she would never see him again.

Every weekend during that long summer, Joyce and Johnny lifted the mobile chair into the car boot before setting off to find a parking spot on the Embankment in Bedford. For Agnes wanted to see again the old walks she'd taken with John as a baby in the smart pram Ted had bought for his new son.

The Embankment gardens, laid out so carefully every year by the Parks Department, were brilliant with summer flowers and the swans that young Robert always loved to feed when he was a child still swam slowly upriver as Agnes brought the mobile chair to a stop at the bench near the Suspension Bridge. There the three of them sat to enjoy an ice-cream cone from the van parked nearby while across Russell Park, children shouted and played in the smart, fenced-in playground near Shaftesbury Avenue and on the tennis courts, energetic young players swung lightweight rackets that had not been invented in Agnes's time at the club in Hitchin.

On many of these visits to the old haunts of Agnes's younger years, they came several times to the bowling green in the corner of the park near Bushmead Avenue, where John had laughed and waved his arms at the solemn, old men in their white panama hats as they walked slowly up and down in that summer sunshine of so long ago.

But now it was Shela whom Agnes came to watch as she played on Saturday afternoons with the other ladies of the club, all in trim white blouses and skirts and red cardigans. And she was comforted at the sight of her daughter restored to health and happy again in her new life with Bill.

On quieter afternoons in the week, Joyce sometimes parked her car in York Street near the park entrance, then walked slowly beside her mother, riding comfortably in the mobile chair as together they visited again the scenes of Agnes's hardest and busiest times in the old house in Castle Road.

The little shop at the top of the street had been Oak's Dairy when Agnes first moved to the area and the big, china urn full of creamy milk, in the centre of the counter, measured carefully into your own jug with a half-pint measure, reminded her always of that old shop opposite her childhood home in London. Was it just time that gave the milk its remembered richness or had pasteurisation really taken all its taste away?

A little further down the street, almost next door to East Hall where that awful air-raid siren had been mounted on the roof during the war, Agnes had queued every Friday outside Bays' Fish Shop for six pieces of cod and a shilling bag of chips. Enough to feed the whole family, she smiled to herself as she thought about red-faced Mr Bays and his mobile fish and chip van which he drove around the streets while his wife and son served in the hot, busy shop. Emily had never really approved of that shop-bought stuff, her daughter recalled with amusement.

And now here they were outside the shop in Castle Road which had been Armstrong's shoe shop where each summer she had bought five pairs of white, canvas, button-up shoes for her little girls. On Sunday mornings, a row of them would appear, carefully blanco'd and propped up to dry on the garden wall, ready for Sunday School held in Christ Church round the corner in Denmark Street.

Agnes smiled to herself at the memory of Joyce's indignation as a twelve-year-old in 1941, when rationing was in full swing and the girl's visits to Harry West's, the grocer on the corner of Bower Street, to collect the family rations in the big, old pram, brought complaints of favouritism from the tired women waiting in the queue.

"I told them we were a big family, Mum. But you should have seen their faces when Nancy West weighed up our rations and now Mr West says I should leave it until nearly closing time before I go next week!"

Across the road from West's, now a wine shop, Agnes noted with surprise, a smart, new "farm shop" sold every conceivable vegetable and fruit you could want, but she remembered it had been Schofield's the greengrocer's where little Mrs Schofield worked all day in an unheated shop selling potatoes from great bins at the back of it and sixpence bought enough for dinner for the family. And Agnes recalled too, the woman's kindness when Beryl went down with the awful acidosis which left her with a swollen belly and legs like matchsticks and Mrs Schofield always managed to find an extra bit of fruit for Mrs Winch's sick child.

Almost opposite to Schofield's, which Gordon Lilley, the young assistant later took over and modernised, was a narrow shop which had been Bell's the barber's and it was here that Ted took all three boys in turn for their fortnightly haircut. John's was only sixpence, recalled

Agnes but by the time Robert came along, the price had gone up to seven times that amount.

Next to the barber's shop on the corner of Pembroke Street, the little sub-post office still sold stamps and stationery but now it cashed giro-cheques and dispensed television licences for the Government. And Agnes thought of those dark days at the beginning of the war when her army pay was late and Mrs Woodward, the postmaster's wife, shook her head regretfully every week for four months when her harassed customer enquired yet again if it had arrived.

"Let's get some cream buns for tea, Joyce."

Agnes pointed across Pembroke Street to the small shop on the opposite corner that had been Ruff's the bakers where on Good Fridays, Emily always bought hot-cross buns for the family from her meagre pension.

"They are as good as I can make," Emily conceded with a smile and Agnes knew it was her mother's way of contributing quietly to the family budget. They were the only shop-bought buns that came into the house from one year's end to another for Emily made all the bread and cakes the family needed until the end of her life.

Agnes sighed at the memory of her hardworking mother as Joyce guided the mobile wheelchair across York Street past the shop that had been the Co-op Butcher's. It was from his shop window that Mr Tye the burly, florid-faced butcher had seen young Joan knocked over outside the little bicycle repair shop in York Street and rushed across to pick the child up and carry her in to her distraught mother in the house across the road at 152. Had that accident, which had resulted in concussion, been the cause of the fainting fits the little girl had suffered throughout her childhood? Agnes never did get a satisfactory explanation from old Dr Chillingworth, she recalled. He probably didn't know the answer himself, she thought, as she glanced back past the old butcher's shop to the premises behind it which had been the Co-op milk depot when the family first came to live in Castle Road in 1936.

Red-haired Mr Burnage was the milkman until 1940 when he was called up for war service and petrol was rationed so that the daily milk had to be delivered on a heavy hand-cart pushed round the streets by a strapping young woman who did the job as well as any man could have managed. When the war ended and the men returned, Agnes remembered with affection, Mr Burnage started on his old milk round again just as if he had never been away.

Across the road on the other corner of York Street, Mr and Mrs Baylis's Ladies' and Gents' Outfitters, where Agnes had managed to buy a length of pre-war, black, pin-striped suiting for a skirt for Emily's funeral, had been taken over by their son, Jim, who now ran it as a successful D.I.Y. business. Such a good friend his mother had been to her old customer who had been left widowed with a young boy to raise alone. For this kind woman was the source of much-needed sewing work for Agnes when she needed it most. And always there was a cheerful word for Mrs Winch from the two shop assistants, Beryl Steele and Marjorie Bodsworth, old school friends of Joyce and Shela.

Moving slowly now past the old house, Agnes smiled as she noticed the brightly-coloured tiles surrounding the porch, which a cheerful Italian family had installed when they moved in some years previously. And she saw that the golden privet hedge had disappeared to be replaced by a modern, brick wall. Much easier to keep tidy, she told herself firmly. Although she had loved that old hedge, for on dark, winter days it stood out from all the others like a beacon welcoming her home from work.

And now here was Linford's old shop on Denmark Street corner and Agnes stopped her mobile chair to look in the window for she wasn't quite sure what the shop sold nowadays. Probably health food or some other stuff which people today didn't seem to be able to live without. And she remembered Beryl's time in the old grocer's shop where the great ginger cat lay in the window basking in the sun and Mr and Miss Linford came in each day in their rickety old car from Swineshead, somewhere out along the Kimbolton Road. A good old-fashioned pair they were, even though their ideas about hairdressing had been proved wrong since her girl left them to make her way up the ladder of success in the beauty business.

Agnes was tired now, but on this summer afternoon with Joyce walking patiently beside her, she wanted to see again all the familiar, loved places of her past and she looked across Denmark Street to the old Co-op

Grocer's shop where she had first registered for grocery rations in 1940.

"Might as well get your divi there every week, Agnes," Ted had advised her. And all the children knew their mother's Co-op membership number, 8300, as they queued with Agnes on divi day at the main shop in Midland Road for the annual payout.

Agnes giggled to herself as Joyce guided her safely across the busy road to the little corner shop where Mr Lawrence had run a confectionery business for many years before he retired soon after the family left the area. Was it Joan that her eldest son had sent across one day to ask Mr Lawrence for half a pint of pigeon's milk that John needed for his model airplane making? And the wise old shopkeeper told the young girl to inform her brother that they were out of stock at the moment but were expecting more in next week if he cared to call in for it himself! And then stood in his shop doorway wagging his finger as the message was delivered to a grinning John and his friends outside 152.

Just behind Lawrence's shop, Agnes could see the two modern houses newly built on the site of what had been Northwood's the baker's old premises. It was from there that Emily had bought the two ounces of fresh yeast every Friday morning ready for the big Saturday baking day when she made bread and scones, ginger parkin and bread puddings to last through the week for the growing family. Agnes could almost smell that hot parkin as it came fresh from the old oven and the thought of her mother's drop scones as she scooped them from the hot-plate ready to be buttered for tea made her mouth water.

And now Joyce walked beside her as she turned back up Castle Road again and here she was outside her old friend's house which she had looked at so many times as she sat in the window sewing for her living when Ted was ill and after he died. The Harrisons had left Castle Road soon after the Winch family moved out in 1961 but Agnes still remembered the friendship offered by the tall man who worked hard in his taxi business and his wife who helped her through many dark days during the war.

On some afternoons the mother and daughter ended up at the old Goldington Road School back gate at the other end of York Street and in her mind's eye, Agnes could see again her youngsters running down the street to school as the bell began to ring at five minutes to nine. For they all knew that if you were late three times in a week it meant the cane from Miss Slater, the strict headmistress of the girls' school or Mr Barratt, the headmaster of the boys' department. One stroke across the hand for the girls and a whack on the backside for the boys. She often wondered which hurt the most but suspected it was the girls' punishment. For Miss Slater always asked which was the child's writing hand before caning the other one, so that turning the pages of an exercise book or an atlas and struggling with knitting needles or a paintbrush for the rest of the day was painful and the hand throbbed all that night and Agnes had to soothe it with witch-hazel bought from Jones, the chemist further along Castle Road.

She noticed now, so many years later, that the old field at the bottom of the playground had been sold off for new houses and she remembered the air-raid shelters built in that field and the weekly gas-mask practice the children endured in those damp, smelly places for up to an hour at a time and how some of the little ones had nightmares about it and always cried when the family slept under the stairs when the air-raid sirens sounded early in the war.

But Agnes also remembered the good times at the school. How her children always had the best fancy-dress costumes at Christmas parties and were the best-dressed in the yearly class plays. For everyone knew that their mother was "good with a needle". And the end of Easter terms, as each of her children learned they had passed the scholarship to the big secondary schools and how proud she had been as she viewed their work displayed in the school hall on Exhibition Day at the end of the school year.

So the quiet summer of grieving passed as Agnes mourned for her boy and at its end she was ready to accept again whatever life had left to give.

It was on an overcast day in October when Joyce and Johnny came to take her the short distance along The Green to St. Mary's Church in Cardington. And as Agnes pulled on her good navy-blue hat and buttoned up the coat she'd made for George's C.B.E. investiture at the palace, she knew that somehow she must be strong for this day when all the family would watch her walk slowly up the aisle to sit quietly in her Sunday seat for John's memorial service.

EPILOGUE

On the china cabinet, the Westminster chime clock that had been one of her ninetieth birthday presents, said almost midnight.

Agnes smiled to herself at her small deception when she reassured Joyce's anxious voice on the telephone an hour ago that she would be in bed by eleven and leaned forward to pick up the order of service where it had fallen unnoticed at her feet.

Her fingers gently traced the outline of John's smiling face on the cover picture before she placed it carefully in the bureau drawer where she kept special birthday and Christmas cards from the family.

She was tired now and her warm bed, already prepared by Joyce in her usual efficient way, was very welcoming as she pulled the duvet up to her chin and reached out to switch off the bedside lamp.

"It's been a long day, Ted," she murmured, for he seemed somehow to be very near in that moment before sleep came.

Tomorrow, she thought, I'll say goodbye to John's girls before they fly back to their distant lives on the other side of the world.

328

And in the little cottage by the green where her treasured photographs stood watch as she slept, life would go on as usual for their Gang-Gang who had always been there for them.

Outside, the lighted carriage lamp over the front door burned on through the dark night as steadily and brightly as Agnes had shone for her family through all the long years.

And in the corner of her bedroom, neatly folded on the old sewing machine, a pile of salon towels waited to be hemmed up for Beryl's shop before the weekend.

I'll run them up in the morning, thought Agnes.

ISIS publish a wide range of books in large print, from fiction to biography. Any suggestions for books you would like to see in large print or audio are always welcome. Please send to the Editorial department at:

ISIS Publishing Ltd.
7 Centremead
Osney Mead
Oxford OX2 0ES
(01865) 250 333

A full list of titles is available free of charge from:
Ulverscroft large print books

(UK)
The Green
Bradgate Road, Anstey
Leicester LE7 7FU
Tel: (0116) 236 4325

(Australia)
P.O Box 953
Crows Nest
NSW 1585
Tel: (02) 9436 2622

(USA)
1881 Ridge Road
P.O Box 1230, West Seneca,
N.Y. 14224-1230
Tel: (716) 674 4270

(Canada)
P.O Box 80038
Burlington
Ontario L7L 6B1
Tel: (905) 637 8734

(New Zealand)
P.O Box 456
Feilding
Tel: (06) 323 6828

Details of **ISIS** complete and unabridged audio books are also available from these offices. Alternatively, contact your local library for details of their collection of **ISIS** large print and unabridged audio books.